HARVARD HISTORICAL STUDIES ◆ 194

Published under the auspices of the Department of History

From the income of the
Paul Revere Frothingham Bequest
Robert Louis Stroock Fund
Henry Warren Torrey Fund

The House in the Rue Saint-Fiacre

A SOCIAL HISTORY OF PROPERTY
IN REVOLUTIONARY PARIS

H. B. Callaway

Harvard University Press

CAMBRIDGE, MASSACHUSETTS
LONDON, ENGLAND

2023

First printing

Library of Congress Cataloging-in-Publication Data is available from loc.gov
ISBN: 978-0-674-27934-6 (cloth)

CONTENTS

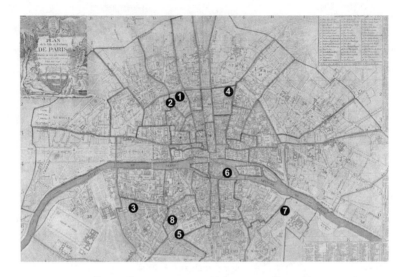

MAP O.I Map of Paris showing approximate locations of key addresses in the text.
Source: "Plan de la ville et faubourg de Paris divisé en ses 48 sections decreté par l'Assemblée nationale le 22 juin 1790." *Credit:* Bibliothèque nationale de France.

1—House of Ange-François Talaru, Rue Saint-Fiacre
2—Domain bureau offices, Maison d'Uzès
3—House of Henriette Becdelièvre, Rue de Varennes
4—House of Madame Blondel d'Azincourt, Rue Notre-Dame-de-Nazareth
5—Berthaud's goat pen, Rue Notre-Dame-des-Champs
6—Home of Widow Planoy, Rue du Cloître Notre-Dame
7—Home of Jean-François Cagnion, Boulevard de l'Hôpital, requisitioned December 1796
8—Property chosen by Cagnion in exchange for his requisitioned property, Rue de Vaugirard

Introduction

IN THE MIDST OF THE FRENCH REVOLUTION, Louise-Perrine Chabanais fled France with her ten-year-old son. Like many nobles, she chose to emigrate as the Old Regime collapsed. She may have gone to the Austrian Empire or to England or to America—these were common destinations. The dossiers containing records of the case only reveal as much as state officials knew, which was that she no longer lived in France. Wherever she went, upon leaving the country she became subject to laws against emigration passed by the revolutionary legislatures. As an émigré, she was considered legally dead. Once her absence had been noted, officials began to carry out the steps to seize her property in accordance with the laws, working within administrations set up specifically to handle the confiscation process. It was all very straightforward—or it should have been, in theory.

Yet a local clerk, writing to his superior, explained that the situation was "*délicate*." Chabanais's son was a minor: unlike his mother, he did not count as an émigré according to the law. With his mother legally dead, the boy was officially considered an orphan and ward of the state. As the clerk succinctly put it, he "has no other defender than the Nation."[1] But although the state was his guardian, officials were trying

I

to seize his inheritance. How, the clerk wondered, should the situation be handled?

Complicating matters further, this quandary over the young Chabanais's legal claim emerged from a tenant's innocuous request for a reduction in rent. Louise-Perrine Chabanais owned a house in the Rue Ville-l'Evêque, not far from the Tuileries gardens. A man named Chartier, who was renting a storefront and an apartment at the address, wrote to the administrators in the Domain bureau explaining that the Revolution had caused him to lose income. He worked for the Comte d'Artois, a relative of Louis XVI's, but the Comte fled the country after the outbreak of the Revolution, and this income had dried up. Chartier asked for a reduction in rent, or a job. As officials examined the details, they discovered that Chartier was only a subtenant. The building was actually leased to a different man, Bosquet. Administrators thus traced the claims on the building from Chartier to Bosquet back to Chabanais, who owned the building jointly with her husband. The husband's death left Chabanais in joint ownership with her son. Granting a discount to Chartier would therefore mean depriving the boy of the value of his asset.

In the Rue Saint-Fiacre, not far from the house that belonged to Chabanais, the fate of another seized house hung in suspense.[2] Henriette Becdelièvre stayed in Paris as her son, a military officer in the Bourbon regime, fled the country. He and his sister were set to inherit the assets of their uncle, Becdelièvre's brother-in-law, a bishop who emigrated to England. Her brother-in-law's assets included a recently built mansion in the Rue Saint-Fiacre, which had been placed under seal and entrusted to the guardianship of a neighbor around the corner. Becdelièvre would fight for years to secure the house and other assets for her daughter, Césarine Talaru. Using public debt that she held, Becdelièvre paid a guarantee in May 1797 to get Césarine's portion of the inheritance released. When the state wrote down the public debt, however, the value of her guarantee was no longer sufficient.

In December 1798, the property was placed under sequester once again. In July 1800, the Domain discovered the tenants in the Rue Saint-Fiacre house owed back rent. Becdelièvre claimed the rent should be paid to her, as it accrued during the time that the house had been released to her. Then, Césarine's brother and coheir was recognized as an émigré, triggering laws against the parents of émigrés that caused Becdelièvre's own house to be placed under sequester. While Césarine's portion of the inheritance should have been preserved, it included undivided assets—such as the house in the Rue Saint-Fiacre—held in common with her émigré brother. Her share could not physically be separated, so it was sequestered alongside her brother's.

The seizure of these two properties crystallize larger issues surrounding the delegation of property rights during the French Revolution. Requiring administrators to untangle interlocking claims on the houses, the confiscation process highlights the varying understandings of property that lawmakers, administrators, and private citizens alike brought to each case. As an asset, a house represented not only a source of immediate revenue—a source of value as a salable good—but also a place to live and a piece of family patrimony. While administrators considered value with an eye to a short-term balance sheet, value for émigré families could unfold over a longer period and could involve habitation rather than cash rent. Ownership of a house concerned not only individual émigrés but also the members of their families who had an interest in it: spouses with joint ownership, children set to inherit, or even elderly family members living there. The interests of these people could be immediate, or could stretch into the future. To seize property from Chabanais, for example, was to seize it from her son. For Henriette Becdelièvre, her brother-in-law's home represented her daughter's future; yet his status as an émigré threatened to leave Césarine with nothing. Becdelièvre herself, with no ownership claim on the house, nevertheless was invested in preserving the asset. Laws limiting emigration targeted individual citizens, but the confiscation process necessarily implicated a broader group of people with claims to the same property.

In both of these cases, the primary property owner was a woman. When male relatives emigrated, women often stayed behind and took responsibility for defending family assets, just as Henriette Becdelièvre did. Women's approaches to negotiating property rights, however, were necessarily oblique, as married women's ability to exercise property rights was limited.[3] Widows had greater freedom to dispose of their assets. Wives could inherit lifetime use of a share of their husband's assets or, as in the Chabanais case, a share of communal assets obtained during the marriage. Preserving and transmitting assets was a family undertaking, one that engaged all members—male and female—even though their claims to formal ownership might differ.

These two cases also illustrate that the clarity of the law did not necessarily translate to clarity in the practice of identifying assets and taking them away from people. While the legal principles of revolutionary property seizure laid out a seemingly straightforward process for administrators who applied them, the complex nature of property itself—whether defined in terms of actual things or claims—and the human relationships that surrounded it could generate surprising conflicts and confusions. Such bureaucratic imbroglios, closely examined, have much to reveal about the way that property claims functioned during the French Revolution. a moment when the legal definitions of property and the political meanings attached to it were in flux.

Redefining Property in the Revolution

Property was central to the revolutionary project of political and social transformation from the beginning. The Revolution itself broke out during a meeting about who owned France's sovereign debt. Among the three constitutions drafted during the revolutionary era, the distinguishing factor was the electoral base, which in each instance was determined by property ownership. Property crops up at crucial moments in the Revolution because lawmakers understood it to be central to the issues of sovereignty and rights that lay at the heart of their agendas.

Before 1789, the king held the underlying ownership of all property in his kingdom. Property rights depended on a person's social status: nobles did not just have more property than commoners; they had a different kind of property altogether. For example, one type of feudal property conferred the right to dispense justice. A venal office in the royal bureaucracy was also considered a form of property, conferring nobility on the person who purchased it. Through membership in a guild, commoners could own a monopoly on the production of a certain product, such as shoes or lemonade. There were many other social categories beyond nobles and commoners: Jews, Protestants, and women, for example, all had special property regimes. The Church owned vast property, and clergy had a special relationship to their property as well. A cleric owned his prebend or benefice but could not sell it or leave it to his (illicit) children, since an underlying claim remained with the Church.

On the night of August 4, 1789, however, members of the National Assembly moved to abolish feudalism. A clear rejection of the Old Regime, the act not only dissolved a major category of property but also constituted a major transfer of property rights: the owners of feudal property effectively ceded ownership of that land to their tenants. While tenants previously had the ability to buy and sell their farms underneath the ownership of the feudal lord, now they effectively became the sole owners of their land. In the fall of 1789, the Legislative Assembly abolished another major category of Old Regime property: it nationalized Church property, on the grounds that only individual citizens—not corporate entities—could own property. The Church's vast land holdings were sold at auction. Finally, the Le Chapelier law of June 1791 abolished trade guilds on the same basis—although guild property, which primarily took the form of monopoly rights to production, was simply dissolved rather than being sold. One by one, each of the major reforms expropriated an entire category of Old Regime society: the nobility, the Church, and the commoners.

The Revolution legally rooted property rights in individuals, not the king, and it made those rights the same for all white men regardless of social status. The king distributed property rights in the Old Regime because, as God's anointed, he was sovereign. Revolutionary legislators, most of whom were lawyers, recognized sovereignty as residing in the people. The purpose of government, in this new system, was only to recognize and protect property—not to hand it out. Property could only belong to one person at a time, and it could only belong to an individual—not to corporate bodies like the Church or trade guilds—because it was individuals who transformed the land with their labor and made it fruitful. This view depended on a social contract understanding of property, most influentially laid out by John Locke in 1689 and Jean-Jacques Rousseau in 1762. In this view, individuals joined together to form government in order to secure their rights to their property and the government's legitimacy arose from the will of the people. The transfer of rights from the individual claimants to the government represented the trust that people placed in public institutions. The duty of government to respect the rights of individuals and to respect private property followed from this transfer.

Echoing the lawmakers themselves, generations of historians understood property reform to be at the heart of the revolutionary project—even as they adopted diametrically opposed interpretations of that project. Through the nineteenth and twentieth centuries, historians debated how sincerely leaders in the Revolution wanted to redistribute property, and considered how successful they were in doing so. In the late nineteenth century, the historian Hippolyte Taine, who represented a trend of scholarship that considered the Revolution to be a protocommunist attack on property, observed, "Whatever the great names, liberty, equality, fraternity, the Revolution decorates itself with, it is in its essence a translation of property, and in this it finds its intimate support, its permanent force, its primary motor and its historical meaning."[4] Roughly one hundred years later, the historian William Sewell, a Marxist historian representing the opposite end of the ideological spectrum from Taine, described the abolition of feudal property as "the holocaust of property of the old style."[5] Both understood property reform to have been at the very core of the Revolution, judging its success or failure in large part on the grounds of how property rights were handled.[6]

More recently, historians of the Revolution have focused on the way reforms to property in the Revolution have shaped modern society. Rafe Blaufarb has argued that the Revolution created the modern social order by separating property rights from political power.[7] Blaufarb departs from the highly political approach to property in the Revolution of earlier generations of scholarship to focus on property as a matter of law. His work still places property, and the reform of property, at the very heart of the French Revolution. In doing so, he considers property as a legal concept whose contents, once defined in law, are more or less self-evident.

One might contrast Blaufarb's approach with that of Rebecca Spang, who studied one form of property, the paper currency issued during the Revolution, known as the assignat.[8] Spang unpacks the assumptions, beliefs, and practices that shaped how people understood money, tracing the implications for the ill-fated assignat. For Spang, law is only the starting point for the assignat; she shows how profoundly the paper money was shaped by perceptions entirely outside the power of lawmakers. As these works have placed issues surrounding property once again at the center of the Revolution, they also prompt the question of definitions: How is property defined, and who defines it?

As the Chabanais and Becdelièvre cases indicate, the law did not answer all questions about how property should be defined and who should own it. Chabanais was legally dead, the means for settling her estate established—and yet in practice, the process of determining who owned what proved messy and uncertain, not least because it forced administrators to choose among competing values. The centrality of property to the social order means that it cannot be studied from the perspective of law alone. Laws set boundaries, but the nature of property itself often defies those boundaries. To understand how property was changed during the Revolution, we must examine what people were doing in addition to what they were saying. In fact, this book argues, administrators, property owners, heirs, and creditors played as central a role in defining property across the course of the Revolution as the lawmakers who proclaimed their vision aloud. We have not fully contended with these other vectors of change, and we have never fully taken the measure of what emerged. Nowhere is this clearer than in the case of émigré property confiscation, which reveals the gap between revolutionary property law, with its vision of how society should function, and the realities of how property already functioned. These realities included emergent forms of property, such as credit instruments and consumer goods, as well as long-standing functions of property that the Revolution did not dismantle, such as patrimony.

Turning the focus to practices reveals how institutions, through the actions of their members, shaped the nature of property and how it fit into the new regime. In particular, administration and the family played crucial roles. Modern democracy, with its emphasis on the state and the individual, tends to occlude the role of administrators. From the perspective of liberal politics, property is a bulwark of individualism. The social contract narrative of democratic popular sovereignty neatly avoids reference to the state as an administrator, concealing the fact that the state decides the contents of rights and who gets them.[9] From Weber to Foucault, modern social theory is extraordinarily suspicious of the state's administrative power.[10] This power is not new, but in the context of modern liberal democracy, administration is portrayed as a nefarious, if necessary, enemy. There may well be something antidemocratic in the figure of the state administrator, but the same rhetoric that has made us suspect them paradoxically has also made us depend on them in new ways. During the Revolution, administrators, if anything, took on a greater role than they had previously played in arbitrating which property claims were legitimate and which were not.

During the Revolution, property also remained enmeshed in family relationships, in the sense that families shared assets among themselves interdependently. The creation of new financial instruments further enabled families to divide property among themselves, sharing layers of ownership to serve their various needs. Marriage and inheritance remained crucial moments for the transfer of property, but also for creating new interdependencies. When parents promised an asset in a marriage contract, or when spouses accumulated assets during their marriage, claims were created. These kinds of connections would continue in the nineteenth century, even as women were sidelined from work and the market. Reforms to family law undertaken in the Revolution had attempted to limit the influence of families, empowering individuals to form and dissolve relationships freely. And yet, individual claims could not be separated out or isolated from the larger web of family claims—in part due to the reform of inheritance law put in place during the Revolution. During and after the Revolution, as the émigré cases will show, family relationships also provided shelter for assets: joint ownership of assets among family members offered a means to defend property against state intervention. This dynamic did not go away in the postrevolutionary era: in the nineteenth century, families provided the capital to mount business ventures, as well as the relationships of credit and trust that allowed them to grow and thrive. For example, many of the nineteenth century's multinational corporations—most notably the international banks—were based on family relationships.

More broadly, the resources of the family as a group provided flexibility in the face of changing circumstances. In practice, the family continued to play a central role in determining who owned what and how assets would be used, long after the attempts during the Revolution to limit its influence.

The Problem of Émigré Property

The relationship between property and social order articulated under the new regime was challenged with particular acuteness by the existence of émigré property owners. Those citizens who left the country during the Revolution, known as the émigrés, were closely associated with the Old Regime aristocracy that resisted the Revolution. The emigration began shortly after the Revolution itself.[11] The Comte d'Artois fled Versailles on July 17, 1789. Within weeks, most of the courtiers at Versailles had fled as well.[12] For the next four years, Frenchmen of all types flowed out of the country in waves.[13] In terms of sheer numbers, most of the people leaving France were clergy and peasants. Considering the makeup of the French population, however, the clerical and noble populations emigrated at a higher rate.[14] This aligned with the popular image of the émigré as an aristocrat hostile to the Revolution.

Emigration intensified at key moments of political crisis, such as the arrest of the royal family on August 10, 1792, and peaked after January 1, 1793.[15] The number of departures also varied greatly by region. People close to the borders, and especially in Alsace-Lorraine and the Moselle, were most likely to cross the border. Emigration from Paris began earlier than emigration from other parts of France, peaking before January 1793. The population of emigrants from Paris also included a larger proportion of nobles and former elites.[16] Both of these trends are explained by the fact that wealth and privilege were concentrated in the capital. By 1793, most French nobles and aristocrats had already left the country. Because elites across France were likely to own property in Paris, they regularly appeared on Parisian émigré lists regardless of where their primary residences were located.

The émigrés collectively owned a great deal of property across the country, creating difficulties for a regime that recognized the links between property rights, citizenship, and sovereignty. Embedded in the rhythm of revolutionary politics, the émigrés embodied everything that threatened the Revolution. They represented internal resistance to the new order, as they voted with their feet and abandoned the Revolution. They also represented external military threats, as they agitated for military action within the Holy Roman Empire and formed their own regiments.[17] Accordingly, concern over their movements grew more intense as the threats they represented became more concrete. Legal measures against the émigrés began within six months of the fall of the Bastille. In January 1790, the Constituent Assembly passed a decree asking civil servants absent without leave to return to France. The following December, the Assembly suspended pensions and interest payments on public debt to anyone who refused to return to France. In June 1791, the legislature began discussing the problem posed by citizens leaving the country. Shortly after, it voted to dissolve the property of trade guilds. Debate on the issue of emigration began in earnest in the fall of 1791, and the first law sequestering émigré property passed in February 1792. Placing émigré property under sequester was a prelude to its confiscation, but already this law went further than previous legislation, which had targeted state officials and imposed fines rather than enacting wholesale confiscation.

From the perspective of revolutionary lawmakers, property—the things people owned—constituted the core problem of emigration. The departure of French citizens initiated what members of the legislature referred to as "the emigration of things," the loss of the money and matériel that émigrés were understood to be carrying over the border.[18] Lawmakers found these departures particularly unsettling because these things were going over the border into the Austrian

Empire, with which France would soon be at war. The regime's major property reforms—abolishing feudalism, nationalizing Church property, and dissolving guild property—operated on an understanding of property as land. But the primary threat posed by the "emigration of things" was property's ability to become liquid and be carried away. Having initiated these reforms with the belief that property rights grounded the contract between individual citizens and their government, revolutionary legislators now faced an unsettling question. What if property owners acted against the interest of their fellow citizens and of the state to whose protection they had entrusted their property?

The seizure of émigré property during the Revolution has been studied extensively, but always from the perspective of redistribution. Studies have focused on the act of transferring of émigré property through sale, with an eye to the social impact of these changes in ownership.[19] The laws against emigration, moreover, have usually been considered alongside the extralegal attempts to redistribute property during the period of extralegal rule known as the Terror—even though the first law imposing a general sequester on émigré property was passed before the Terror, under the constitutional monarchy.[20] While these studies have offered important insights into the treatment of émigré property, the far-reaching operation of the confiscations invites other kinds of questions about the process and its impact.

Indeed, confiscation from the émigrés was not the only instance of revolutionary expropriation. The Church, the Old Regime trade guilds, and owners of noble forms of property were expropriated as well, in larger numbers and to a greater value than the émigrés. The confiscation of émigré property is distinct from these other forms of expropriation, however, in three key ways that distinguish its significance beyond the measure of its value or the number of people directly affected by it. First, émigré property encompassed all forms of property: land, investments, and personal property. This distinguished it from guild property, comprised of monopolies, and feudal property, which included rights more than land tenure. The capacious nature of émigré property made it unwieldy and difficult to confiscate. Unlike feudal dues or guild monopolies, it could not be dissolved by fiat. It had to be found and carried away or, in the case of real estate, locked up.

Second, émigré property belonged to individuals as individuals. Feudal, Church, and guild property belonged to its owners because of their membership in a social caste; these were legal categories of property that preexisted the Revolution. Church property, which represented a far larger confiscation project than émigré property, belonged to an institution. Émigré property was no different from other forms of private property, except that it belonged to members of a novel legal category created during the Revolution. In fact, the reason emigration was seen as a threat to the Revolution was that the émigrés were understood to be property owners. If any quality united émigrés as a group, it was as much their status as owners as it was their departure from the country.

Finally, émigré property as a category was created during the Revolution. This makes it an actor's category: a concept used by historical actors and understood by them to have meaning, as opposed to one used by historians to make sense of the past. From the beginning, émigré property was a loose and capacious category—owing in large part to the ambiguities around defining "property" more broadly. Did property refer to rights or assets? Did it include ownership of the self and artistic productions? To attempt to pinpoint property's many possible forms is to bypass the important fact that the term's elasticity made it a powerful conceptual omnibus. The émigré confiscation process involved both political debate about the nature of property rights and also the painstaking administrative processes of identifying what people owned and taking those things away. It was difficult to execute because ideas of property as a political right and property as an asset kept bumping up against each other, beginning with the very text of the first decree allowing confiscation. The way that revolutionary legislators defined the category of émigré property, and the reasons they gave for treating it as a coherent whole, ultimately reveal a great deal about what they thought constituted property and what function they believed it should play in the polity.

This book uses the process of expropriating émigré property to illuminate how lawmakers, administrators, and private citizens alike understood the nature of property during the Revolution. The seeming incongruousness of the confiscations, which absorbed a great deal of governmental and legislative energy, should not encourage us to set them aside as an anomaly. Rather, it should encourage us to ask a new question: What understanding of property must lawmakers have held for émigré property confiscation to have seemed like a reasonable idea? This is not a story about changes to the nature of property law over the course of the Revolution: although thorny and contested, the confiscation process did not tangibly impact the legal definition of property over the course of the Revolution. Instead, the story of émigré property illuminates heretofore obscured tensions alive within those definitions of property articulated by lawmakers, in the early reform years of 1789–1791 and throughout the Revolution.

Transformations of Property in the Eighteenth Century

Approaching property rights from the perspective of practices, as opposed to law, encourages us to consider French revolutionary property policy less as a rupture with Old Regime practice and more as an array of competing commitments negotiated by individuals on the ground. There was far more continuity between Old Regime and revolutionary practices than the law proclaimed. This was, first, because customary law remained the base of French law. Second, property ownership continued to depend on webs of connections beyond the relationship between citizen and state. The boundaries of law left a wide margin for action, including practices that departed from the intentions of the law even as they remained legal. This is not to say that nothing changed; on the contrary, property went through important transformations over the course of the eighteenth century, with implications for the application of revolutionary reforms to property.

From the perspective of practices, the transformation of property during the French Revolution is a story that begins at least in the 1680s.[21] The events of 1789, as disruptive as they were, should be seen as a continuation of the successive ruptures that took place over the course of the eighteenth century. While lawmakers' axiomatic definitions of property indicated a clear rupture with the Old Regime, they also belie the fact that even Old Regime attitudes had already been informed by at least a century of evolution in broader European conceptions of property. Long before the new regime in France passed a single law, the definition of property, in the sense of what property was, underwent significant changes across northern Europe and America. For hundreds of years in Europe, the rich lived off rents and nobility was synonymous with large portfolios of land. Economic change in the eighteenth century, however, brought new forms of property to Europe, including new types of credit instruments, consumer goods, and stocks. At the same time, existing forms of property—notably, ownership of enslaved people, itself a new and radical understanding of what property could be—came under scrutiny.[22] Democratic revolutions brought about monumental legal and political changes, creating egalitarian social orders based on equal rights and instituting popular sovereignty. There were new things to own and new ways of owning things, as well as a new understanding of the significance of ownership for politics and social relations.

Eighteenth-century observers noticed these changes and considered them to be significant.[23] The type of property that people owned and traded—whether land, credit, or merchant wealth—was understood to shape their values and character. Not only this, but the type of property that made up a nation's primary source of wealth would shape the character and even the future of that nation. Much more was at stake in the emergent field of political economy than wealth alone. British and French political economists, including Adam Smith and François Quesnay, identified land as a salutary counterweight to more troubling forms of property. Agriculture, many believed, generated a more stable kind of wealth than commerce. Literally rooted in the ground, it did so by inspiring the right qualities in the people who engaged in it. In contrast to feudal lords, who lived off revenue, farmer-owners on small plots were considered more efficient and more virtuous. Commerce—the source of financial wealth—was associated with luxury, which was understood to corrupt and weaken nations that indulged in it. A nation of merchants and financiers would encourage outsize borrowing by the sovereign, increasing the problematic tendencies of government; sober, diligent landowners would, in contrast, defend their freedoms against royal overreach, effectively limiting the problematic tendencies of government.[24]

Yet while political theory and political economy identified land as a crucial bulwark against despotism and corruption, land was simultaneously losing its economic hegemony. Likewise, financial wealth took on a dominant political role just as it was coming to be seen as a threat to political stability. During the eighteenth century, commercial and financial investment steadily surpassed land as the most significant source of national and individual wealth, with profound political consequences. This was not entirely a coincidence. During the reign of Louis XIV, public credit—the bread and butter of financiers—made it possible for the British and French governments to borrow huge sums of money, which they used primarily to wage war against one another.[25] Financiers maintained close ties with the Crown through personal and patronage networks, provoking further anxiety from intellectuals concerned about the integrity of public life.[26]

The period in which land lost its dominance as the source of wealth and political influence was also the great moment for theorizing labor on the land as the source of property and, through it, popular sovereignty.[27] By the time the Revolution broke out, discussion about property had been going on for a long time. The speed with which the Constituent Assembly produced the Declaration of the Rights of Man and Citizen, the preamble to a new constitution for France, reflects the influence of this debate on the revolutionary leadership. That is, when the Revolution broke out, people who had been involved in intellectual debate already had a good idea of what they thought the problems with French society and government were, and how to fix them. These ideas were based on their beliefs about what property was or should be, not necessarily on the reality of how property was changing. Their ideas are, obviously, of great importance, as they shaped the new regime. But the gap between their ideas and other aspects of property to which they may have paid less attention is equally important.

The Émigré Dossiers

The gap between the political articulation of property and the practices surrounding property was pronounced in the French Revolution. Recovering this gap requires a genealogical re-creation of the processes by which property was constituted and used, as well as the forms of imposition and resistance through which the concept of property took shape over the revolutionary era. The core source base for this project, therefore, is a series of dossiers documenting émigré property seizures in the city of Paris. These dossiers were composed by officials in the Domain bureau, the local authority responsible for coordinating property seizure, as they attempted to apply the law and interacted with property owners, tenants, creditors, and family members. Each dossier compiles the administrative correspondence relating to a given property and its owner, with letters between the director of the Paris Domain bureau and his staff constituting much of this correspondence. While the Domain bureau initially depended on the Ministry of Finances, it also worked closely with Paris municipal authorities. Oversight of the local bureau switched back and forth between the Ministry of Finances, which assumed overall responsibility for émigré property, and the regional government of Paris, which handled the émigrés themselves. Today, the dossiers are held by the Archives de Paris. The archives of the Ministry of Finances were destroyed by fire in 1871, and most archives of the Domain bureau were destroyed with the archives of the city of Paris when the Hôtel de Ville burned in the same year. While some additional material relating to émigré property seizure survived the Hôtel de Ville fire along with the Domain dossiers, overall the records of property seizures in Paris are incomplete.

The incomplete nature of the Paris archives presents a challenge. Because so much material was destroyed, and because the dossiers that remain are by nature fragmentary and elliptical, it is difficult to generate a coherent picture of seized property in the city. The archive, for example, does not lend itself to a systematic citywide study of the sale of seized property. Moreover, the most complicated cases are necessarily overrepresented in the archive. The simplest cases generated the least paperwork and are nearly invisible in the archive. Meanwhile, problematic properties produced the thickest dossiers recording endless administrative obstacles. Cases generated correspondence when administrators faced uncertainties and needed to consult with each other on how to proceed, as in the Chabanais case. Frustratingly, the correspondence frequently breaks off before revealing the resolutions, if any, to the problems raised therein. Once a property was sold, it no longer generated correspondence—essentially becoming invisible in the archive. The émigré dossiers are a flawed source base, but this does not make them a useless one.

The dossiers, although somewhat disorganized, are quite rich. Gathered into a composite, the pieces from many different dossiers offer an exceptional window into the process by which officials seized—or attempted to seize—émigré properties. While it is generally not possible to follow a single case from start to finish, we can re-create both the individual steps and the process as a whole by layering the dossiers into a mosaic of sorts. The narrative certainty of a single case study, however, is at least as artificial as a reconstruction of the process from dozens of separate dossiers. This is because the officials themselves handled the business of the Domain in the same way that we are forced to consume it: pieces here and there, snapshots of one case and then another, returning to a forgotten case months later to take the next steps, after many others had intervened. This is likely why the director fiercely enforced procedural discipline, as Chapters 3 and 4 will show: doing so made it easier to pick up a case midstream and remind oneself of what was happening.

Yet before examining what is representative about the dossiers examined in this book, it is important to understand the ways in which they are exceptional. For this book, 116 dossiers were selected, representing all dossiers handling real property filed under the letter *B* in the "Ancien ordre" of the Paris Domain archive.[28] The choice of surnames beginning with the letter *B* is borrowed from demographers, who favor this letter because it comprises about 10 percent of the French population and does not overrepresent aristocrats or foreigners.[29] The "Ancien ordre" dossiers contain primarily material beginning between 1792 and 1794 and running through the first decade of the nineteenth century; the "Nouvel ordre" dossiers, for the most part, contain material from the Napoleonic empire.

It is difficult to estimate what proportion of the total number of dossiers this subset represents. The organization of the dossiers is chaotic, and there is not a firm count of the total number of properties seized in Paris.[30] If one assumes, on the basis of Monin and Lazard's *Sommier,* that somewhere between 1,600 and 2,000 properties were seized in Paris, and the dossiers group issues around a single address or set of addresses such that no property appears to have more than one dossier associated with it, a selection of 116 dossiers should represent

5–10 percent of the total. As we will see below, however, there are deeper issues with the dossiers that render them, in all likelihood, unrepresentative of broader patterns.

Only dossiers containing real estate were retained in the selection. The initial focus of the project was real assets (real estate) because the seizure of physical assets seemed to be the most visceral and contested aspect of the process. Over the course of the research, however, it became apparent that the distinction between real and personal property—essentially, between land and other forms of property, such as investments, loans, and movable goods—was artificial at best. Although choosing to focus on real property risked the possibility of underestimating the importance of financial instruments, it in fact only served to highlight the significance of investment property in émigré portfolios. The ways in which this is the case will be unfolded in the chapters that follow.

One might imagine that excluding the dossiers that handled only financial assets meant cutting out an important, unique part of the source base. There is likely little difference, however, between the dossiers that contain real assets and those that do not. This is because most of the émigré owners without real assets in Paris likely owned real property elsewhere in France. It is extremely difficult, even impossible, to reconstruct a full picture of these assets. As we will learn in Chapter 1, there were no public records of property ownership in France until 1791. The problem of reconstructing émigré patrimonies bedeviled administrators overseeing émigré policy. Even aside from the issue of financial assets, however, the dossiers do not come close to presenting a representative sample and, thus, do not support a study of patterns of property ownership. The selection methods used make it possible to glean a broad sample from across the source base, controlling against clumping and thematic sorting. (At some point dossiers were grouped by theme, so that, for example, all the dossiers dealing with rug auctions were in the same archival carton.) Fortunately, however, the representativeness of the selected dossiers is not a problem for our purposes.

Another category of asset is excluded from the sample, namely colonial property—in the sense either of assets located in the French colonies, or credit contracts linked to colonial business ventures.[31] Such assets likely played an important role in many Parisian portfolios, but they are almost entirely invisible in the Domain records. The absence of these assets highlights the limitation of these sources as a means of measuring the scope and composition of assets. An entire category of property, enslaved people, who were treated as property by French law, is absent from the present study as a result. The Domain sources provide a great deal of insight into the practices of property ownership—the comportments of owners and those they interacted with—but the absence of the full spectrum of property is a limitation of the source.

Seizure of property in the French colonies was carried out by a different administration, the Minister of the Marine. This point reflects the official French position at the time, that the colonies were fundamentally separate from France. This position existed alongside an approach to property that tended to divide and separate various types rather than to understand all forms of property to be interlinked; this was the approach adopted by revolutionary legislation and administration. This book will demonstrate the limitations of such an approach, breaking down the logic that allowed colonial assets to be walled off, even as it is limited by the sources that logic produced.

Even if the sources were complete and had been fully sampled, the information in any one source is not itself generalizable. It is important to note that the émigré dossiers from Paris do not represent the broader population, for a number of reasons. First, the dossiers overrepresent the most unusual and difficult cases because these were the likeliest to generate correspondence. Second, the dossiers are limited to confiscations in the city of Paris. These cases are not necessarily reflective of how seizures were conducted more broadly across France, as the amount of property seized and the political context of seizure varied by region and locality. Moreover, Paris is an outlier among outliers: urban property was unusual in late eighteenth-century France, and the capital contained a unique concentration of the nation's wealth. The émigrés who appear in the dossiers owned apartment buildings and elegant mansions in the most expensive quarters of Paris. For many of them, these Paris holdings were just a fraction of far larger provincial wealth, which mostly remains invisible due to the regionally segmented nature of the confiscation process. Even the "normal" Parisians caught in the net of émigré confiscations do not particularly resemble other Frenchmen, because they lived in the country's largest urban center, where they witnessed firsthand a disproportionate share of the political events of the Revolution.

The émigrés themselves were also outliers by nature. Émigrés tended to be wealthy and aristocratic, setting them apart from the French population generally. They were court nobles, military officers, financiers, and magistrates. Happily, they are not the only people who appear in the dossiers. But they appear in numbers that far surpass their share of the French population. Their experience of the Revolution was also rather different from that of most, as they not only chose to flee the country but also ran afoul of revolutionary authorities. Though many people resisted the Revolution and many were unfortunate enough to be targeted by revolutionary laws, these experiences can't be considered the norm. Very little about the émigrés' experience reflects that of other French people in the revolutionary era. The dossiers document outlier cases of property seizure among the outlier population that was targeted in the first place, in a location that is unlike others.

Yet precisely because they are outliers, these sources offer a particularly illuminating window into the heart of revolutionary property reform. For example, legal sources have been particularly fruitful for historians because crime is, paradoxically, revealing of the norms and assumptions that govern a society.[32] Similarly, spectacular cases can offer insight into general attitudes in a way that more mundane matters do not.[33] What is shocking or out of the ordinary reveals what is normal and routine, because the unusual or transgressive forces people to articulate what is standard in a way that would be difficult without a negative example. As the cases of Louise Perrine Chabanais and Henriette Becdelièvre begin to illustrate, the challenging, unusual nature of the questions raised during the confiscation process led administrators to articulate values they may not have under less unusual conditions. Similarly, the exceptional nature of the seizure process identified and linked together people and their property to an extent that is difficult to find in other sources. This is because administrators had to piece together patrimonies and trace family trees in order to figure out who owned what, and also because owners engaged in maneuvering either to protect assets or to take advantage of opportunities presented by the Revolution.

The dossiers also invite us to consider the role of gender in the seizure process. While most of the lists that identified émigrés do not reveal information about gender, women are present in the dossiers created during the seizure process to a striking extent. Families often left together, and in fact, the regime later would seek to draw the younger generation back to France with conciliatory laws. In 1793, children under ten were exonerated from being counted as émigrés; the same law extended the opportunity to return to France without penalty to girls under fourteen.[34] As Louise-Perrine Chabanais's case shows, that when women fled, they could be targets of the émigré confiscation laws if they owned property. Chabanais was a widow at the time of the confiscation: her husband, Claude-Théophile Colbert-Chabanais, died in September 1789. Other women, like Henriette Becdelièvre, appear in the records because they stayed behind to guard property while their relatives joined the military or fled the guillotine. Becdelièvre was already a widow; when a married woman remained in France and her husband emigrated, her property would not be confiscated, but half of any assets she shared with her husband would be, along with whatever belonged to him by lineage. Wives of émigrés often guarded real assets by living in them, and they held claims of various kinds on their spouse's property. As Chapter 5 will show, upon marriage, women were more likely to receive cash or nontangible property claims as opposed to real estate titles. Similarly, widows could be granted use of their husband's assets for their lifetimes. Understanding property to include a range of forms, as well as the various kinds of claims that could be made on them, makes women's ownership more visible—although, as we will see, women's ability to exercise property claims often required skillful navigation of law and administration.

Organization of the Book

The structure of this book is meant to reinforce its methodological turn from legal to social history. In the first three chapters, I examine the key groups of people involved in shaping émigré property law and negotiating the property seizure process: lawmakers (in their roles as both jurists and politicians), administrators, and the émigrés themselves. Chapter 1 introduces the political vision of the lawmakers who articulated property policy; Chapter 2 examines the émigré laws specifically and considers their relationship to the political goals of the Revolution writ large; and Chapter 3 pieces together the seizure process as administrators attempted to carry it out in practice. These three chapters draw on an array of printed and manuscript sources, including laws, legislative debates, and administrative documents produced during the seizure process.

In the last three chapters, I turn to the practices of property ownership in the revolutionary period, examining what people owned and how they made use of it, as these practices are revealed by the seizure process. These chapters read the dossiers from the Paris Domain bureau to understand how owners engaged with property. Each chapter approaches the dossiers from a different perspective. In Chapter 4, I focus on property in the social context of its use, tracing the property negotiations in a single dossier (that of Henriette Becdelièvre) and considering the forms of value it constructed. Chapter 5 turns to property in the context of the family, finding a tension between the ways families mobilized assets strategically and the moralizing approach that lawmakers took to family relations. Finally, Chapter 6 examines property as a financial tool. Here, a series of cases drawn from the dossiers show that, in contrast to political rhetoric that emphasized land ownership, real estate was not a more sought-after form of property but rather fit into an array of types of assets that owners and other parties mobilized and leveraged. These three successive readings of the sources reflect the layered uses of property that ultimately made confiscation such a complicated and difficult process. Of course, these social uses of property overlap with and inform one another. Chapter 5 focuses on family relations, but a family also figures at the center of Chapter 4. Chapter 6 foregrounds the potential of assets to be leveraged for credit, but Chapters 4 and 5 also feature examples of property being leveraged. My aim, in taking this approach, is to use these successive readings to generate a deeper understanding of property's many functions and how they can intersect—not to claim that these functions are distinct or isolated from one another.

While the book begins with the definitions of property offered by law and policymakers, its goal is not to privilege these perspectives but rather to undermine them successively over the course of the chapters that follow. First approaching property as a legal matter, much as the revolutionary lawmakers themselves did, the book then follows the process they set in motion—one that swerves *away* from the law, into the administration it created and the practices that officials sought to grasp and enact. In this way, the organization of the book itself demonstrates the limits of law as a tool for understanding the nature of property. If the law is a gateway to this story, it also conceals important tensions among the uses and functions of property that the émigré confiscations are well positioned to illuminate.

The Legacy of Revolutionary Property Reform

This is a story of the French Revolution, but to the extent that the regime of property formalized in the revolutionary era is still in effect, it is a story that continues today. This book concludes with the Civil Code of 1804, which established the terms of property that, in France, are still in force—most notably, in Article 544 of the Code, that property rights are attached to individuals and are absolute, within the limits of the law. As we will see, however, the Civil Code did not answer fundamental questions about the nature of property so much as it formalized ambiguities in operation during the Revolution.

The regime of property rights put in place by the French Revolution became the basis of modern democratic government in France, and it also became the central source of political conflict in that country in the nineteenth century. Property defined the way people thought about justice, social relations, and legitimate authority after the Revolution, regardless of whether they approved of private property. Because contestation around property rights is coeval with modern democracy, it is especially important to attend to the circumstances surrounding the creation of those rights. Property rights, as they were established in the Revolution, were contested almost from the moment they were made law.[35] The socialist thought of Marx, Proudhon, and others primarily critiqued bourgeois property relations, which were understood to have been a product of the French Revolution.[36] At the heart of these critiques lay the charge that the Revolution solidified protections for property owners and cemented in place a system of inequality that allowed for the exploitation of those without property.

Contestation around property rights was not limited to France. Property rights were exported with European colonialism, generating new conflicts and ambiguities. In the case of the British Empire, histories of India and Bengal have already brought together legal history with cultural and social history to reveal the slippages in European property rights as they were imposed in those places.[37] In North Africa under French colonial rule, administrators bracketed out family law, allowing multiple legal regimes to coexist when it came to administering property for colonized people versus colonizers.[38] And yet, legal regimes allowed for greater elasticity and ambiguity than the politics of colonialism would tolerate, as administrators sought to assert sovereignty through control of property claims.[39] Colonized people used the courts to challenge colonial administrators, relying on European property law to defend their claims.

The questions raised by the property reforms of the Revolution are still active. The reforms to property rights in the French Revolution paralleled reforms in the United States and elsewhere; individual rights and a regime of private property underpin modern liberal democracies broadly. As property rights have been enshrined in modern liberal political communities, the foundational questions that dogged property rights at their revolutionary birth have not gone away. There is still a broad field of possibility within property rights, which modern democracies continue to explore. Intellectual property law is still testing the boundary between the claims of an individual and the interests of society. When is a discovery, such as a new medicine, so vital to public welfare that property rights become unethical? New technologies have raised a whole host of property issues, as questions of privacy and bioethics frequently resolve into questions of ownership of one's personal data or one's body. In addition, property law recognizes the right of individuals to abuse their property, but the question has arisen whether the public interest may place limits on the amount of pollution an individual can produce. Finally, modern governments have long maintained a right of expropriation. Under conditions that continue to be defined in law, democracies can seize the property of individual citizens.

The émigré confiscation process offers the opportunity to examine the origin point of property rights in the revolutionary regime from a new perspective, one that highlights contestation and innovation. Property rights have never been purely a legal matter; they engage assumptions about social life—family relations and relations between citizens—and cultural assumptions about what property is or should be, who should have it, and the uses to which it can be put. The Revolution aspired to go beyond France and to be universal, creating an order based on equality and rights that would be the same for all people and based on humankind. But what it built was particular and conjunctural—situated in a time and a place.[40] The dossiers of the émigrés bring the historian back to this particularity, in the hopes that understanding it more deeply will shed light on the social and political forms it generated.

Property Law in Revolutionary Society

THE AIM OF THE REVOLUTION, expressed by its leaders, was to dramatically rupture the order of the Old Regime. Legal reform was integral to this process of reconstituting French society, and property played a key role in the major legal reforms of the Revolution from the start. The revolutionary National Assembly abolished feudalism, which at its core was a property regime, on the night of August 4, 1789. The Declaration of the Rights of Man and Citizen of 1789, in turn, recognized property as a foundational right belonging to the people. Today, legal scholars use the term *ancien droit* or "old law" to refer to the legal regime of the Old Regime; the term points to the significance of the legal rupture that the Revolution brought about. This understanding of revolutionary law as being characterized by rupture is shared by historians of the Revolution. Rafe Blaufarb, for example, has argued that the legal reform of property was the signal achievement of the Revolution, establishing a "great demarcation" between old and new regimes.[1]

Yet even as revolutionary law remade French society, it did so according to assumptions about property law and social relations carried over from the Old Regime. Lawmakers embraced the notion, established by natural rights theory generally and social contract theory specifically, that the individual is the bearer of rights. At the same time, they held on to the notion that members of society are interdependent, linked together in particular by the shared space of the public domain. Revolutionary property law did not merely mark boundaries, delineating what belonged to whom. Rather, property law made property itself the instrument of social reform. The way that lawmakers and politicians defined property under the law says a great deal about the kind of society that they sought to build.

Revolutionary law is widely understood to have introduced a tension between individual and society: individuals became the bearers of rights, but democracy placed new requirements on communal social life.[2] On the one hand, property became an individual right: vested in the owner alone, property rights cannot be infringed except in very particular circumstances. On the other hand, property also linked the individual citizen to the community, abstractly through the social contract and concretely through voting rights and property taxes.[3] Maintaining a balance between the rights of the individual and the claims of the community is crucial to democratic society; when democratic states violate the rights of their citizens, they cease to be democratic. And yet the solution cannot be to eliminate the tension. In the French Revolution, at least, lawmakers sought to serve both purposes through their legal reforms, and they carried out this intention, notably, in their property policy—as we will see in this chapter.

The customary law of the Old Regime accommodated new ways of defining property with great elasticity, recognizing that social relations—which were structured in part by property rights—evolved over time. In 1789, the revolutionary National Assembly dismantled the social order framed by Old Regime customary law, but it did not entirely eliminate the underlying legal traditions. While enshrining the individual as citizen and legal subject, revolutionary lawmakers recognized that citizens continued to belong to deeply rooted networks of social interdependence and mutual benefit. This tension between new and old played out in property law, where the idealized relationship between the citizen property owner and the state was often complicated by the fact that property continued to mediate a range of other relationships.

This chapter will explore two crucial areas where old and new ideas about property were uncomfortably synthesized in revolutionary law. The first area is legislation on authorship and public lands, where a tension emerged between the individual and the community—that is, between recognizing the claims of individual authors and defending the community's interest in the free circulation of ideas. Laws governing property transfers, mortgages, and taxation, meanwhile, reflect a second tension between transparency and privacy—that is, between the transparency of ownership information that facilitated political and economic life, and the privacy of this information that personal life and reputation required. These cases highlight the ways in which the Revolution did not so much break with the past as rearrange it. In some regards, property rights continued to serve the same constitutive political functions they did in the Old Regime; in others, property rights took on crucial new purposes in revolutionized society. Property was meant to be an individual right and yet also was linked to community interests. What was new about the right to property that emerged from the Revolution was its plasticity—that is, its ability to serve multiple and potentially conflicting purposes at the same time.

Old Regime Corporate Society

Property rights in the Old Regime were governed by customary law, a set of long-standing principles that guided legal outcomes.[4] Different regions of France had their own customs, making the country an enormous patchwork of jurisdictions. Often, however, the customary regimes informed and cross-pollinated each other: a jurist in one area might look to another to see how customary tradition handled a given issue if his own was "mute" on it. The relationships between different customs were guided by a loose hierarchy: those that had been compiled extensively had authority as a reference for regions with a less well-articulated custom, and, in cases of uncertainty, Paris custom took precedence over all others. This legal decentralization was possible, in part, because France did not have a written constitution. What it did have was a constitutional tradition that governed the relationship between the king and judicial authorities. As a divine right monarchy, this tradition was informed by theology, which centered the person of the king and emphasized the cooperative, interdependent nature of society. The monarchy was also feudal in origin, meaning that the king was the most powerful lord, a position that stemmed from his property holdings and the wealth they generated.

Customary law broadly gave shape to French social relations in Old Regime feudal society.[5] It also guided the distribution of property and determined what types of claims were recognized as property. The king was sovereign over all property but recognized ownership privileges of lords. Lords, in turn, retained fundamental claims to property even as they ceded the physical possession and the use of it to tenants, who could buy and sell it among themselves. In this system, possession was only one element of ownership, and ultimately it was the weakest: the farmer who possessed a plot of land was only a tenant, even though his lease might be a perpetual one. The array of entitlements attached to ownership were described as privileges, not rights, since they were granted at the king's pleasure. Beyond possession, they included the ability to hunt, to keep pigeons, to collect certain types of taxes, to display a coat of arms, and to administer justice on one's lands, among other things. As this rather heterogeneous assortment suggests, some of the privileges of ownership were connected to the use of the land, and others allowed the owner to engage in activities associated with his social position.[6] This was because in the feudal system, the kind of ownership claims a person could make depended on his social qualities. The entitlements that came with the ownership of noble lands were limited to nobles; until the eighteenth century, a commoner who bought a piece of land that had such privileges attached to it could not exercise them.[7]

Customary law shaped more than just property relations. It framed an entire feudal social order, of which different kinds of property ownership constituted only a part.[8] The various tasks that, together, ensured communal survival were divided among different classes of people. In this system, articulated in the twelfth century, society was analogous to a human body, much as the community of faithful within the Catholic Church was imagined to take the form of the body of Christ.[9] The king represented the head, and other parts of society represented the different body parts.[10] Each part of the body—each social group—was understood to have a distinct role to play in order to ensure the proper functioning of the whole. The three primary groups, or orders, were the clergy, the nobility, and the common folk: those who prayed, those who fought, and those who worked the land.[11] The separate bodies or corporations that made up society had access to different types of property, according to their purpose.[12] The nobility had access to the privileges of lords, while the other two orders enjoyed their own forms of property. The Church held vast quantities of land that came into the possession of particular bishops and priests during their careers but still belonged to the Church as a whole rather than the individual. Trade guilds held monopolies granted in letters patent from the king; rural commoners had access to feudal leases on nobly held lands. For the Church, as for guilds, membership in the corporate body granted access to the property. In every case, membership in a social order or caste determined the type of property—whether feudal, guild, or ecclesiastical—one could own.

Continuity and Rupture in Revolutionary Law

If property defined social and political life in the Old Regime, it was also through property that the old order was overthrown in the early months of the Revolution. Feudalism was ended in a single evening as members of the Assembly who held feudal privileges stood up one by one and renounced them on August 4, 1789.[13] The now-iconic events of this night reflected a series of overlapping imperatives. On the one hand, members of the Assembly renounced their individual privileges in favor of a common goal. Giving up their special status, they put themselves on the same footing as the rest of the population and made equality of rights possible. On the other hand, their actions also contributed to a profound change in property rights, as the interdependent model of the Old Regime was rejected in favor of individual ownership. The decision to abolish feudalism initiated a massive transfer of ownership: property that had technically belonged to feudal lords and was perpetually leased to tenant farmers became the sole property of the tenants when those lords renounced their claims.[14] An action taken in the name of the common good brought individual property rights into existence. Every person would be granted the same rights, regardless of social standing, and each person's political status was determined by his individual identity as a citizen. The continued existence of a legal regime of enslavement, of course, was a glaring exception to revolutionary citizenship.[15]

In reforming property rights, lawmakers proceeded with the goal that citizens should be free to dispose of their property as they wished—without any limitations or obligations of the kind imposed by royal privilege. This idea was provocative and new, explicitly contradicting the interdependent nature of Old Regime property. In the Old Regime, for example, a person could own a piece of land but not the rights to hunt game that he found on it. Likewise, he could write a lengthy treatise on a subject of general interest but be prevented from publishing it. In this sense, the revolutionary legislatures took what we might call today a liberal approach to property: they believed that everyone would benefit if landowners and entrepreneurs could pursue profit freely.

For example, when members of the Legislative Assembly abolished feudalism on August 4, they immediately gave owners of real property the right to hunt on it. This meant, functionally, that nobles who had previously pursued game with guns and hounds across tilled fields would no longer be able to do so. While a committee later revisited the issue, ultimately the principle held. In July 1791, landowners were also given mineral rights for their property. Under the Old Regime, the king had retained claims to any wealth found underground. Perhaps most importantly, owners of agricultural property were "freed" from collective obligations that governed what they could plant, when they could harvest, and whether they could fence their fields.[16] Overall, such legislation broadened real estate rights to give owners more discretion over the use of their land and broader claims to its produce.

Some lawmakers expressed concerns that in a system based on equality, liberated from the hierarchies of the Old Regime, people could become selfish.[17] What if a spiteful landowner chose to set fire to his wheat fields, to the detriment of the public grain supply? These concerns were not new; ensuring a stable supply of bread was a concern of the Bourbon monarchy. The Old Regime had carefully policed the production and sale of grain and flour, and this operation continued during the Revolution.[18] This was also true of butchers and the meat market.[19] These concerns, however, represented a clear minority. Most lawmakers believed that greater freedom for property makers would serve the public interest. In this, many of them were influenced by a movement of economic thought known as physiocracy, which maintained that allowing property owners to use their possessions as they wanted would increase agricultural efficiency, generating wealth for the state. The idea that property owners were in a special position to benefit or harm the public would also prove influential in shaping attitudes toward the émigrés, as Chapter 2 will show.

The irreconcilable tension between the rights of the individual and the interest of the community has been taken as a sign that the core values driving revolutionary reform were dangerously flawed.[20] A system that recognizes limitations on the individual in the name of a vague "public good" must inevitably, this argument runs, degenerate into an oppressive, dictatorial system such as the one instated during the Terror. This insistence on clear lines between individual rights and the community, however, reflects a liberal ideal of personal freedoms that has never existed in any modern democracy.[21] In fact, it is exactly in the fraught space between the rights-bearing citizen and the regulating state that modern democracy took root and flourished.[22]

While the Revolution introduced the radically new political identity of the citizen, citizenship depended on an existing understanding of the interdependence of individual and society. In dissolving the privileges that had separated members of the different estates, lawmakers created a nation of citizens who shared a common cause and common rights. The entwinement of individual and community interests is elegantly demonstrated by two legal concepts that were defined during the Revolution: rights of authorship and rights of the public domain. Both concepts were established specifically to balance the interests of the individual with those of the community, a fact that distinguishes them from other types of property regulated by lawmakers. Both deal with the open space or "town square" of free exchange that lawmakers understood to be essential to democratic society. Each poses a paradox. Property laws around authorship recognized an individual's right to control the flow of their own ideas, but also limited that right in favor of the public interest, on the grounds that new ideas served democratic debate. Public domain law attributed ownership of common public spaces to the state—though in a regime of popular sovereignty, it is arguably nonsensical and even outright problematic for a disembodied entity to exercise property rights. In the first instance, individual rights were limited in favor of the public interest; in the second, for the same reason, a community interest received recognition reserved for individuals. Both areas of law recognized an unusual individual property right on the grounds that it serves the public interest to do so.

Authorship: A New Kind of Property

Property law was engineered by French revolutionary lawmakers to produce desirable social outcomes, designed from the start to foster certain types of behavior. The case of copyright law offers an especially clear example of how lawmakers' aims for the new social order shaped their definitions of property, as copyright was designed at once to encourage individual genius and to harness it in service of the open debate on which democracy depended. In 1791 and 1793, the Constituent Assembly and Convention passed landmark laws on authorial rights. Together, the laws gave the authors of literary and dramatic works a right of property in their creations. On the one hand, this embrace of copyright law exemplified the Assembly's prioritization of individual rights: copyright empowered an author to assert their rights against others who might want to make use of the work. On the other hand, the Assembly was careful to limit those rights. Property law thus not only recognized ideas as property but also sought to establish their natural limits.

The idea that an author "owns" their work depends on a particular idea of authorship that emerged in Europe during the eighteenth century. Before the Enlightenment, ideas had never been considered property. The Enlightenment, however, fostered a new reverence for genius that treated the artist as an exceptional, unique individual. Isaac-René-Guy Le Chapelier, the influential member of the Legislative Assembly who drafted a report on literary property for the body, described literary works as "the most sacred, the most legitimate, the most unassailable, and . . . the most personal forms of property."[23] By describing creative work in this way, Le Chapelier aligned himself with a relatively new understanding of authorship. The legal scholar Jean Domat likened the author's creation of a literary work to the divine act of creation. The comparison notably suggests that the author is acting like God, rather than responding to divine inspiration. This view reflected the emerging prioritization of the individual, as well as the secularizing emphasis on man's capacity for progress and innovation.[24] The human spirit was deemed capable of producing original and beautiful ideas. It was at this time that the idea of the genius took hold—the singular, boundary-breaking individual who could push all of humanity forward with his insight and creativity.[25] The idea of literary works and inventions as property developed from this view of creation as an intensely personal act, connected to an individual's unique interiority.

Revolutionary jurists acknowledged the claims of authors and inventors in tandem, recognizing the close relationship between these two figures.[26] Patent, however, was driven less by a reverence for genius than by recognition of the state's interest in encouraging the creative energies of individuals. Inventions had the power to improve lives and transform society.[27] The Crown actively encouraged individual innovation by offering prize contests and even contracting with inventors to develop useful things.[28] This interest in fostering ideas was not purely utopian: industrial competition with England added a geopolitical dimension to the business of ideas.[29] Being the first to develop a new technology gave a nation an edge over competitors, as other nations would be forced to import a desirable new commodity.[30] British industrial spies had stolen the technology to weave silk from the factories in Lyon, and after Britain developed the technology to produce printed cottons, Parliament banned imported cloth from India. Fostering new ideas was a state interest, but it was also a specifically national one.

When it came to copyright, French printers initially made the case that authors should have a property right in their work. Through the mid-eighteenth century, the monarchy policed printing by licensing a small number of printers and holding them responsible for the material they produced. Tight control of printing made rights of authorship moot in practice, as printers paid authors for manuscripts and then prosecuted anyone who pirated them. By the middle of the eighteenth century, however, licensed printers began to face increased competition from illicit sources. Underground printing thrived, partly in response to the huge demand for popular works, and partly in response to royal censorship, the other key element in the control of printing.[31] In a set of lawsuits, printers championed the rights of authors as a way to fight piracy and defend the investment they made when they purchased a manuscript legitimately.[32] They argued that it was in the public interest to make sure that only high-quality, genuine texts made it to market.

In the 1760s, French authors began to assert their rights against printers, changing the nature of the conflict and, accordingly, reorienting the public interest. Most notably, in 1761, the heirs of the fabulist La Fontaine sued his publisher for the right to his works.[33] Having fought to establish perpetual authorial rights, the printers' guilds suddenly faced the possibility that they could lose the rights to a manuscript they had purchased when the author died. Tireless litigation between printers and authors ensued, until the king responded with a royal decree in 1777. The decree confirmed that an author's rights were perpetual, but only allowed them to be ceded for the lifetime of the author. The decree was intended to increase the circulation of useful knowledge in printed works. By allowing heirs to renegotiate contracts with printers after an author's death, the decree made it possible for books to be reprinted that might otherwise have gone out of circulation.

Both authorship and invention were compared to a laborer who, upon working the land, earned a right of ownership in its fruits.[34] The lawyers and commentators who made this comparison evoked the theory of John Locke, who was associated with the idea that labor generates property rights. When they evoked Locke's laborer, lawmakers essentially suggested that all forms of property were fundamentally the same and protected by the same rights. But at the same time, the law gave authors more limited recognition than other property owners. The claims of authors did not have the same status as other forms of property, because unlike other property claims, authorial rights were not perpetual—they expired after the author's lifetime plus ten years.[35] This recognition of creative works as a form of property and simultaneous limitation on that property right makes clear that the Assembly did not develop property law in the abstract. On the contrary, property law was crafted according to the role it played socially in structuring human relationships under the new regime.

It is important to recognize that authorial rights took on new political importance during the Revolution. Since the reign of Louis XIV, the Bourbon monarchy had sought to control the circulation of ideas through censorship.[36] During the early years of the Revolution, from 1789 to 1791, revolutionary leaders embraced—at least in theory—a more open model of public discourse. The free circulation of ideas was a fundamental value of revolutionized society, because access to ideas was an urgent matter of public interest.[37] For the people to be represented, they had to talk to each other—Rousseau's model of the general will, for example, assumed extensive, open debate. Furthermore, revolutionary leaders prized the free flow of ideas as the surest means of shaping public opinion and guarding against encroaching despotism. The abstract entity of "public opinion" had enormous power in this new democratic context as a kind of proxy for truth.[38]

The shape that copyright and patent took in revolutionary law, then, must be understood within its political context. On the one hand, the value the National Assembly placed on the free circulation of ideas was a logical extension of the abolition of guild property, as free circulation directly challenged the power of the printers' guild. On the other hand, maintaining certain protections for authors through copyright law was meant to inspire greater public expression. Practically speaking, public opinion was expressed in a healthy marketplace of newspapers and political pamphlets. From the smallest points of conflict to the greatest matters of governance, open discussion and debate were considered the means for arriving at just solutions. Perhaps counterintuitively, the best way to protect public debate was to guarantee authors the means to earn money from their work, granting them a right of property in their manuscripts.

Copyright law protected the rights of the individual, but only because those rights were understood to serve the public interest. Limits were placed on the individual's ability to exercise copyright specifically in order to keep ideas in circulation. Other forms of property are perpetual, meaning that they can be passed on from one generation to the next. This is an essential aspect of property: no one buys a chair, a painting, or a house with the assumption that it will revert to the state in fifty or one hundred years. While lawmakers could have treated authorship in the same way, as a perpetual right, the possibility of an author keeping unlimited control of an idea in perpetuity seemed too obviously against the principles of democracy. Much as Old Regime customary law had formulated property rights to serve the community and not simply individual property owners, revolutionary property law functioned as the handmaiden of the state in its quest to resolve the conflict between individual and community interests. Revolutionary copyright law offered one solution to this conflict. Faced with the same tension between property rights and public good, lawmakers would find a different solution when it came to public lands, known as the public domain.

Public Domain: A "Traditional" Form of Property Made New

Authorship rights navigated an area where property reached an extreme of individualism, reflecting the thoughts and ideas that a person generated in their own head. The counterpoint to this intense personal relationship between owner and property is the public domain, the wide-open space where nothing is owned and ideas are freely exchanged. It is a metaphor that also has a concrete form, in the roads, waterways, and open spaces that are shared by everyone. But who is "everyone"? In the Old Regime, these types of property belonged to the Crown; in the Revolution, they became the property of the state. But while it is fairly simple to imagine the Crown owning land, as the inalienable property of the monarch, it is less easy to understand who constitutes the state in a regime based on popular sovereignty. What does it mean for the people, as an abstract entity, to own something?[39] The fate of the royal Domain modeled the ambiguous relationship between the sovereign people and the individual citizen.

When the National Assembly declared itself sovereign in the summer of 1789, it shifted sovereignty from the Crown to the nation. It was not immediately apparent, however, how the people, as both the unified sovereign and individual citizens, could coexist. For example, although the people were sovereign, they could not be consulted *en masse*. To solve the problem of how to make popular sovereignty work in a state as large as France, the Abbé Sieyès had worked out a justification for representative government—although this solution was not without its own drawbacks.[40] Would representatives be free to exercise their reason, or must they follow their constituents' wishes? In addition, according to social contract theory, the root of sovereignty was property rights. How could people who owned nothing exercise sovereignty? The Constitution of 1791 addressed the problem by creating different tiers of citizenship, based on tax brackets, and granting additional voting rights and the ability to stand for election to those in higher tiers—but this seemed to violate the principle of equality.[41]

When the people assumed sovereignty, they also assumed ownership of the royal Domain: both the royal lands that belonged to the king and the public lands that fell to the Crown, such as navigable waterways and roads. At the origins of French kingship in the eighth century, the king was considered a feudal lord who dominated the other Frankish lords. As such, he owned vast fiefs in his traditional stronghold of the Ile-de-France, the extraordinarily fertile region that encircles Paris. As sovereign, the king also retained dominion over the entire territory of France and ownership of public lands such as roads, navigable rivers, certain types of riverbanks, and public squares. The relationship between the king as a landowner and the king as sovereign was uneasy. Jurists compared the king's relationship with the Crown lands to a marriage, in which the property that one spouse brought to the union could not be disposed of or inherited by the other. The king was sovereign, but he did not really own the sovereign domain.

During the Revolution, the relationship between the sovereign and the Domain only became more problematic. Popular sovereignty depended on the idea that the people were the ultimate proprietors of the nation. Beginning with the renunciation of feudal property on August 4, the National Assembly limited property rights to individuals, on the grounds that only individuals could be members of the sovereign. Accordingly, the guilds and the Church had lost their corporate property. The relationship of the people to the Crown lands after 1791 bore an uneasy likeness to the relationship of the Church or the guilds to their property under the Old Regime. That is, if only individual citizens could own property, then how could the abstract entity known as the people own the Domain?

The Constituent Assembly took pains to eliminate any doubt surrounding the status of the Domain. The law that formally recognized the new, national, Domain described the nation's ownership of it as "the most perfect that one could imagine, because there exists no superior authority that could modify or restrain it."[42] The unspoken comparison was to the royal Domain, which had been limited. And yet, the law implied that the ownership rights exercised by citizens—which could be limited by law—were also less perfect. This was the crux of the paradox posed by sovereignty: it was a power seated in the people, and yet it was capable of dominating any one citizen. The people were sovereign, as a whole, but any one person could not exercise that sovereignty and, on the contrary, was subject to it.

Nevertheless, the Domain served a vital function. Shared ownership and administration of common spaces served the common interest. The Domain also encompassed the state fiscal apparatus, since public property included financial assets in addition to real estate. The Domain modeled the curious absence at the heart of popular sovereignty— unlike the royal domain, owned by the king, the people as an entity could not properly own property; and yet, there was no other owner besides the people to reasonably own shared public lands.

In the case of public property, as in the case of intellectual property, revolutionary law offered an initial answer to profoundly thorny questions: How should private property be balanced with public interest? What can be owned? Can ideas be private property? If waterways should not be private property, then who owns them? In these areas of the law, there could be no hard line between individual and community, private and public. Protecting the interests of one served the interests of the other. Yet extending the status of property to these categories was also an awkward exercise. Each new form of property required special justification, including the claim that they were better than other forms of property. Le Chapelier maintained that authorial property was "the most perfect that can be conceived of," a sentiment expressed almost identically in the Domain decree.[43] He compared the right of authorship to the relationship between a parent and a child, suggesting that the integrity of the claim was not only unassailable but even self-evident. The right of the Domain, based on the priority of the state's claim to property, similarly went without justification; it was taken as self-evident that certain types of land should be held in common. The Assembly's approach to authorial rights depended on the political value attributed to the circulation of ideas; their approach to the Domain depended on the long-standing expedient of reserving common spaces from private ownership. While imperfect as forms of property, both served essential functions in the minds of the lawmakers who granted them legal protections.

Competing Imperatives of Publicity and Respectability

When lawmakers established property as an absolute right attached to the individual, the consequences of this move were not self-evident. Lawmakers shaped property rights in accordance with the kind of society they wanted to create, namely, one in which individuals met each other as equals and exchanged with each other—in public debate and in the market—in a context of transparency. For authorial rights and the public domain, achieving this goal meant extending the range of things that could be called property to include copyrighted ideas and public lands, two categories that fit badly into the model of individual property rights and yet were deemed essential to constructing a public space for democratic exchange. In addition to deciding which types of property would be recognized, revolutionary lawmakers contended with another set of issues regarding transparency. The link between property and citizenship elevated the importance of information about ownership, as participation in civic life depended on how much property a person owned. Democracy required transparency.[44] And yet, long-standing legal traditions identified the nature of property as fundamentally personal and intimate.[45] The demands of publicity competed with the interest of families and businessmen, who did not want the details of their assets laid bare for all to see. Once again, revolutionary reforms layered a new value (transparency) onto an existing value (privacy) without eliminating the latter. This divided individual citizens' political lives, which were expected to be open and transparent, from their personal lives, which existed in a realm of privacy protected by a legal shroud of secrecy. Successive revolutionary regimes, from the Constituent Assembly through the Directory, insisted on the importance of property owners to the regime. By placing property requirements on voting rights, each regime sustained a practical need for the state to have information about property ownership. But they variously valued the competing claim for privacy, resulting in reversals and amendments to the reforms that instituted transparency: tax and mortgage law, as well as measures for public land surveys and registration of property transfers.

As the citizen took shape as a political entity, citizen-owned property took on a new public character, connecting its owners to the polity.[46] Political rights, such as standing for election and voting, were linked to property ownership in law.[47] Lawmakers argued that property owners were the best suited for responsibilities requiring a public interest, because property—in their view—raised its owners above petty, private concerns. Owning property tied individuals more closely to the state, because it gave them an interest in the survival of the regime that guaranteed their property. This was expressed positively in the theory of representation, outlined by Sieyès and used to justify the limited suffrage established by the Constitution of 1791. Acting as a representative placed a particular demand on individual citizens, as representatives were understood to represent the interest of the entire citizenry, not simply their own interests or even those of their constituents.[48] By extension, people who did not own property were seen as less committed to the regime. This argument was made by lawmakers in favor of nationalizing Church property in the fall of 1789.[49] Church property, lawmakers claimed, could be distributed to people who had no property in order to stabilize the revolutionary government.

The Directory government replaced the Convention in 1795, after the fall of Robespierre in July 1794, ending the radical period of the Revolution. Directory officials maintained that property owners were better suited to participate in public life than those who did not own property, although they offered different explanations as to why. When

François-Antoine Boissy d'Anglas presented the draft of the Constitution of 1795 to the legislature, he emphasized that property owners were the best educated and the most interested in public affairs; it was logical that they should vote and serve in public office, because "we should be governed by the best."[50] After outlining the excesses in which the propertyless could be expected to indulge should they be given the power to legislate, he noted that "a country governed by the propertied is in the social order; one where those without property govern is in the state of nature." While the Constituent Assembly suggested property was a natural right when it nationalized Church property, the Directory approached property as the product of law. This approach was inherently more conservative, because it justified inequalities of property; if property is a natural right, then everyone is entitled to own some.

As he outlined the new Constitution, Boissy d'Anglas drew a clear distinction between citizens and noncitizens by joining fiscal responsibility and virtue. Nonvoting citizens should still pay taxes, following the principle that "every member of society should contribute to its expenses, however limited their wealth."[51] Conversely, he explained that bankrupts should lose their civil rights because they "are debtors to all of society as a whole; they have betrayed the first duty imposed by it, that of respecting engagements; they are presumed to be acting in bad faith."[52] The language of debt, betrayal, and bad faith offered a counterpoint to the fiscal contribution, fidelity, and frank honesty of the citizen.[53] He concluded that "it is in this way that you establish that emulation of honor and virtue that is the foundation of republics."[54] By this account, making information about assets public was essential to distinguishing the worthy citizens from the unworthy.

The tax code paralleled the limited suffrage regime in this regard, placing the same special responsibility on property owners. In fact, it was by paying taxes that one became an elector, as the property requirements for voting were based on tax brackets.[55] Under the Old Regime, taxation existed in the form of a levy imposed by the king. When sovereignty shifted to the people, taxation became a contribution that citizens were expected to make in support of the polity. The Revolution also introduced a key technical shift in how taxes were assessed. Where the Old Regime had relied on a mix of direct taxes, caste-based levies, and periodic special contributions to fund wars, the National Assembly created an indirect tax based on wealth.[56] Citizens would contribute to the expenses of the polity based on their revenues, with wealthier citizens paying a larger sum.[57] The indirect wealth tax introduced a new wrinkle into the relationship between property owners and the polity. This new tax system measured revenue, but the various rationales for why property owners were more invested in the polity all assumed that property equaled land. New taxes introduced in 1791 targeted non-land assets and businesses.[58]

The revolutionary value of transparency also impacted the operations of credit. In the Old Regime, mortgages were privately contracted between borrower and lender. The system relied on goodwill to prevent borrowers from taking out multiple mortgages. This system had been the target of royal reform in the decades preceding the Revolution, but these were quashed by notarial interests that stood to lose business. Concerns about the publicity of liens appeared in the instructions sent by local assemblies with their representatives to the fateful Estates General of 1789.[59] Mortgage reform would provide greater security to lenders, who would be able to verify whether a property had existing liens before accepting it as collateral. This would make it easier for borrowers to leverage land for investments, facilitating the circulation of credit.

These measures only became more pressing during the Revolution, because the abolition of feudalism made it easier and more desirable to mortgage property. Eliminating the claims of feudal lords reduced the number of ownership claims on real assets by putting them exclusively in the hands of tenants. In addition, freeing these assets from perpetual obligations made them more valuable and easier to sell. The Constituent Assembly debated how to create a public mortgage registry in 1790 but never arrived at a decision.[60] Such a system could work in a variety of ways, each of which would benefit the borrower, the lender, or other lien holders. A borrower who took out a mortgage could designate a specific piece of property for the loan (an option known as *hypothèque spécial*) or apply the loan to all property equally (*hypothèque général*). In June 1795, the Directory finally passed a law reforming the mortgage system under the *hypothèque général* model. The claims of wives and minors were also adjusted: while they had an automatic preemptive claim against any other creditors under the Old Regime, the 1795 law took away this legal privilege. By the time the law took effect in November 1798, however, the system had been reformed again: borrowers would now be required to designate a single property for mortgage, rather than all of their property as a whole; and the claims of wives and minors were reinstated.

The Directory also sought to change the way that property transfers were registered. A public register of property transactions would further secure lending, as it would allow lenders to verify that a borrower actually owned the property being mortgaged or sold. In the Old Regime, property could be transferred by private contract or—in Normandy, when inherited in the direct line—with no contract at all. The only way to know what a person owned was to ask. The Directory's attempts to reform property transfers fared even worse than its halting attempts at mortgage reform. Property transfers had historically required a far broader shield of secrecy than mortgages, which would ultimately win out over the Directory's efforts to introduce new levels of transparency.

A whole range of claims to secrecy characterized the treatment of property under the Old Regime, including, but not limited to, property transfers. These claims were both rearticulated and broadened in revolutionary law and the Civil Code.[61] Such secrecy protected the personal and financial affairs of families, as well as merchants, whose credit depended on their reputation for solvency.[62] Under the Old Regime, families were understood to have a right of privacy known as *secret des familles* or *secret des patrimoines;* individuals also enjoyed an interlinked *secret de la vie privée.* These rights to secrecy extended well beyond property, broadly protecting the private acts of the individual. To use an example often cited by modern jurists, an heir cannot obtain information about bank transactions undertaken by a dead benefactor, as they could reveal maintenance payments to a lover—information protected by the *secret de la vie privée.*[63]

The Revolution introduced revenue-based taxation, as opposed to fixed levies; but taxing people based on their capacity to pay meant the state had to have knowledge of revenue. Lawmakers in the Revolution and into the nineteenth century expressed reservations about instituting an income tax on the grounds that people would have to declare revenues to the state for taxation, and the state would have to verify this information, reaching into the private affairs of citizens.[64] Much as taxes on salt or windows and doors were hated in the Old Regime, they did not require individuals to reveal their private dealings to fiscal authorities.

Secrecy in private affairs protected a person's reputation, and commercial secrecy operated on the same principle. Credit was understood to be a fundamentally private concern, based on a relationship between two people who through their own judgment decided to trust each other.[65] The *hypothèque* attempted to facilitate those judgments by laying bare each party's existing obligations.

While the political uses of property demanded transparency, an individual's property was also intimately connected to their private life, family affairs, and business dealings in ways that demanded privacy. The power of secrecy was so strong that the Civil Code undid revolutionary legislation creating public mortgage registers, dropping the curtain of secrecy anew over family wealth. But while the state dismantled the mortgage registry and obligation to make property transfers public, it maintained its ability to pierce this shield of secrecy. Taxation continued to rely on declarations of revenue, in which individuals were expected to lay bare to the state their private financial operations.[66]

The state's hesitation over the publicity of property came down to the tension between, on the one hand, the private character of property as both a piece of family patrimony and an investment and, on the other, its public character as a token of citizenship. It was the attribute of lineage, shrouded in the secrecy of family affairs, and of the businessman, trusted at their word; but it also became an attribute of the citizen, frank and open, taking their place in the public square. Property could not serve these two antagonistic functions at once. Simultaneously, property played a third role as security against debt. Different types of credit made different demands of property, requiring either full disclosure or a veil of discretion. Consistent across all these functions, however, was the image of the respectable property owner. He could be trusted to form an independent opinion in politics and to honor his debts; he was a responsible patriarch and a sober guardian of his family's wealth. He had to do many things at once, more than was perhaps possible. This tension between transparency and privacy is, of course, not limited to French democracy. It is one with which modern democracies continue to struggle today, made more complicated by new technologies that compromise privacy even as they promise social benefits—from DNA databases to mapping to medical data. The way that revolutionary lawmakers grappled with these issues, first committing to transparency and then recognizing the value of secrecy, is illuminating. The tension between the two could not be resolved; the requirements of democratic society meant keeping the tension alive.

Conclusion

Very few of the laws passed during the Revolution endured. So few, in fact, that legal historians refer to revolutionary law as *droit intermédiaire*—not revolutionary, but intermediate, in between the Old Regime and the Civil Code of 1804. Today, the Civil Code, not the law of the revolutionary period, is hailed as an enduring landmark in the history of law. In the most difficult situations, however, the Civil Code did not provide any more definitive a solution than revolutionary law did. It was not until the 1950s, for example, that either the Domain or the public mortgage register took the form they have today. In these cases, the answers provided by the Civil Code were no less intermediate or provisional than those provided by revolutionary law.

The Revolution did introduce profound change, of a different order. Members of the National Assembly made a powerful statement about the ability of the law to initiate social transformation. Legal reform, their actions showed, could fundamentally change society: at the stroke of a pen, all Frenchmen became equal under the law. Belief in the transformative power of the law endured throughout the Revolution, although legal transformation itself masks a deeper continuity. While the layers of feudal ownership were legally replaced by individual rights, property continued to serve many different functions and secure the same broad array of relationships as it had under the Old Regime. Abstract or concrete, public or private, the terms of ownership depended on both the object and the owner, as well as on the relationship of the owner to other individuals and to society at large.

Reforms to property as a legal concept had a transformative effect on French society, but these were effected within a social and economic context that was itself marked by continuity and change. As a result, revolutionary property reform did not yield a coherent shared social vision, but rather layered differing expectations and assumptions on top of each other. Individual citizens remained profoundly connected with the people around them: business associates, family members, friends. These webs of connections were marked by varying expectations and protections around property rights, which at times tugged in opposite directions. On top of this, lawmakers manipulated property law to fit particular agendas as they made decisions about property in a charged and constantly changing political context.

Nowhere was the significance of politics to decisions about property law more apparent than in the fate of émigré property owners. Faced with the political challenge of emigration, lawmakers debated for years over how to respond. They took action as the settlement between the king and the revolutionary legislature began to collapse. And yet, the émigré issue gave lawmakers the opportunity to articulate and apply their ideas about the responsibilities of citizen property owners to the state. Contingency may have pushed them to act, but it did not prescribe the form that action would take. Indeed, lawmakers crafted a solution that fit their understanding of what property rights should be. In this sense, if the present chapter has approached revolutionary property law as the product of politics, in the sense that property rights were shaped to serve certain political ends, Chapter 2 will approach émigré policy as a matter of property law.

The Émigrés and the Politics of Property

THE EARLY LEGAL REFORMS of the Revolution aimed to create equality by investing individuals with rights; lawmakers sought to redefine property in ways that reinforced this society of equals. The decision to confiscate property from people identified as émigrés seems like a radical departure from this agenda. Indeed, lawmakers were motivated to take action against emigration by the political context they found themselves in. And yet, lawmakers took some pains to justify their measures in legal terms. The legislative response to emigration makes visible a variety of underlying assumptions about the political value of property ownership. Lawmakers considered property ownership to be a crucial aspect of citizenship, such that property owners had special duties to contribute to the prosperity of the nation. The prospect of property owners behaving in antisocial ways was particularly threatening to lawmakers, because they considered the actions of individual property owners to have political and economic significance for the nation as a whole.

The émigré confiscations, to the extent that they draw the attention of historians, are generally viewed as part of the period of radicalism known as the Terror.[1] Laws against the émigrés did harden during this period, which lasted from 1793 to 1794, but confiscation was already underway. Property confiscation, in other words, was not a consequence of the Terror.[2] This is an important distinction. During the Terror, which formally suspended the Constitution of 1792, any laws passed were avowedly extralegal. The lawmakers who framed the émigré laws, however, explicitly addressed the legality of such measures, placing them in continuity with revolutionary property policy.

Émigré property confiscation has also been linked to redistributive social policy in the Revolution. Lawmakers did entertain the idea of redistributing émigré assets to the propertyless, as they had considered doing with Church property. They did not, however, follow through on this idea. But like their decision to seize émigré property, their abortive move to redistribute it expressed a fundamental tension between two understandings of property: as a reward for deserving citizens, on the one hand, and as an asset with a cash value, on the other. Revolutionary leaders, in other words, understood property rights to have an important political function in the new order: property carried a moral valence and had to be placed in the right hands. Property rights also carried an important economic function, as the means to bring about new social projects. In practice, these imperatives could fit together well, if property owners contributed to economic prosperity through their activity. But they could also clash, if property owners did not put their property to good use or engaged in uses that lawmakers disapproved of, such as leveraging it for credit. The laws around émigré property confiscation were taken seriously and show that revolutionary property policy was motivated not by a titanic clash between liberalism and communitarianism but rather by an array of commitments that sometimes aligned with and sometimes contradicted one another.

Three legislatures under three different regimes passed laws relating to émigré seizure: the Legislative Assembly under the constitutional monarchy (1792), the Convention in the First Republic (1792–1795), and the upper and lower houses of the Directory (1795–1799). Each of these bodies had unique dynamics and faced particular political challenges, but tracing émigré policy reveals assumptions and preoccupations that extended across them. The initial law allowing property confiscation was debated and passed by the Legislative Assembly in the winter of 1791–1792, a particularly crucial period of political decomposition. The constitutional monarchy collapsed just six months after the law was passed. The Directory government established in 1794, meanwhile, was more conservative on property rights than the previous two regimes. Yet members of its legislatures did entertain the idea of canceling émigré debt in order to free their property of liens, a move that would have entailed a massive redistribution of wealth from émigré creditors to the state.

Each of the legislatures that handled the confiscation process ultimately opted to maintain property rights, while fretting about the consequences of allowing property to fall into the wrong hands. In each case, a basic defense of property rights was tempered with the conviction that property owners should be the right sort of people. Property in the right hands would be a great boon to the nation, creating prosperity and forming a virtuous citizenry. Allowing property to fall into the wrong hands, however, could lead to injustice and malfeasance. The present chapter will proceed in three sections: first, with an account of the first law sequestering émigré property, passed in the final months of the Legislative Assembly; second, by looking back to the decision to nationalize Church property, made by the Constituent Assembly in 1789, and then looking forward to the laws organizing the sale of émigré property passed by the Convention; finally, with a consideration of the treatment of creditors of the émigrés by the Directory government.

The Émigré Threat

The high-profile departure of "Mesdames," the king's aunts, in February 1791 captivated attention and "spread alarm among the people."[3]

The women were linked to a supposed conspiracy to take the Dauphin (heir to the throne) out of France, a sign of royal resistance to the Revolution.[4] The émigrés also began to coalesce into a military threat, as the Prince de Condé began forming an army at the border with the intention of invading France and reestablishing the Old Regime. Impending belligerence at the borders along with the high-profile defection of Mesdames spurred the Constitutive Assembly to form a committee responsible for drafting a law addressing the émigré issue.[5] The problem was that it wasn't clear that anything could be done to stop the émigrés from leaving. The prospect of limiting free movement was highly contentious, and the Legislative Committee of the Assembly warned that such a law would be "against principles and . . . a true dictatorship."[6] Those for and against a law aligned along existing cleavages between the Left and the Right of the Assembly. Members of the Cordeliers Club and more radical Jacobins wanted to punish the aristocrats who were undermining the Revolution, while those more sympathetic to the king sought conciliation and, above all, preservation of the public order.

A few months later, the political landscape shifted again. Friction over revolutionary reforms finally ignited on June 21, 1791, when Louis XVI and his family attempted to join the emigration and were apprehended in the town of Varennes, near the border of the Austrian Netherlands.[7] Supporters of the king in the legislature passed off the episode as a kidnapping, but no one was fooled. Ire toward the émigrés inspired a set of new, harsher laws punishing emigration. A law dated June 21 closed the borders to exit, and a week later a new law reiterated the ban, with an exception for merchants who obtained passports. In July and August, a pair of laws ordered that anyone absent from France must pay triple their usual tax burden.[8]

Over the fall and winter of 1791–1792 domestic politics continued to deteriorate, elevating the profile of the émigré issue in both the Assembly and the popular press.[9] War looked increasingly appealing to the

Jacobin Club as an exit from political factionalizing and distrust of the king. The émigrés, symptomatic of both internal perfidy and external menaces, offered a satisfying target. It was in these conditions of a newly elected legislature and an increasingly fragile political entente that legislation against the émigrés began in earnest.

In August 1791, the Legislative Assembly voted on a law requiring all French citizens to return to France. In the fall, the Assembly undertook debate about further measures.[10] The path to a law was hardly clear: as Jacques-Pierre Brissot, one of many to speak against a law on emigration, pointed out, "If I violate the law, you have the right to punish me: but if I renounce living under this law, its empire over me is finished."[11] Lawmakers struggled to find a logic that could make emigration a crime. Various proposals presented two quite different lines of reasoning. Some discussed the harm caused by the émigrés in economic terms, while others framed the crime using an understanding of duty that relied on the social contract. If emigration was about citizens and their right to free movement, it was also about money—and property—from the beginning of the debate.

Emigration constituted a financial crime to the extent that émigrés were believed to be taking money and goods with them over the border. Lawmakers discussed the *"émigration des choses"* alongside the *"émigration des personnes."* Pierre-Philippe Baignoux, a member of the Left, and Mathieu Dumas, a member of the Feuillant Party (which supported the constitutional monarchy), used these categories to point out that people could not be controlled like land or produce—they must be left to move freely.[12] Others took a different approach, arguing that neither the movement of people nor the movement of commercial goods could be impeded. Pierre-Edouard Lemontey, who would himself flee to Switzerland in 1793, pointed out that it was impossible to stop the movement of cash, and that attempting to stop the movement of arms could lead to *"facheuses représailles"* (damaging blowback) with trading partners.[13] Blaise Cavellier distinguished between matériel, which he believed should be limited, and other *"marchandises,"* which should be "imported or exported without permission or formalities."[14] The exit of goods was potentially as dangerous as human departures; emigration was an economic problem as much as a political one.

Some legislators believed that the outflow of cash in émigré pockets caused harm that would reverberate widely in the French economy. Claude-Emmanuel Pastoret, who was seated on the right of the Assembly, argued that emigration was a crime not because the émigrés themselves were dangerous but because their actions inflicted real harm on society. Money, as "the sign representing the produce of the earth, and the means of transmitting this," needed to be circulated through society from the rich to the poor, for whom it was "the guarantee of property and of future consumption." By taking their money with them, wealthy émigrés carried off the "salary" of the "poor man."[15] The idea that rich landowners circulated wealth through society via the wages they paid to poor laborers was distinctively physiocratic. The economic doctrine of physiocracy held that all wealth stemmed from agricultural surplus; commercial wealth was simply the circulation of agricultural wealth through society. The key to increasing state revenue, then, was to increase agricultural production. Physiocracy itself was almost intentionally obscure, but the core of its argument— that land was the source of wealth—rang true for many influential politicians.[16]

Although the legislators had different ideas about how to stimulate the economy, the dire state of French finances was readily apparent to all. A sovereign debt crisis and the attendant threat of royal bankruptcy was the proximate cause for the outbreak of the Revolution. Since then, the financial situation had only worsened. The hated Old Regime direct taxes had been abolished and the tax base restructured, decimating receipts.[17] France had declared war on the Austrian Empire, incurring the heavy costs of mobilization. Usually the solution to financing war was to borrow, but the fiscal crisis destroyed the Crown's creditworthiness.[18]

The government owed more than most people thought it could ever repay, was not collecting what it should have been in taxes, and was facing an enormous increase in expenses. From this perspective, the prospect of French citizens damaging the economy by taking wealth out of the country posed a profound threat to the budding nation.

As they discussed the issue, lawmakers also focused on the moral qualities of the émigrés, drawing on overlapping ideas of moral value from eighteenth-century literature and religious thought. Pierre-Victurnien Vergniaud, a Girondin or, one might say, member of the Center Left, described the inevitable fate of the émigré, wandering the Earth, "remorse in his heart and shame on his forehead, becoming forever the dregs of all peoples."[19] The image recalls Cain, cursed to be a fugitive and a vagabond, bearing the mark of his dishonor on his forehead. Jean-François Crestin cataloged the "species, the moral character, and the conduct of these fugitives." The émigrés shared the traits of "fugitives inspired by the same prejudices, in thrall to the same pride, deluded by the same hopes, sustained by the same obstinance." The idea that the émigrés were driven by pride suggested a misplaced sense of honor.[20] For Crestin, the émigrés' actions confirmed their character: "They have led the king to the most false, the most dangerous undertaking," presumably a reference to the royal family's attempt to flee France in June 1791. In his view, the émigrés had already begun to "beg for help against their homeland, from all the despots of Europe." Worst of all, they were guilty "of seducing, of betraying, of corrupting peaceable citizens."[21] This final note of seduction and corruption, torn from the pages of a novel, highlighted the moral turpitude of the émigrés in the language of Enlightenment sentiment.[22]

Emigration by members of the military and princes of the blood—social categories with a clear duty to serve—particularly alarmed lawmakers. As debate generalized to include emigration by all citizens, however, a duty to serve was expanded to apply to all citizens.[23] Existing laws condemned military deserters, but the Assembly heard new reports of mass desertion.[24] By the end of October, discussion of the scurrilous lack of virtue among émigrés, soldiers, and civilians alike had escalated to accusations of outright treason. The language of civilian obligation appeared most clearly after a petition from the Jacobin Club pointed out that "the enjoyment of rights necessarily imposes duties."[25] Antoine-Louis Albitte, who would subsequently join the Mountain (the radical Left of the legislature), reflected the general direction of debate when he moved that "these men, unworthy of bearing the name of Frenchmen, should be deemed despicable [infâme], incapable of ever bearing arms for their country, and should lose the rights of active citizens."[26] The measure exactly paralleled the punishments being proposed for military deserters. In Albitte's mind, emigration had become tantamount to desertion.[27]

The parallel between duties of service and citizenship informed the two most influential proposals presented in the legislature. First, Nicolas Caritat, Marquis de Condorcet, repurposed the language of duty to construct the crime of emigration. He proposed a system of oaths, inspired by the view that, in addition to an "obligation morale" grounded in "these sentiments that a noble and appreciative spirit maintains for his country," citizens were bound by "strict obligations."[28] Specifically, a citizen who left his country had a duty not to act against it for the period during which he "could use against his country means that he received from it, with which he could do more harm than a foreigner." Given this moral obligation, French citizens abroad would be invited to take an oath of allegiance to the Constitution in order to maintain their citizenship while outside France. Alternatively, they could simply swear not to bear arms against France for a period of two years. Those who took this option would be considered foreigners and "could not return to their rights as active citizens except by the same means required of any foreigner."[29] Those who refused to take either oath "will be supposed to have hostile intentions; indeed since they will have refused to disavow them, one could, without injustice, deem them guilty of such."[30] The oath not to bear arms explicitly paralleled the military, which already required such a commitment from soldiers ending their service. The system put citizens in the same position as civil servants or soldiers by assuming that they could, for a specific window of time, have information that could hurt the state.

Vergniaud improved on Condorcet's system by reframing the idea of duty such that émigrés could be deemed guilty without the cumbersome apparatus of an oath. Vergniaud reasoned that the social contract conferred benefits and protections on citizens in exchange for certain commitments, much as the military conferred a salary on soldiers in exchange for their commitment to fight. In the state of nature, man was free to do anything he liked. Upon entering society, however, "man contracts relations with other men, and these relations become so many modifications to his natural state." This concession of liberty was worthwhile because "as the immortal philosopher observes . . . it's less a true alienation of liberty and life, than a means man adopts to better preserve each of these."[31] He did not need to specify that the "immortal philosopher" was Rousseau. Given the protections the nation granted to individuals, "when a nation deems it necessary to its tranquillity to require the assistance of its members, it's a sacred duty for them to pay the tribute of blood or fortune that she requires." If an individual were to refuse such a request, "by his treason, he has broken the social compact." As a result, "the society to which he is unfaithful, no longer owes him any protection, either to his person, or to his property."[32] The proposal did not require an oath, because it assumed that citizens had already made the equivalent of an oath by joining the polity.[33]

The idea that the émigrés had broken the social contract was already circulating when Vergniaud brought it to the floor of the Legislative Assembly. A letter from a regional official in the Isère department had been read on the floor of the Constituent Assembly in October 1790, accusing *"les émigrants"* of "an infraction . . . against the social compact."

It went on to posit that liberty "is essentially inseparable from the obligation to serve the Homeland."[34] In June 1791, a group of concerned citizens in Poitiers sent the Committees of Finances and of the Constitution a letter complaining, "the infraction against this essential part of their obligations is not compensated for in any way . . . these thefts from the State must be repaid, property must stand in place of the person."[35] Petitions and letters to the legislature generally expressed a particularly rabid brand of patriotism; the arguments they made cannot be deemed to have been mainstream. Similar ideas, however, had even been raised before on the floor of the Constituent Assembly, a month after the letter from Poitiers was sent. Bertrand Barère, who would go on to preside over the trial of the king and serve on the Committee of Public Safety, spoke on "measures of Police to be taken against the emigrants." He maintained that "the social compact being established, it is no longer the citizen's place to withdraw himself from a society so holy, so necessary, as long as the homeland is in danger."[36]

Still, both Vergniaud's and Condorcet's proposals were among the more extreme of those proposed in the fall of 1791. Brissot advocated a measure that would punish only functionaries and royal princes who did not return to France, leaving others to come and go freely.[37] None of the proposals went so far as to demand a general sequestration of property; even Vergniaud's proposal only reimposed the triple tax assessment. The measure that was actually passed declared all émigrés to be under suspicion of conspiracy against France and called for the sequester of the revenues of any princes who failed to return.[38] The king applied his royal veto to the decree in short order. The émigré problem continued to hang over revolutionary politics.[39]

The members of the Legislative Assembly returned to the émigré question in the winter of 1791–1792 with renewed vitriol. This time they asked the Committee of Legislation to draft a sample bill to sequester the property of the émigrés, meaning that the state would draw the revenue from the property but not take ownership of it. The report that

Mathurin-Louis Sedillez presented on February 9, 1792, used the same language of contract that Vergniaud had invoked, explaining that "every political association is in reality a contract that produces reciprocal obligations between the State and its members."[40] The proposed decree did not go as far as Vergniaud's proposal on a crucial point. Where Vergniaud concluded that the émigrés had broken the social pact, the Committee suggested that citizens who were absent without cause should simply pay the triple tax burden that had previously been put in force, "as an indemnity for the personal service that every citizen owes the State."[41] But the Assembly was committed to sequestering émigré property. The proposal that won out repeated Sedillez's language of contract but imposed sequestration—without mentioning citizenship.

The punishment was not the only element that the Assembly changed. The wording of the clause about indemnity was also changed, with significant implications. The law justified the measure "considering that it's essential to assure the nation the indemnity that is due it for the extraordinary costs incurred by the conduct of the émigrés."[42] Subsequent legislation clarified that the indemnity was "due to the nation because of the war."[43] In other words, the crime of the émigrés was not simply that they left. It was that they took their money with them. As Jean-François Blanchon rather histrionically put it, the émigrés "have carried off your gold, have sucked out your essence, have pumped your blood."[44] His words suggested that by withdrawing their own money and leaving their own fields fallow, the émigrés deprived those who stayed behind of wealth as well. Vergniaud's use of the social contract had invoked the citizen's moral duty to aid the nation. But the language of indemnity recast the citizen's duty as one of economic productivity and wealth production. The Legislative Assembly, after theorizing property confiscation in terms of the social contract, had ultimately seized property as an indemnification for war expenses—an approach that recognized property as a financial asset rather than a sacred token of membership in the polity. The two qualities—financial asset and token of membership in the polity—were inseparable in the theory of the crime.

The evolving legal basis for the émigré laws clarified the centrality of property to the status of the émigré. The initial law described sequestration as an indemnity for the military expenses the émigrés forced the government to undertake. Around the time that émigré policy shifted from sequestration to confiscation, new laws began to refer to the émigrés in moral terms, as guilty of a "shameful desertion" and of being "bad citizens."[45] But a central facet of that desertion, brought out in the debates, was the *"émigration des choses"* that the émigrés drew in their wake. The purpose of the punishment—sequester and, ultimately, sale of property to indemnify the nation—assumed that the perpetrator had some amount of wealth that was worth taking. The émigré was bad because he was using his property for evil.

In fact, from a practical perspective, only people who owned property could be enrolled on the émigré list. The administration of the émigré laws relied on local authorities and neighbors to identify émigrés in their midst by denouncing any property owners who were observed to be absent from home. The more property a person had, the more likely they were to be absent from any one place at any time. Accordingly, people with properties in multiple, distant places were quickly reported absent. The assumption that an émigré was a landlord, not a tenant, was reflected in the émigré lists themselves, which contained a column for the *"situation des biens"* of each émigré—the name of the community where the person's property was located. Further, individuals who were unlikely to own anything were explicitly excluded from émigré status. The law of 22 nivôse III (January 11, 1795) excepted from the émigré list "workers & [agricultural] laborers . . . who habitually work with their hands." Servants who followed their masters abroad were not granted a universal exception, but they were protected from losing their wages when their master's property was put under sequester.[46]

Because lawmakers positioned property ownership as the defining characteristic of the émigrés, they also necessarily implied that the émigrés were male. Most women, married or single, could not own property in their own name. Married women's relationship to their property was indirect: they had a claim to shared spousal assets, which would revert to them upon their husband's death, along with their dowries, but did not control either.[47] The émigré was understood in relation to the citizen, who was male, owned property, and generated wealth for his own account and for the nation. Of course, widows like Louise-Perrine Chabanais did own their assets directly, and they could be punished as émigrés when they left the country. Wives who stayed behind tried to defend their assets by claiming a widow's portion. After the Convention legalized divorce, women who stayed behind had a new tool to separate and defend their assets. These strategies, however, ultimately highlight the way property owners were assumed to be male.[48]

"Des braves défenseurs de la République"

The prospect of the émigrés' property offered lawmakers, in the immediate, the means to address France's significant sovereign debt and to fund the war. But it also offered the possibility of resolving the problem of social inequality that had presented itself from the fall of 1789. In addition, émigré property could resolve the economic inefficiencies that overly large parcels of land were perceived to cause. The hopes for émigré property were expressed before the émigrés themselves were even constituted as a legal category, and they reflected an ongoing conversation about how property should be distributed in the polity. The goals of paying off the sovereign debt and providing the landless with property were, by definition, mutually exclusive. But, along with theories about the benefits of small holdings, they both depended on the idea that property ownership served a larger purpose, and they employed the rationale that property should not languish in the wrong hands. This section shifts from the justifications for the law sequestering émigré property to debates about what to do with émigré property once it was taken. In doing so, it looks back to 1789 before picking up the narrative in 1792, after the transition from the Legislative Assembly to the Convention in September 1792.

From the earliest months of the Revolution, lawmakers expressed concern that political equality could not be achieved as long as profound inequalities of property continued to divide rich from poor.[49] The argument had been made, during the nationalization of Church property, that the vast ecclesiastical land holdings could be made available to the poor. From this point of view, nationalizing and selling Church property would serve "to diminish the number of individuals who, owning nothing, for this reason are less committed to the public cause [*la chose publique*], and are dangerous in times of calamity or foment."[50] The problem of landless citizens had also come up in the debates over the Constitution of 1791, which imposed property requirements on voters.[51]

The decision to confiscate émigré wealth echoed, in some ways, the decision to nationalize Church property, voted by the Constituent Assembly in the fall of 1789. Much of the debate over Church lands revolved around whether selling them would actually retire the public debt: while advocates of nationalization claimed that it would, opponents defended Church property on the grounds that it could never raise enough money to do so.[52] When the Constituent Assembly voted in favor of nationalization, it justified the decision by pointing out that only individuals—not intermediate bodies like the Church—could own property under the new order. Members of the Assembly thus were motivated both by the knowledge that the sale of Church property could raise needed funds for the state and by the conviction that the Church could not be allowed to own property because it was not a legitimate member of the polity.

The legislation to confiscate émigré property was accompanied by rhetoric that treated land as a reward for deserving citizens. This rhetoric was used negatively in denunciations of the émigrés, and positively in affirmations that émigré lands be made available to deserving citizens who had little or none. The law that called for seized émigré property to be sold urged that émigré lands be sold in small lots, "in view of multiplying the number of small Proprietors."[53] Property should be made available to each destitute head of household.[54] It should be used for the payment of pensions to soldiers and their families.[55] These calls framed property redistribution in terms of either sale or rewards for specific groups. Wholesale redistribution of property was so far from the agenda of any of the legislatures that the mere discussion of it was made punishable by death. The idea was expressed only in coded references to the "Agrarian Law," a phrase that evoked a policy of property redistribution in Ancient Rome.[56]

The idea that a more equal distribution of land would lead to greater prosperity and social stability depended on economic theories that emphasized privately owned agricultural enterprise as the key to wealth. Such theories had been invoked to justify selling the royal Domain, since "real property holdings, turned over a general administration, are struck with a kind of sterility," whereas in private hands the same lands drove commerce and industry.[57] There was a subtle difference between this line of reasoning and the political argument for a polity of citizen landowners, however.[58] Economic theory inspired by physiocracy assumed that some would own land while others worked for wages. Private ownership of land was essential, but widespread ownership was not. An opponent of the plan to nationalize Church property had complained, "One pretends that this operation will be useful to the State, because it's advantageous to increase the number of small owners who drive industry. But can the kingdom be made up of owners alone?"[59] A similar idea later appeared in the émigré debates, when, in 1791, Pierre Paganel argued that abandoned émigré lands were lying fallow, such that "the constant increase of emigrant land-owners leaves . . . idle and without subsistence an equally increasing number of industrial citizens [*citoyens industriels*]."[60] A polity of land-owners was advantageous politically, but not necessarily from an economic perspective.

The text of the law on the sale of Church property expressed the mixture of motivations that inspired it. The opening lines of the decree explained, "The sale of National Domains is the best way to extinguish a large part of the public debt, to inspire Agriculture and Industry, & to procure the growth of the general mass of wealth, by dividing these public lands into private property that is always better managed, & by the possibility that this provides to many Citizens to become landowners."[61] In addition to paying off the public debt, the sale of Church property would spur industry by putting the lands into private hands, and it would make land available to those who had none. These were heavy expectations, and some were mutually exclusive. Paying off the public debt meant selling the lands for more than the landless could afford, so both goals could not be met at once.[62]

Support for expanding property ownership throughout the population had an immediate political expediency. Fears that peasants would attack property owners had motivated decisions in the legislature since the night of August 4. After the abolition of feudalism and the nationalization of Church property, peasants began felling trees in the forests previously protected by these institutions.[63] After the decision to sell émigré lands, abutters of properties under national administration pulled up fences, expanding onto lands left fallow.[64] Confiscating property was politically dangerous, as it could encourage property violations, but it could also be turned to enormous advantage, if seized lands could be distributed to the peasantry. Everything that was said about the future of émigré property, and all the policies enacted, were shaped by the knowledge that such policies would have a direct impact on what was happening in the countryside.

The laws to confiscate émigré property and then to sell it passed in the final months of the constitutional monarchy; when the Convention government was seated after the declaration of the First French Republic in September 1792, it could have done what was not done with Church property and taken steps to make émigré assets available to the poor. As the means of addressing the wealth gap were placed within reach, however, the Convention backed away from such a measure. Though the rhetoric surrounding property became strident, the actual protocol for the sale of émigré property became more conservative. The laws governing land sales changed repeatedly and were not uniformly applied.[65] The few provisions favorable to peasants, such as the division of land into small parcels, were applied so narrowly as to be illusory.[66] Coupons worth 500 livres were promised to destitute families, but the inflation of the assignat and the presence of speculators with deep pockets rendered the coupons that were distributed essentially useless. Other provisions actively impeded peasants from participating in the sales, such as the centralization of land auctions at the county seat rather than at the properties themselves.

In June 1793, just before the moderate Girondins were purged from the Convention—one of the moves that marked the beginning of the radical Terror period—the Convention passed a law definitively stating the principle for the sale of émigré property. The law stated that "the real property of the émigrés will be sold to the best offer and last bidder."[67] This measure was reiterated exactly one month later, in a decree that restated and expanded the existing sale legislation. The same had been true for Church property, which despite early optimism had been sold with an eye to maximizing revenue rather than expanding the propertied classes.

In February and March 1794, at the height of the Terror, the Convention passed a particularly punitive set of laws known as the Ventôse decrees. They called for property to be seized from all suspects of political crimes and redistributed to the poor. It's not clear, however, why the decrees called for a separate list of suspects whose property should be seized, when the revolutionary government had spent three years setting up an administration to handle confiscations. The language of the decrees, which called for redistribution but gave no details, seems strikingly sketchy in contrast to the hundreds of laws detailing the procedure for identifying émigrés and seizing their property. It is not surprising, given this, that the decrees were not widely applied.[68] The sentiment they expressed, however, did not differ all that greatly from earlier émigré legislation.

"La bonne foi"

The émigrés left behind thousands of debts, large and small, which became the responsibility of the state when their property was seized. The question of whether to honor creditors' claims, and to what extent, was debated as an issue of property rights. The claim of a creditor to a borrower's wealth was effectively a claim to property. It also engaged numerous parties with competing priorities, including the creditors themselves, the family members of émigrés, and the Treasury. Debate around how to handle émigré debt engaged questions of deservingness, much as the debates around what to do with Church and émigré property had. The issue of debt, however, scrambled the parameters for measuring who was deserving. This is not necessarily to imply that lawmakers were disingenuous; the point is that debate around the disposition of property was animated by moral calculus, even as the outcome of this calculus shifted or became obscure.

As the gavels fell on émigré property auctions, and as clerks scratched out columns of figures in their account books, it became increasingly clear that the value of émigré estates would not equal the demands being placed on them. If émigré creditors were satisfied to the amount of their claims, the whole value of the property would be swallowed up. Émigré estates had lost considerable value since 1789. Many émigré portfolios contained feudal property and public debt, both of which had their value gutted over the course of the Revolution. In addition, the discredited and devalued assignat hurt the sale of émigré property, which did not command the prices at auction that Church property had. On top of this, buyers felt squeamish about the idea of purchasing the property of private owners who were likely to return.[69] Lawmakers understood these latter devaluations in particular as a potential liability for the state, which creditors could claim had destroyed their collateral.[70]

The Convention government first addressed the issues posed by émigré creditors in the provisions of March 1793, and their status continued to be revised throughout the Revolution. Initially, the law required émigré creditors to sue for their debts, and only allowed presentation of claims on debts contracted before February 1792. The law of 1 floréal III (April 20, 1795), passed under the Directory government, revised the status quo by converting private émigré debt to public debt. Creditors would no longer have to sue for their debts, but they would be paid in various forms of paper, including certificates to buy *biens nationaux,* shares of public debt, or assignats. They could expect to receive about a third of the value of their claims.[71] In April 1795, the policy was revised to cover only émigrés who were not "in bankruptcy [*faillite*] or notoriously insolvent." The phrase "notoriously insolvent" reflected how difficult it was to determine the state of an émigré's finances, as debt from a single émigré could be scattered all over the country.[72] Within Paris, determining a person's solvency had its own challenges. As René Eschasseriaux pointed out, "We know that with the exception of those who had a certain display of fortune or of renown, these borrowers were either unknown, or barely known."[73]

Suspicion characterized the attitude of lawmakers toward creditors generally. In the spring of 1795, the Convention began to debate returning property to the heirs of those condemned by the Revolutionary Tribunal. One argument against such a policy was that reducing the amount of property underwriting the assignat would further damage the value of the revolutionary paper currency. François-Antoine Boissy d'Anglas took the opposite view, arguing "good faith, that is the basis of credit." The real reason for the decline of the assignat, he maintained, was "the delay you are making in being just toward the families of the condemned."[74] It was a rhetorical flourish, but the attitude he expressed—that property claims should be resolved with an eye to the intentions of the parties involved—influenced a great deal of revolutionary financial policy. The particular formulation of *"bonne foi"* (good faith) itself reflects the self-consciously gentlemanly, bourgeois respectability revered by the men of Thermidor, the interim period between the fall of Robespierre and the beginning of the Directory government.[75] More specifically, it was an attitude shaped by the sovereign debt crisis. The financiers who benefited from excessive royal borrowing were viewed as bloodthirsty intriguers, and public debt was considered a "source of calamity for the human race."[76]

Debt, however, engaged a much broader set of interests than those of the financiers who had brought low the monarchy. Debt could be speculative, as in investment in tontines or the taking out of life annuities on third parties, but it was also a reliable source of investment for thousands of ordinary men and women.[77] Already in the fall of 1792, as the property seizure process began, lawmakers were aware of creditors' claims and the complexities they could pose for émigré assets. Commitment to honor émigré debts reflected lawmakers' awareness of how deeply individual debts were enmeshed in commercial networks, which operated on negotiable instruments. These networks followed the flow of trade across the nation, as "the merchant in Bordeaux ships his wines to his correspondent in Nantes, who sends them on to a wholesaler, this merchant to retailers, the retailers to consumers; the merchant in Marseilles does the same for his oils & soaps; the one in Nantes for his sugars & coffees; and so on: letters of change and promissory notes pile up, circulate, pass from hand to hand."[78] The interdependence of these networks meant that a general default by émigrés could cause chaos throughout French society, as the effects cascaded over artisans and merchants across the nation. Lawmakers were well aware of the economic significance of borrowing, and the law reflects this awareness. Émigré creditors were granted six extensions on the deadline to declare their loans, from the winter of 1794 through March 1801.

When the state inherited in place of an émigré, however, it placed limits on its own responsibility for any debts. In December 1794, all the debts against the émigrés were converted into public debt, to be registered in the *Grand Livre de la Dette Publique*.[79] As a result, claims would be discounted and repaid in paper against the state. The law included a crucial provision, however: claims would not be honored against borrowers who were "in bankruptcy or notoriously insolvent at the moment of confiscation." The state would not be held responsible for repayment beyond the means of the original borrower. It also meant that creditors of émigrés would be forced to accept a discount on their claims, or might be denied payment entirely if the émigré in question was found to be insolvent.

The social politics of credit were complicated, because credit networks were overlapping. The same individual might owe money to wealthy speculators charging a high rate of interest, to family members charging no interest, and to local tradesmen.[80] In Paris, where the credit market was particularly active, the wealthy might have occasion to borrow from the poor.[81] Similarly, tradesmen who provided goods and services on credit could find themselves holding the debt of wealthy elites. The image of a rapacious notary helping his client take on debt may have reflected a certain reality, but the worthy sansculotte tradesman did so too. Further, some loans were secured against mortgages— these were likely formally contracted *rentes* (annuities)—while other debts might have no security other than the reputation of the borrower.[82] Separating the deserving from the undeserving could not be accomplished easily when creditors had already been sorted into a legal hierarchy based on the priority of their claims.

The social politics of credit contrasted sharply with the social politics of land, because the deserving and undeserving were not so clear. The poor man who deserved a plot of Church land might also be the creditor of an émigré—a reality that made it difficult to denounce creditors unilaterally as a bloodthirsty lot. In a speech that urged the hastening of the liquidation process, Pardoux Bordas sketched a portrait of "good sansculottes, who for a long time have been asking the Convention for favors that will dissipate their poverty and prolong their old age."[83] He estimated that 600,000 people had an interest in émigré debt. They wanted their claims on émigré assets honored. By the fall of 1794, the term "sansculottes" not only signaled patriotism but also contained the threat of social unrest.[84] Canceling the émigrés' debt would mean redistributing wealth from these worthy creditors to the families of the émigrés. This was not an expropriation that any revolutionary government wished to contemplate, even though, for reasons of the national Treasury, it would be desirable to make émigré debt go away so that the properties could be sold for profit.

Émigrés were also creditors. When the state took over their assets in these cases, it was the state itself that stood to gain or lose as contracts were liquidated. In the eighteenth century, the *rente viagère* was a common investment tool and a means of making structured payments. Lending at interest was illegal until the reform of October 3, 1789, so contracts in the form of these annuities, with interest folded in as a lump sum, were extremely common. They posed a special challenge in the émigré context, however, as the terms of the *rente viagère* extinguished debt upon the death of the beneficiaries. Many émigrés were receiving payments on such instruments, and the borrowers argued that since the émigrés were civilly dead, the *rentes* should be canceled. Using civil death as a proxy for actual death also helped resolve the practical difficulty of securing information about the health and welfare of émigrés who had left the country. The borrower's obligation depended on the lender proving the borrower was alive; "without this proof, the borrower is discharged from their obligation; and in the case of the Émigrés, how probable it is that such proof is physically impossible."[85] Unilaterally canceling all *rentes viagères* on émigré heads, however, would deal a further blow to the state, which would lose the potential revenue. In 1793, the émigré laws explicitly allowed for the *rentes* to continue to be collected, and administrative practice reflects that this was done.[86] When the émigrés were the ones in the position of creditor, then, the republic not only honored their claims but extended them beyond their legal limits.

In October 1796, under the Directory, the Council of Five Hundred returned to the question of *rentes viagères*. A special commission established to study the issue recommended that the *rentes* be paid according to a fixed timetable, regardless of whether the émigré could be proven alive or dead. For political purposes, the émigrés were dead; for fiscal ones, they would be reanimated. Objections to the proposal cited the property claims of the lenders. As Francois-Toussaint Villers put it, "Show us what is just, and stop presenting financial measures that are always contrary to the most simple principles and the most incontestable rights of property."[87] In decisions about émigré assets, the legality of a given transaction repeatedly competed with the perceived merit of the beneficiary.

Questions around the redistribution of property in the Revolution were taken up from the dual perspectives of fiscal expedience and social justice—such was the case for Church property and for émigré property. These dual motivations were problematic enough, but on top of everything, they were based on the flawed belief that property could be redistributed cleanly by taking it away from one entity and giving it to another. As the issue of credit illustrates, the interests involved were interlocked and the deservingness of any party contingent and situational. The political rhetoric that stated property should be in the hands of deserving patriots could not be squared with the legal and fiscal realities of the market.

Conclusion

In the estimation of revolutionary leaders, the émigrés had committed a crime by depriving the polity of their wealth. In turn, the Legislative Assembly reasoned, they deserved to have their property taken from them. While property confiscation was certainly an expedient way to punish citizens who were themselves absent from the country, expediency was not the only reason that lawmakers pursued this strategy. The émigré laws were motivated both by economic opportunism—the desire to capitalize on émigré wealth—and by the philosophical belief that seizure was the logical consequence of the émigrés' choice to breach the social contract.

The account of the émigré laws that has been given here is unorthodox in its light treatment of the distinctive political context of each of the revolutionary legislatures. The outflow of citizens toward France's enemies became increasingly problematic as the revolutionary regime stalled in the face of royal prerogative; the hardening of the émigré laws under the Convention occurred in the punitive context of the Terror; the possibility that émigré lands could be used to indemnify the poor became policy as the political influence of the sansculottes workers of Paris reached its acme during the Terror. But to interpret each of these stages purely within its proximate political context is to miss the consistent set of assumptions that undergirded all of them. These politically distinct regimes shared a belief in the transformative power of property relations: if the right people owned property, under the right conditions, then society would function as it should and political stability would be ensured. Moreover, all three regimes acted on the idea that while property rights must be guaranteed, an important way to ensure the solidity of those rights was to remove property from those who used it improperly—among them, the Church and the émigrés. The polity could thrive, these men believed, only if property were put into the hands of those who deserved it.

The dual motivation expressed in the drafts of the 1792 sequestration law does not seem so odd or accidental when situated in the long arc of émigré property policy. The law was based on the idea that citizens had a moral duty to their nation, following a logic based on the social contract, but the language of the law itself only referenced the economic damage done by the émigrés. This pairing of a moralizing view of citizenship with a focus on property as primarily an economic tool ran through the émigré laws. These were not really separate threads: émigré policy reflected a kind of moralizing view of the economy, in which assets placed in the right hands would generate prosperity for all, whereas assets placed in the hands of the wicked would lead to idleness and debt. This wasn't a fully developed theory; it remained at the level of association. But this essentially unexamined assumption that property should belong to the righteous, and the corollary that property—land, specifically—could make its owners into the right kind of citizens, would continue to appear during the Revolution as lawmakers continued to elevate land over other forms of property. It would crop up in family law as it intersected with émigré policy, in the form of an emphasis on deservingness and persistent equation of property relations with moral bonds—as we will see in Chapter 5.

In one sense, the legislature's approach to property was practical: each regime sought to use confiscated property to retire the debt and stimulate the economy. However, their understanding of émigré property failed to account for the practical realities of property ownership at the end of the eighteenth century. The legislative debates about émigré property, which had initially focused on cash and goods being exported by the émigrés, settled instead on land. Lawmakers conceptualized émigrés' assets as land, and specifically as land unencumbered by debt. They were blindsided when it turned out that émigré property was heavily leveraged. Assets taken from their owners dissolved when the absent owner was found to be insolvent. Even estates that were sufficient to cover debts were complicated to liquidate: émigré debts were not fully extinguished for decades; the Restoration monarchy continued to legislate on the issue after 1815.

It was not sufficient, of course, simply to mandate property away. Various claims had to be identified and disentangled before ownership ties could legally be dissolved. This work depended on an expansive administration, which is perhaps the hallmark of property confiscation during the Revolution. Chapter 3 examines the methods by which émigré property was identified, linked to its owners, and then legally alienated from them.

The Hands of the Nation

T HE TEXT OF THE FEBRUARY 1792 law placed émigré property, rather evocatively, "under the hand of the nation." One might imagine that the nation had only one hand available, as the other was busy wielding the sword of the law, with which it was also menacing the émigrés. In any case, this fanciful personification of the nation concealed lawmakers' discomfort with recognizing the role of administration in the new regime. In the nineteenth century, the German philosopher G. W. F. Hegel would envision administration as an exalted interface between people and state. In the idiom of revolutionary ideals, however, the law was supposed to act directly on the people without any intermediate authority interposing itself. Representatives in the revolutionary legislatures were deeply suspicious of administration and sought to limit it to the greatest extent possible. Their ideal of representative government was based on a direct relationship between the people and the state, making illegitimate any authority that intervened between the sovereign people and their representatives.[1]

Far from ushering in an enlightened era of small government, however, the Revolution has long been associated with the development of modern bureaucracy. Alexis de Tocqueville, the great chronicler of

French administration, viewed the Revolution as a period of unprecedented state centralization that was in continuity with the intentions
of officials in the Old Regime.[2] His association of the revolutionary state
with expanding administrative authority matches the interpretations
of the great historians of administration, Max Weber and Michel
Foucault. Both diagnosed bureaucracy as a particular characteristic of
modern state power; Foucault traced the origins of the disciplinary
power of the state to the Revolution specifically.[3]

In his multivolume work, *The Human Comedy,* novelist Honoré de
Balzac offered another interpretation of the growth of bureaucracy.
Unlike Foucault and Weber, Balzac focused on bureaucrats themselves, whom he portrayed as human beings deeply enmeshed in the
life of the office, playing their parts in an interpersonal drama unfold-
ing across the administrative hierarchy. Far from cogs in a rationalized
machine, Balzac's characters are impetuous, gossipy, and prone to
leaving work in the middle of the day. Balzac was not a social scien-
tist, of course, but he was admired for his realism and uncanny grasp
of the social dynamics of his time. If Weber and Foucault portray
bureaucracy from the abstract perspective of the institution, Balzac
reminds us that an administration is only as efficient as the people
who staff it.

The procedures of émigré confiscation were so fragmented across
the government that one might reasonably believe they were intended to
fulfill a revolutionary aspiration to hobble administration. Separate
authorities handled émigré real estate and émigré credit obligations;
these authorities partially overlapped with those that handled Church
property. Credit obligations were managed nationally, whereas physical
property was managed locally. Instead of intentional inefficiency, however, the administrative structure of property seizure seems to reflect the diverse forms that property took: real or personal, buildings,
things or papers. Property was not treated as a body of assets, but rather
as a set of discrete categories. As a result, papers relating credit obligations

were warehoused and the highly leveraged status of real property came, as we have begun to see in Chapter 2, as an ugly surprise.

The fragmented nature of the confiscation process is paradoxical, because the image of the nation laying its hand on émigré property implies a transparent relationship between people and their things. Law-makers attempted to create such a relationship, as Chapter 1 has shown. Mortgage registries and publicity of property transfers were supposed to support the link between citizenship and property by making it possible to know who owned what. Even with these measures, however, ownership was not transparent. While the aspirations that lay behind the property seizure law were vast and symbolic, the reality involved raking through the contents of a stranger's house. Identifying the property of émigrés required judgment and expertise on the part of administrators. It was not so much the hand of the nation that acted as the hands of the nation, plural, in the form of hundreds—thousands, more likely—of officials working for the state.

This chapter examines administration from the perspective of the set of tasks carried out by administrators. In other words, the pages that follow adopt the position of examining the work that administrators do and the effects of this work, within the context of the Domain bureau's attempts to confiscate property.[4] The focus is on the operations of individuals, as opposed to the institution of administration and its relationship to the state and to government—its subject is administrators rather than administration.[5]

Under the Old Regime, the relatively disorderly customs of property title fell outside the purview of the state. There were no public registries of property, and property was not taxed as such. Property title depended on human relationships, and continued to do so through the Revolution. Title was proved by showing that you obtained a property legally and that the person you obtained it from owned it legally. As a result, title to a property was, physically, a bundle of old documents. The law of title, including the methods for proving it, remained unchanged in the Revolution. Thus, tracing title required the work of people skilled at parsing the various types of contracts that could be used to prove title. Revolutionary law, however, brought ownership under the scrutiny of public administrators responsible for creating inventories and reconstructing chains of title. Property titles thus came under the purview of the state in an unprecedented way—although it is important to remember that the state itself, far from a disembodied source of power, was ever embodied by the officials who conducted its administrative work.

Administrators closed the gap between lawmakers, who did not necessarily take the practicalities of title into consideration when they passed laws, and the operations of property owners. Day to day, they used their judgment and knowledge to apply the law to the circumstances they encountered. This meant that while the legal structure of the confiscation process was complicated and constantly evolving, administrators carried out their work in much the same way over the revolutionary years. The seizure process was riddled with obstacles both legal and practical: reading the correspondence of the officials who carried it out, one might be surprised that any seizures at all were successfully completed. To the extent that they were, those results are a testament to the skill of the administrators themselves.

The Domain Bureau

Administrative procedures to carry out revolutionary property confiscation began in 1790 with the nationalization of Church property. In 1792, France became a republic, leading to broad administrative reorganization, and émigré property began to be confiscated. Even though émigré property represented only a fraction of the quantity of Church property, the émigré confiscation process was more complex and engaged a broader swath of government administration. This was partly because the émigrés had to be identified before their assets could be seized, and partly because their assets were sold in smaller lots. In addition, the émigrés were private citizens, a fact that brought its own complexities: émigré properties were generally full of belongings, and, often, occupants. Emigré families resisted confiscation however they could.

When Church property confiscation began in 1790, a committee of the Constituent Assembly—the Committee of Alienation of the National Domains—oversaw the nationalization of that property. The process was carried out by authorities in the Ministry of the Interior at the level of the District and Department, corresponding to the municipal and regional levels.[6] Another committee, that of Domains, helped with oversight. In 1791, a financial administration, the Caisse de l' Extraordinaire ("Special Fund"), was created to handle the process in place of the Committee of Alienation. The Caisse continued to handle the sale of *biens nationaux* and management of the revolutionary paper currency, the assignat, as émigré property began to be confiscated.[7]

After France became a republic in 1792, the Committee of Legislation became the most involved in émigré affairs, through its oversight of civil and judicial administration. The Ministry of the Interior and the Ministry of Police, which would become the Ministry of Justice, worked together to gather information about absent citizens and formulate official lists of émigrés. The émigré lists were produced by individual municipalities, ratified by the departments, and then distributed to the Ministries of the Interior, of Justice, of War, and of Public Contributions (which would become the Ministry of Finances).[8] The émigré list enrolled the names of people who were absent from their homes; correspondingly, a list of émigré property registered properties that had no owner present in France. However, at least in some areas, the lists of people were created retrospectively from lists of property. The Convention ordered each municipality to list all properties "situated in its territory, belonging to persons that it does not know to be currently domiciled in the Department."[9] The phrasing of the law oddly avoided the émigrés themselves, pointing to the lack of a relationship between these complementary lists. The list of émigrés did not generate the list of property; instead, properties were identified by the absence of an owner.[10]

The Caisse de l'Extraordinaire operated until January 1793, when its functions were attributed to the Treasury. At the conclusion of an auction of émigré property, the proceeds were initially deposited with the Domain receiver locally and passed to the Caisse de l'Extraordinaire. When the Terror government took shape in the Year II (1792–1793), oversight of property sales shifted to the Commission of Finances (rebaptized the Commission of National Revenues).[11] Within the Commission of Finances, the newly created Administration des Domaines Nationaux assumed oversight of the sale of the *domaines nationaux*— an umbrella term that included Church and émigré property, in addition to former Crown property.[12] The Administration gradually received its form and mandate over the following months.[13]

The Paris Domain bureau handled the local confiscation process, from the identification of émigré assets through their sale within the city of Paris. It was part of the Régie National de l'Enregistrement, Timbre, Hypothèques & des Domaines Nationaux. The Régie itself was part of the Ministry of Finances and then the Treasury. Initially, the bureau existed within the Ministry of Finances; in 1795, under the Directory government, it was moved into the Department of Paris, the regional government for the capital.

Similar bureaus operated across France, but the Paris Domain bureau was considerably smaller than its counterparts in the other regions, or Departments, of France. The reason for this discrepancy was the particular place of Paris in the Revolution. Since the summer of 1789, the municipal government of Paris took an active role in revolutionary politics. In 1791, France was divided into departments, each one composed of districts. Paris, however, became its own department. It had no district mediating between the regional and local levels. As a result, officials in the national government, either in the legislature or in the Ministry of Finances, played a more direct role in Paris property seizures. Elsewhere in France, national officials communicated with officials at the regional level; but in Paris, they communicated directly with the director of the Paris Domain bureau.

Across France, the liquidation of émigré financial assets and liabilities was handled separately from the administration of real property. This was because émigré property was sold free of liens, which the republic took responsibility for settling up to the value of the assets.[14] Outside Paris, this administrative work was handled by the Departments, under the aegis of the Ministry of the Interior, much in the way Church property had been managed. In Paris, however, the liquidation of émigré assets was separated from that of émigré liabilities. Moreover, both functions were removed from the Department administration to the Treasury. Ostensibly, this was done because the Paris municipal administration was too busy with other matters; it may have been a result of the Convention government's punitive stance toward the city of Paris, or simply a reflection of the large quantity of financial assets held in the capital.[15] Finally, in April 1795, the liquidation process was centralized nationwide in a single bureau in Paris.

The Régie and the other offices of national government concerned with émigré confiscation went through constant reorganization over the revolutionary period.[16] From 1789 through the late 1790s, the structure of the Régie changed about every two years. The number of overseers (régisseurs) at the head of the Régie fluctuated. The name of the authority itself changed, to Agence Nationale de l' Enregistrement et des Domaines in the Year III (1794), then back to Régie, and then finally in Year XI (1802) to Administration Générale de l'Enregistrement et des Domaines. In 1793, the Administration Générale des Domaines Nationaux operated separately from the Régie within the Treasury. Also in 1794, oversight of the Registration and Domain divisions in the city of Paris was separated and entrusted to two separate directors. In the ten years that followed, the Paris Domain bureau saw four different directors. The receivers in each arrondissement turned over at a steady rhythm.

The changing organization of revolutionary administrations reflected real changes in the attitude of the government toward administration itself, in addition to responding to the needs of the confiscation process. Already in the waning years of the Old Regime, from about 1750 onward, the king in his council began to rely more heavily on input from administrators as opposed to his ministers.[17] During the Revolution, the abolition of venal offices brought previously independent administrators into the state hierarchy.[18] The early years of the Revolution slowed, if not reversed, the trend toward a larger and more independent state administration. The Constituent Assembly was very hostile to administrators. Ministers were not allowed to send interpretive instructions to their employees until the Directory.[19] Even so, during the war years of 1792–1794, the number of administrators ballooned. Overall, the revolutionary period witnessed a large and durable expansion in the number of administrators.[20]

The formal differences in administration between Paris and the provinces don't fully reflect the difference of scale in the work the Paris office undertook. Consider that in the department of the Gironde, the property of 334 émigrés was sold; in the department of the Cher, the property of 84 émigrés; and in the Côtes-du-Nord, the property of 606 émigrés.[21] In Paris, around 1,000 émigrés had their real assets seized. The high proportion of nobles and general concentration of wealth in Paris also meant that in qualitative terms, the dossiers must have been more complicated than in the provinces. Differences in patterns of property ownership would also influence the kinds of problems that administrators tackled: Paris had very little arable land, but many rental buildings filled with tenants, which meant a larger number of individual parcels on the same surface area, and the greater difficulties of dealing with people versus empty land.

The city of Paris was home to the offices of its own Domain bureau, and also the offices of the central government that handled the confiscation process at the national level. The offices were dotted around the city in a variety of former Old Regime administrative buildings, Church property seized in 1789, and, in later years, former homes of émigrés.

The Régie de l'Enregistrement occupied a building in the Rue de Choiseul, the financial quarter on the Right Bank, not far from what is today the Opera Garnier. It had been built in 1678 by a nobleman who had to sell his venal position in the Chambre des Comptes, part of the Old Regime financial administration, to pay off his gambling debts. He did not, however, sell the house. His son-in-law, the royal falconer, inherited it and rented it to the chief of police, the famous Jean-Charles-Pierre Lenoir. It was sold and then replaced with an apartment building in 1779, which was rented and then sold to the king in 1786. At this point, the predecessor authority to the Régie moved in. No longer the Hôtel de Choiseul, it was known as the Hôtel de la Régie Nationale.[22]

The Administration Générale des Domaines Nationaux occupied offices in the sumptuous Hôtel de Calonne, in the Rue Neuve-des-Petits-Champs, throughout the Revolution. This building also served government purposes in the Old Regime, lodging visiting ambassadors before housing the royal fiscal office of the Contrôle; it became the seat of the Ministry of the Interior in 1792.[23] The national office for the liquidation of émigré debts, when it was created, moved into the same building in the Rue Neuve-des-Petits-Champs. Previously, the Paris office for liquidation was located in the former seminary of the Order of the Holy Spirit (Ordre du Saint-Esprit) on the Left Bank, near the Pantheon on the edge of the Latin Quarter.

When authority over the Domain bureau shifted from the Ministry of Finances to the territorial authority, the Department of Paris, operations moved into the Maison d'Uzès in the Rue Montmartre, a ten-minute walk east (fig. 3.1). Formerly called the Hôtel d'Uzès (aristocratic homes in Paris bore the descriptor "hôtel," meaning, simply, a large and

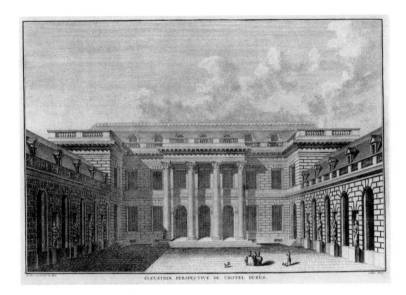

FIGURE 3.1 Facade of the Maison d'Uzès, seat of the Paris Domain bureau 1794–1796, seized from the Duc d'Uzès, attributed to the architect Claude Ledoux. *Credit:* Harvard Fine Arts Library.

important house), it was seized from the duc d'Uzès.[24] Finally, the Domain—along with the financial administration of what was now called the Department of the Seine (formerly the Department of Paris)—moved into the Rue Neuve du Luxembourg, now the Rue Cambon, just west of the Place Vendôme. The building, also seized from an émigré, held the offices of the director of the Paris Domain bureau as well as his residence.[25]

The physical locations of these offices reflect a mishmash of old and new. Existing sites of Old Regime authority were turned over to new administrations, and newly acquired buildings, equally old, were pressed into service. The buildings present a veneer of stability and age—some of them dating back to the seventeenth century—and yet their ownership and rental histories tell a different story. These buildings saw a procession of administrators, owners, and tenants, even in the brief period preceding the Revolution.

Their physicality offers a useful counterpoint to the grand, abstract facade of power presented by administration as an arm of state power. These were buildings on streets in neighborhoods around Paris, where people commuted to work (or, in the case of some administrators, where they lived alongside their offices). They highlight the provisional, cobbled together nature of revolutionary administration—offices hastily repurposed and interrupted by periodic packing up of papers and shuffling of employees as offices changed locations. They point to the immediacy of the relationship between administrated and administrator, in the sense that émigré homes could become offices for people doing the work of seizing émigré homes.

Applying the Law

Administrations were meant to carry out the confiscation process as it was articulated in the law, and that law was voluminous and evolving. As a briefing from the Committee of Legislation acknowledged, "Numerous laws have been made on the émigrés."[26] So much legislation was issued that an Émigré Code was compiled to track it all. It was the only legal code produced by the Convention—a fact that attests to the volume of legislation and, perhaps, to the perceived importance of penal law or, by analogy, honor as an aspect of citizenship.[27] The Code might have helped keep track of all the legislation, but officials had a hard time getting their hands on it. One official requested additional copies from the minister of justice in March 1796, explaining, "Just one copy of the émigré code per bureau is not enough, I think at least two would be necessary." The minister replied curtly, "One must suffice, economize."[28] In addition to the laws governing émigré policy that appeared incessantly throughout the period, circulars from the national Régie arrived in local Domain offices during the Directory at a rate of more than a dozen per month.[29] These letters announced new regulations or provided details on how existing regulations should be applied.

To some extent, these problems of ever-evolving and inaccessible codes were not new, though the Revolution surely exacerbated them. Already in the 1780s, administrators in the Régie faced a "multitude of regulations, judgments, & council rulings, many of which at first glance seem to imply a contradiction."[30] To help them sift through it all, officials could turn to third-party handbooks that distilled complex legislation into a dictionary of procedures. The revolutionary version, compiled by Desormeaux, went through four editions between 1789—when it was still keyed to the Old Regime—and 1802, suggesting it was popular.[31] Officials had a particular interest in staying abreast of the law, as they were held personally responsible for failure in carrying it out.[32]

The attribution of authorities was complex enough that even the director of the Paris Domain bureau occasionally made a mistake. After writing about a matter to the supervisors (régisseurs) of the Régie, he learned that he had addressed the wrong authority. The régisseurs wrote back in a gently chastising tone, "It is not at all for our office, Citizen, to handle the recovery of sums due by suppliers for advances made under ministerial orders to them on contracts they have not yet executed. The law of 4 March 1793, referenced in a letter from the Commissioner of the Executive Directory to the Departmental Administration, of which we sent you a copy, on 19 pluviôse, outlines the steps undertaken by the National Treasury."[33] The response is rather Kafkaesque. How could someone be expected to keep track of all these regulations and authorities? A particular understanding of the administrator's role with respect to the law, and of law itself, lay behind these directives.

To some extent, employees in the Domain may have been able to rely on career knowledge of administration to help them navigate their work.[34] There are no extant personnel records for the Paris Domain, and for most employees there is no consistent way to find given names, making it perilous to try to identify officials across archival series. Old

Regime personnel records do contain references to people who could perhaps be the same as those who signed the documents in the Paris Domain bureau.[35] Yet the only certain identification that can be made is that Gentil, director of the Paris Domain bureau from 1791 through 1795, previously held the position of verifier, an ascension that at least suggests he could have begun his career under the Old Regime in a lower position.[36] It seems likely that some employees carried over from the Old Regime, given that at least some of the work of confiscation was deemed at the time to be specialized. For example, the work of making inventories of émigré credit liabilities was shifted from the Sections of Paris to the Domain administration when it was deemed that the Section officials did not have the necessary knowledge to read the documents.[37] Paris was divided into forty-eight sections (also called districts) during the Revolution; the main qualifications for positions in the Section administrations were residency in Paris and demonstrated political loyalty to the Revolution. The Domain officials who took over making the inventories, on the other hand, had to be skilled in reading financial documents, whether or not they had worked for the Old Regime.

Whatever their previous experience, employees in the Paris Domain office could rely on administrative procedures to guide them in their work. These procedures are physically apparent in the written record: in letters to the director, Domain officials always began with a paragraph that summarized the case in question. In the heading of the letter, they would write the unique number that had been assigned to the case. They also set the margin halfway across the page, allowing the director to draft his response directly on the letter and hand it off to a clerk for recopying (fig. 3.2). When one verifier skipped the obligatory summary preface and dove directly into his business, the director scribbled curtly in the margin, "You need to recall the facts and establish a rationale."[38] He did not address the substance of the letter. In addition, employees checked each other's work, from reviewing documents to re-tallying arithmetic.

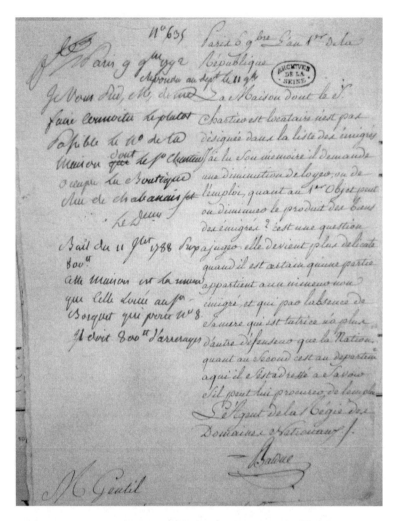

FIGURE 3.2 Example of a piece of the Domain director's correspondence with his response to an employee's letter drafted in the margin; from the dossier of Louise-Perrine Chabanais. *Credit:* Archives de Paris, DQ10 708 Chab.

Overall, the correspondence tells a remarkably smooth, stable story, in spite of the challenges posed by the process. Issues are raised and handled; properties are taken into administration, inventoried, emptied, and sold. Given the changing attributions of the different authorities and their various addresses, it is rather surprising how efficient work seemed to be on the ground. In this sense, an irreconcilable tension existed between the view of the confiscation process at the national level and the one from inside the Domain bureau and its various outposts around Paris. Lawmakers and officials bemoaned, in reports to the legislature, the chaos of the confiscation procedure.[39] Meanwhile, employees showed up for work every day. As challenging as the work was, as chaotic as the process may have been at times, it was the job of the employees to carry it out, and they did so.

Lists and Inventories

In Paris, information about émigré property arrived piecemeal through reports from municipal authorities and denunciations by neighbors. In June 1794, the director of the Paris Domain bureau learned that officials in one of the bureau offices near the Panthéon had received a denunciation from a neighbor about a property belonging to "one Bretignières de Courteille, émigré." He in turn wrote to the president of the Department of Paris, who agreed that he would "add this property to the next list of émigré property."[40] On another occasion, the director wrote to the Department administrators that the émigré Bernard owned property in Paris, even though it wasn't mentioned on the émigré list.[41] In these situations, the Domain uncovered property that it did not previously know about but that belonged to people already on an émigré list.

Simply gathering accurate information about who was an émigré and what they owned posed challenges throughout the Revolution. In fructidor of the year 11 (September 1803), the administrators of the

Domain—the supervisors at the national level of the Paris Domain bureau—received a letter from the commissioner of the 3rd Arrondissement denouncing the heirs of Nicolas Bouthillier, who had left "a large inheritance" to relatives in St Petersburg and Strasbourg. The commissioner warned that "it's time the government acted since this large inheritance is on its way and . . . the relatives are in a position to dispose of it without saying anything."[42] Nicolas Bouthillier and his wealth proved to be a hoax, as did the author of the letter himself. Cornebize, the Domain receiver for the 3rd Arrondissement, wrote to the director, "Lebrun who signed this letter is in no way known in the title he claims as superintendent of the 3rd arrondissement." Cornebize reported that even the police commissioner had never heard of such a person.[43]

The Domain initially had good reason to believe that the letter was true, as information about émigré properties could come directly from officials at the neighborhood level. In another case, the director of the Agence du Domaine National forwarded a letter to the Paris bureau from a tenant who complained that he did not know to whom to pay his rent because his landlord had disappeared. He wrote, "This individual who lived in the same street, in the house next door to the one in question, has been absent for several months. The revolutionary committee of the Fontaine-Grenelle Section placed seals at his house, and by all accounts I consider him to be an émigré."[44] It's not clear whether the Section committee had yet informed the Domain of what was happening—it was only the conscientiousness (or meddling) of the tenant that brought the matter to the director's attention.

Once émigré assets had been identified, officials moved to formally take possession of them. Buildings were visited by officials from the municipality of Paris and the local neighborhood authority, the Section committee. If people were living in the building, they paid a guarantee. If a building was empty, seals were placed on the doors so that no one could remove anything before the contents could be taken to a warehouse. A guardian—often a neighbor or building staff—would be appointed to make sure the seals remained intact.[45] The Directoire du District would send an official, accompanied by two representatives of the municipality, to draw up an inventory.

The lists of émigrés and property with absent owners prepared by the municipality were only the first in a series of inventories that marked the confiscation process. Commissioners from the city and from the Domain bureau prepared inventories of the contents of houses, as well as subinventories listing only carpets—if the house had enough of them—or household items reserved for daily use. Inventories tracked fixtures and other built-in aspects of a house separately from the removable contents. The concierge responsible for a seized building that had been rented to tenants prepared an inventory of refuse left behind when a tenant moved out in the middle of the night.[46] This list, in particular, has the quality of a snapshot; one can almost picture the dirty cloths and faïence plates scattered around the empty room. And yet unlike a snapshot, which would capture objects within the coherence of a room, the lists of émigré belongings offer only a jumble.

Lists and inventories—of people and of things—represented a good deal of the work product of officials involved in the confiscation process. They highlight, as such, the first, major challenge of property confiscation: identifying owners and enumerating their property. They also seem to encapsulate the administrative zeal of the Revolution, whose officials sought to enumerate, to an extent never before attempted, the people and things of France.[47] Inventories, of course, were not new; they were a staple of notaries' work. In certain kinds of inheritances, a notary would be retained to create an inventory of the deceased's assets, including an exhaustive list of everything in their house. But in the context of the Revolution this existing tool, the inventory, was transformed—deployed on a new scale and for new purposes. They are also a good metaphor for the way revolutionary administration was supposed to work: direct, immediate, factual. The hand of the administrator is almost invisible, simply transcribing what it is visible. But their neatness belies the complexity of administration, as they fix in time people and objects that could, in fact, move or be moved freely.

Receivers and Verifiers

Much of the work of the Domain office took place after properties had been identified, but before they were sold. This period could stretch on for years, as officials investigated complex ownership arrangements or simply managed tenants in buildings that were not yet up for sale. In this work, the director depended on the receivers, who sat in offices distributed around the city. In the Bouthillier case, the director received information from his supervisors at the national level, as well as from the receiver, who could verify facts on the ground. There were six receivers for the twelve arrondissements. They received payments—such as from buyers of émigré property—and collected information.[48] The turnover in the job was fairly regular, with five to seven receivers serving in each arrondissement over the period 1793–1806, a rate of roughly one every two years. This was more or less on par with the turnover rate for directors, of whom there were five over ten years.

Receivers fielded inquiries and requests from residents in their arrondissements, reported information up the administrative chain to the director, and in turn executed the director's orders. Citizen Bellet triggered this two-way process when he requested that repairs be made to the house he was renting near the Place des Vosges, in the Marais. In October 1801, the director, Eparvier, drafted a formal order for the prefect determining that the repairs should not be made because the house had been released to the owner, named Mauléon-Savaillant, or his heirs—and they were the ones who should be doing the work.[49] He noted that his information came from one of his architects, Lelong, who had learned it from the local receiver, Durant. After the prefect

had issued the order, Eparvier wrote to Durant and told him to inform
Bellet that the prefect had rejected his request. In November, Bellet
returned to Durant's office to renew his entreaties. He explained that
the wind had blown down a chimney, and conditions had gotten so bad
that his tenants were withholding their rent.[50]

The problem, it turned out, was that even though the house had been
released from sequester and Mauléon-Savaillant struck from the
émigré list, no heirs had actually come forward to claim the house.
Durant tried the request from a new approach, asking the director,
"Wouldn't it be useful to consider this house abandoned, since no one
has claimed it, and reintegrate it to the National Domain?" The apparent absence of the owners posed a problem, as the repairs needed to be
done as soon as possible. A month later, in January 1802, the prefect also
wrote to the director, questioning whether the owners had ever really
taken possession of the house. The prefect noted that "subsequent research has given me no information that any such order lifting the sequester on the house exists. . . . It's indispensable that I should know
in virtue of what authorization the administration of the house could
have stopped." Eparvier scribbled a note at the bottom of the letter that
a reply was unnecessary because the date had been found. Mauléon-
Savaillant was struck from the émigré list in April 1801, and the prefect
issued a release order for the property in April 1802.[51] A few days after
the release order, the director wrote again to Durant, scolding him that
he had granted the release to Mauléon-Savaillant too soon: Durant
had done it after the émigré had been removed from the list, rather
than waiting for the official release order from the prefect.[52] It seems
possible—even likely, given the late date of the prefect's release order—
that Durant's intervention on behalf of Bellet was what prompted
the prefect to notice the missing order and issue it. Ultimately, then,
his activity at the local level brought the case back to the attention of
the director and the prefect.

Perhaps the most striking aspect of this affair is that it primarily concerns management of a rental property, and only peripherally seems related to property confiscation. And yet, the ownership of the house and the legality of its confiscation became crucial issues in determining whether the Domain should pay for the repairs. The receiver handled the responsibilities of a landlord but also monitored the sequester and confiscation procedures that would determine who the landlord was. Ordering repairs on a chimney was, in this way, just as much a part of the confiscation process as placing seals on the doors of a building or preparing paperwork for a sale.

Receivers also took deposits of émigré documents, which were pulled out of sequestered homes or handed over by notaries. Anyone holding émigré business papers was compelled to turn them over by the law of August 23, 1792. Notaries handled finances for private individuals, and accordingly they were directed to declare any assets they held that belonged to émigrés. Similarly, creditors of émigrés had to register their claims. Commissioners from the Paris municipal government could also turn over papers they pulled out of émigré houses that went under sequester. These flows of information helped to form an account of each émigré's assets and liabilities, a crucial step toward liquidating their estates. The receivers sent the documents, in turn, to the liquidation office that handled émigré credit and debt.

Deposits of émigré papers included a wide assortment of documents of varying importance. A deposit might include several contracts constituting annuities, the inventory and damage report of a rented apartment made at the lease signing, and receipts from merchants for payment in exchange for goods received.[53] Some of the documents were themselves property titles, such as the annuity contracts; others testified to liabilities, such as rent due. Like real property, they came to the attention of municipal authorities and, through them, the Domain primarily via word of mouth. Unlike real property, however, paper assets could be lost, hidden, or misplaced. Without the paper, the assets essentially did not exist, whereas the paperwork for a building could be backfilled under duress—there was no doubt that a piece of real estate existed.

A verifier assisted and corrected the work of receivers, doing deeper research when necessary and checking over the receivers' accounts. Bignon, a verifier in the Domain bureau, wrote to the director in April 1799 that the amount listed for an annuity for Claude-Antione Beziade and his wife seemed too low. He examined the register and determined, "It's obvious there is an error. It's obvious that in writing out the division the copyist made a fault, today recognized, in stating 1379.65 instead of 1879.65." Following the error to its source, ever needle-nosed, he found that "this fault can be found in the record of the division, which I verified, and until this record is rectified the treasury will make difficulties about making the necessary amortizations." The error had become official record when it was recorded in the estate division, so it could not easily be fixed. But, Bignon had found a solution: "If you would be so kind as to explain this error to the Department, I am given assurances that on the basis of your letter, it will be rectified."[54] Another verifier, Delacourtin, checked over some accounting done by the receiver for the 3rd and 4th arrondissements, Cornebize, because the work "seemed unsound to me in its base."[55] Neither Bignon nor Delacourtin credits their discoveries to any special perspicacity. Bignon's repetition of the phrase "it's obvious [il est évident]" reflects, on the contrary, that the error was obvious. Delacourtin, meanwhile, didn't find a mistake in some arcane element of his colleagues' accounting—the problem was in the very "base" of the thing. One might imagine that the men downplayed their findings so as not to imply wrongdoing on the part of the colleagues who prepared the documents in question. In any case, rooting out such errors was their job.

Even with notaries and business partners making deposits, Domain officials had to crisscross the city to fill in missing paperwork needed to prove a title and legally transfer ownership. This work also fell to the verifier. The letters of the Domain are filled with reports by verifiers who traveled across town to dig through a notary's or a clerk's records in search of a necessary piece of information about a property. Bignon visited several notaries to find out the origins of a large covered market belonging to the Boulainvilliers family. He proudly reported to the director that "my search was not in vain" and proceeded to enumerate the various private notarial offices and public records depositories he had scrutinized, naming an array of notaries and offices around Paris: "Instead of waiting for a dispatch from the clerk, I went to Rondonneau's office where I got a copy of the letters patent of the establishment. . . . From there I went to Citizen Preignon, successor to the Porte d'Auteuil, where the sale of the market was made in 1779. . . . I didn't find the act of adjudication made by the Commissioners for Robit. I had already gone to the National Archives near the Palace of the 500 [legislative chambers], where I couldn't find the titles with the specifics mentioned above, but we found a considerable trove of papers."[56] He was not always so lucky. In a letter on a different case he admitted, "I vainly searched for a long time for the annuity contracts. . . . I didn't find any trace of them in the public depots, nor with the Receivers, nor at the Department archives."[57] His predecessor Moncuit, another verifier, faced the same challenges: seven years earlier, he went on a hunt for papers that yielded results only after a false start. As he recounted to the director, "I was at Citizen Dorez's office (which is no longer Rue du Paradis, but Rue de Cléry, near 85 Rue Montmartre) to get the papers that he had."[58]

Paper Property

Paper lay at the heart of the confiscation process, in the form of property titles. It was the only way to know that some forms of property existed. Even for real estate and personal property, paper played a crucial role. The seizure process attached a given piece of property to a particular person and transferred unwieldy physical objects—large houses, furniture—onto a piece of paper that could be slipped into a dossier and filed. Still, managing the papers, figuring out which documents were important, and extracting critical information from them all required skill on the part of administrators. The volume of paper itself also became a real challenge in executing the work of confiscation. Indeed, the documents themselves could hinder the Domain's ability to collect the value of a contract, as sorting through mountains of paper required an enormous amount of skilled labor. In a report on the state of efforts to liquidate émigré debts made in June 1796, a representative in the Directory legislature described how contracts had poured in from notaries and others before the first deadline for declaring claims against émigrés. These documents had been stockpiled into the former monastery of the Order of the Holy Spirit in the Rue Lhomond, near the Pantheon. They had not even all been registered, as the titles had been "carried in haste and in a mass." As the documents were too numerous to manage, the only solution was to "stack them up in the bedrooms . . . since then these titles have been almost forgotten, or, if someone has occasionally attended to them, it was only to move them without precaution or order."[59]

These papers were still being inventoried after the offices responsible for émigré paper assets—credits and liabilities—had moved out of the Saint-Esprit building and into the Maison d'Uzès. The work of sorting through it all caused an employee in the Archives Bureau to have a nervous breakdown. The employee, a man named Lienard, was confronted by two supervisors about taking too many breaks during his inventory work. Losing his cool, Lienard turned on Bardin, one of the officials, and "called citizen Bardin a *j . . . f . . .* [*sic*] and after a string of insults each more crude than the last, and after many threats, including that he would throw him out the window, upon the observation by [Bardin], that all these insults wouldn't prevent him from doing his duty, and that as to the rest, there was a saying that 'thieves hate to hear the dogs barking,' [Lienard] grabbed a chair and chased Bardin, who went down the stairs."[60] The altercation took place in front of ten witnesses, "who remained silent spectators of this scandalous scene." A little over three months later, Lienard got his job back. Was the bureau too overwhelmed to dismiss someone skilled enough to read the material, no matter how unstable he might be?

Interminable and voluminous as they might have been, the documents themselves played a crucial role in separating owners from their property. They served as the link between the highly conceptual operation of transferring ownership from one entity to another and the relentlessly physical operation of taking away a person's belongings. They recorded the actions of the architects, bailiffs, receivers, and other personnel in the confiscation process, imbuing those relatively banal actions with the weight and timelessness conferred by documentation. The many official reports (*procès verbaux*) created by officials effectively served as proof that they had carried out an action. A justice of the peace made a report to certify that seals had been placed on a sequestered building, and a bailiff made one each time he served papers.

Property owners, for their part, could create oral contracts—a source of difficulties for the Domain. When Moncuit, the verifier, arrived to collect documents from the notary of the widow Berbis-Desmailly, a man named Dorez, he replied that he "always handled affairs in confidence and without any receipts on his part."[61] It was possible to eschew paper because ultimately a debt and the interest paid on it depended on the agreement between the borrower and the lender. The contract formalized this relationship but was not required to create it. Moncuit collected what papers he could from Citizen Dorez, and wrote to inform the director that he had received them. The director wrote back, horrified that he had not properly registered the documents: "I cannot conceive how you could receive the papers without making a record."[62]

He demanded that Moncuit come back to his office in person "without delay to take back these items, you must feel that it is indispensable for your responsibility and to avoid any future claims that you arrange with Citizen Dorez to make an inventory together." In requiring Moncuit to go back to the person who had provided the material and create an inventory with him, the director was effectively asking him to replay the original receipt of the documents. Important actions could only be considered to have taken place if a record was made of them. Under this fastidiousness lay a truth about property ownership. While there was no doubt that a building existed, it could not be owned without paperwork to connect it to a person, and it could not be confiscated without a paper record either. Given the historical nature of title, chain of custody became important—hence the need to create a receipt for the papers, as this could prevent documents from being lost and, potentially, authenticate their source.

Of course, paper, while essential, was not always sufficient to maintain ownership. Some forms of property, such as company stock, could require an ongoing relationship to remain valid. After Antoine Brochet de Saint-Prest was condemned to death, the Domain confiscated his interest in a coal mine. It turned out, however, that the mine held weekly shareholder meetings. Someone needed to attend and represent the interests of the Domain.[63] The director recommended sending a man named Lecouturier, the cashier for the mine shareholders' corporation and the person who had told the Domain about Saint-Prest's shares in the first place.[64] All the same, paper remained the crucial first step.

The property seizure process required specific knowledge on the part of the people carrying it out. To keep the process moving, personnel in the Domain office exercised expertise and discretion as they identified and read the papers that related to property transactions. However, there was no single method for identifying émigré property. Sometimes, assets were declared by a contracting party; other times, the paper was pulled out of an émigré house. In yet other situations, a third party reported knowledge of a relevant transaction. Even with the paper in hand, additional steps might be necessary, such as attending a meeting or securing additional papers or goods themselves. Perhaps unsurprisingly, the officials themselves did not frame their work in these terms. They rarely made the exercise of their own judgment explicit, deferring instead to the disembodied ideal of the republic. Whereas the nation had the use of its hands to achieve its ends, the republic exercised that more dispassionate resource, interest.

The Interest of the Republic

Considering the errors, fruitless searches, and hostile work environments that characterized the confiscation process, it would be possible to conclude that administrators had no idea, really, what they were doing. But property *did* change hands through their efforts. Officials made sense of the laws and orders, and sooner or later they laid their hands on the right papers. They exercised expertise and good judgment to answer cascades of questions: How should a given individual be categorized, and which corresponding set of procedures should be applied? Which in a series of successive laws was the relevant one to be applied? What was the best means of meeting the clear imperative of the émigré laws, that confiscated property should be made to produce revenue? To answer these questions, administrators consulted "the interest of the Republic." The phrase implies an appeal to authority, but in fact it reflected a judgment passed by an individual. In contrast to the kind of state authority it seems to invoke, the authority exercised through this phrase was generally wielded by officials at the local level.

From the early days of the Terror through the Directory, directors in the Domain bureau spoke of "the interest" or "the interests" of the republic when encouraging subordinates or superiors to take action. In some situations, the phrase acted as a shorthand for whichever procedures were required in a given case. When Gentil learned that local officials had made off with the armoires and hardware from yet another building, he asked the Agence National du Domaine to "take the measures that the interest of the Republic requires to restore these effects."[65] In another case, he explained to his superiors, "I did what the interest of the Republic prescribed."[66] Though the sources most often reflect the Paris director's use of the term, he was not the only one to invoke this language. The minister of finances also did so, suggesting it was in fairly widespread use among administrators.[67]

Broadly speaking, the term could serve to justify administrative activities. Gentil told Balduc to proceed with auctioning the produce from an émigré garden, reminding him, "the interest of the Republic requires the greatest speed."[68] This same interest was consulted to determine whether new leases should be signed for a large covered market belonging to the family of an émigré named Boulainvilliers before the building could be sold. The Department wrote to the director, "Awaiting this decision, the interest of the Republic and that of the Boulainvilliers heirs requires that the property not remain uninhabited."[69] In these cases, the interest of the republic appears self-serving, as the director and the Department seemed to use it to lend authority to their own point of view.

When used to justify actions, the interest of the republic took on the quality of the spirit of the law, able to trump the letter of the law. Theoretically, the Paris bureau needed authorization from the Department to sign a lease on a sequestered property. In reality, however, the director urged his subordinates to go ahead with rentals before authorization came through. When he learned of a property belonging to an émigré that had not been included with her other goods on the émigré list, Gentil wrote to the Department asking that it be entered. He added that "in the meantime I prescribed to the Receiver of the Régie all the dispatch that the interest of the Republic requires." The president of the Department assented in the same language, telling Gentil, "In the meantime I authorize you to undertake all the duties prescribed to you by the interests of the Republic."[70] The fixity of the formula suggests habitual usage, a sort of wink and nod that, in this case, allowed both parties to sidestep the fact that the actions in question contravened the procedures set in place by the law. The interest of the republic, not the mandate of law, was invoked to justify these actions.

Each time an official invoked the interest of the republic, he made a judgment call. When the director learned that a canon of the Cathedral of Notre Dame de Paris, Bochard de Champigny, would soon be included on the émigré list, he immediately wrote to the local receiver where the house was located and to the agent for rentals. He took this action because, as he explained to the Department, "I thought it necessary to prescribe the appropriate measures to obtain the advantage required by the interest of the Republic." As in other instances, he chose to act before Champigny's property had been recognized and registered on the émigré property list. He explained to Balduc, the agent in charge of rentals, that "authorization from the Department isn't necessary for me to take advantage of their assets, unless the owners are only accused of emigration and have not been placed on the émigré list." Given that the émigré in question had already been placed on the list, "it's enough that on your opinion I alert the Domain, but you can always go on ahead and take the measures required of you by the interest of the Republic. You should remember these instructions for similar cases."[71] To justify that he had remained within the boundaries of the law, Gentil had to parse its terms carefully. Significantly, he used the episode to establish a policy, giving Balduc instructions based on his interpretation.

The building presented further complexities, because Champigny owned only seven-eighths of it; the other eighth belonged to his sister. The administrators of the Department reminded the director that "by the terms of article 16 of the law of 8 April 1792 the Régie is charged with taking possession of assets that are shared and undivided with émigrés."[72] The Domain would take over administration of the entire house and pay the sister her share of revenue. Even the relatively simple act of taking possession of a house, which represented just the tip of the iceberg within the confiscation process, required careful attention to the specific details of the case so that the proper laws could be selected and applied. The administrator's habit of citing the law and the interest of the republic could be seen as excessive dependence, the officials acting as automatons who simply applied the statutes they received. But if the choices that officials made about which law to follow or whether to "go on ahead" of the law were obvious, then the motivations behind any given decision would not have to be cited so consistently.

The use of "interest" to justify actions is especially intriguing because the concept did not carry particular political weight before the Revolution. The word "interest" appears in Jean Bodin's influential *Six Books of the Republic,* first published in 1576, where it referred both to abstract benefit and to interest payments on debt. These references do not shine much light on the revolutionary usage, however, and this is not surprising. The basis of Old Regime monarchy was not interest but will, and the phrase "le roi le veut" (the king wills it) carried ultimate power.[73]

The word "interest" appears more frequently and significantly in republican political theory, but even here it does not rise to the importance given it by revolutionary officials. John Locke used it in the *Second Treatise,* in crucial chapters discussing the extent of government powers in the Commonwealth.[74] It also appears, with particular significance, in Rousseau's *Social Contract.* Here, Rousseau argued not only that society is rendered necessary by the opposition of individual interests but also that common interest is the basis of legitimate government.[75] The concept of will is more strongly associated with Rousseau, however, in the sense of the general will, and the word appears about three times more often than "interest." The revolutionary usage puts more weight on the term than could be drawn from Rousseau alone.

Whatever its origin, Domain officials were not the only ones to invoke the interest of the republic in the revolutionary years. The phrase appeared regularly in parliamentary debates from the beginning of the First French Republic in September 1792. It appears with particular intensity around the trial of Louis XVI in January 1793, when lawmakers used it frequently to discuss whether the king should receive the death penalty. It appears periodically in legislative texts, from the beginning of the republic in 1792 through the Directory and Consulate years, primarily in military and administrative contexts: "the interest of the republic requires that their work be executed without confusion," or "to take the measures that the interest of the Republic requires." The same phrase, in the same context as the one used by employees in the Domain, appears in a decree ordering two members of the Convention to visit the army in the north, take action in the interest of the republic, and report back.[76] This usage evokes both urgency and a certain vagueness—it's not clear exactly what needs to be done, but someone must figure it out and do it as soon as possible.

Did the Domain officials learn the usage from lawmakers? It may have originated from a third source. Whatever the case, it appears to have been far more prevalent in administrative contexts than legislative ones. In the correspondence of the Domain, the phrase captures the tension administrators faced, between following the letter of the law without deviating, on the one hand, and finding solutions to situations the law did not predict, on the other.

Conclusion

Old Regime customary law concerning title continued to apply in the revolutionary era. Property titles continued to depend on human relationships, most importantly the relationship between contracting parties, but also the relationship between the Domain official and the émigré, engaged at times in something resembling a game of cat and mouse. And yet the Revolution created a radically new context in which these rules were applied, establishing the ideal of an orderly administration in which laws flowed down from the national level and were applied seamlessly by administrators. In the context of property seizure, this meant that administrators—people making decisions—took on particular importance, as they were capable of bridging the gap between old and new, to adapt old rules to a new context.

Tocqueville's account of centralization focuses on local administrators' loss of autonomy. Balzac's portrayals of bureaucrats show them to be ineffectual. But from the perspective of the seizure process, it is striking what incredible authority local officials came to wield. They determined who owned what, and took things away from people deemed to own things in the wrong way. By this account, the Revolution represented an extraordinary extension of state power. Property rights became a symbol of the individual citizen's rights against the state, but at the same time, the state became the final arbiter of those rights in a more far-reaching, day-to-day way than ever before. The Bourbon monarchy could take things away from people, but it did not bother itself with registering property or scrutinizing title. The work of Domain officials, verifying property title on an enormous scale, represented a stunning invasion of the state into a realm where it had not gone before—a realm that, as Chapter 1 showed, was explicitly shielded as private, outside the purview of anyone but a narrow family circle. Their work had this effect because the seizure process was a strictly legal one—it was neither arbitrary nor extralegal.

It is customary to identify the emergence of separate public and private realms in the eighteenth century.[77] Where one's personal status determined one's political rights under the Old Regime, the democratic revolutions of the eighteenth century separated the public realm of government from the private realm of wealth and family. Property, however, remained a crucial bridge between these realms. On the one hand, property was closely related to citizenship. Consequently, as Chapters 1 and 2 demonstrated, lawmakers sought to establish greater transparency around property ownership. The relationship between property and citizenship was made possible by the émigré laws, which inverted the principle of popular sovereignty by taking property away from bad citizens. On the other hand, it remained extremely difficult for administrators to find out what someone owned if that person did not want the information revealed. The key to all the Domain's difficulties in taking possession of émigré property was that the émigrés resisted, either actively, by sending property titles to relatives, or passively, by leaving their papers in a mess and keeping track of debts orally. The case of émigré property does not reflect a separation of public from private so much as a struggle between these realms for control of property.

The result of this struggle between lawmakers and émigrés was the empowerment of administrators as the arbiters of property. Karl Marx sneered at Hegel's naive idea that administrators play a crucial role as mediators between the state and its citizens. He argued instead that bureaucrats simply served their own interests.[78] Neither position entirely captures what was going on in the Domain. In "the interest of the Republic," one might well find the thinly veiled interest of administrators themselves, seeking an expedient solution or putting forward their own views. But just as lawmakers' quest to achieve transparency brought property more tightly under the surveillance of the state, so also the administrators' self-serving ballet achieved something unintentional: the veil of secrecy that had shrouded property was lifted, and administrators were largely successful in separating émigrés from their assets.

As we have seen already, however, émigré property was heavily leveraged. The confiscation process separated émigrés from formal ownership of assets, but this was not the only way to be connected to an asset. Possessions were caught in a web of relationships connecting the owner to their creditors. The following chapters will consider the ways that owners—and others—could be connected to property. The Revolution layered new significance onto existing functions of property in politics and society. The uses of property also evolved and expanded over the course of the eighteenth century, as a result of economic and cultural shifts.

Césarine's Inheritance

CÉSARINE TALARU WAS MEANT to inherit from her uncle, a bishop with no children of his own. Her uncle, like many clergy, refused to swear an oath of allegiance to the Revolution and instead emigrated. The inheritance seemed to be lost, seized as the property of an émigré, until clergy assets were released toward the end of the Convention government. Once again, her mother, Henriette Becdelièvre, hoped that Césarine might inherit her uncle's property, including his house in the Rue Saint-Fiacre. But Césarine's brother, an officer in the army of Louis XVI, had also emigrated. Because he was her coheir, his status meant that any indivisible assets—such as a house—would be placed under sequester until they could be liquidated. Once again, her inheritance seemed to be snatched away.

Henriette Becdelièvre worked tirelessly to secure her daughter's intended assets, but her own relationship to her émigré son placed those assets under threat. As the parent of an émigré, Becedelièvre saw her own property placed under sequester, nullifying the guarantee she had provided the revolutionary state in order to get Césarine's assets provisionally released. As the status of each of her relatives changed, so too did the shape of Césarine's future. The evolving body of émigré law created cause for hope and brought fresh troubles. Césarine in the Rue Saint-Fiacre each remained the same, moving closer together or farther apart as policy changed and Césarine's relatives lived or died in law.

This chapter focuses on the contents of a single dossier, following the property of the Talaru family—and Césarine's inheritance, in particular—across the course of the Revolution. Paying close attention to a single dossier gives the opportunity to see the operations of administrators across the seizure process, and puts their actions into the context of a particular array of assets that composed a family's patrimony. The opportunities for the Domain to translate these assets into cash varied depending on the nature of the asset and the relationship of the asset to its owner. In this way, the different facets of a single case highlight the conundrum of value that seizing émigré property raised. The Talaru family's dossier is an especially instructive focal point because it draws together a variety of types of assets: personal property, real estate, and financial obligations. It also involves two generations of a family: in this case, Ange-François Talaru and his brother, and the younger generation of Césarine and her brother. The family dynamic is further expanded by the presence of a widowed spouse, Becdelièvre, in the same generation as her husband and brother-in-law, but working on behalf of her children. Finally, the case shows an extensive back-and-forth within the Domain and between the Domain and the family, represented by Henriette Becdelièvre.

In tracing the interrelationship of persons and things through a single dossier, the chapter aims to illuminate the varying forms of value attributed to property by both émigré families and administrators, and the challenges of translating one form of value into another. The monetary value of many of the Talaru assets depended either on the Talarus' social status or on personal relationships with tenants—factors that made it difficult for the Domain to convert them into cash. Becdelièvre's continuing efforts to secure the release of her daughter's inheritance from state sequester were eventually successful in part because of this interdependence of asset and owner. Her efforts also succeeded because the changing émigré laws offered new opportunities for her to challenge the state administration of the assets, even as these and other revolutionary laws also sometimes made the negotiations more complicated for her. The forms of value at play in this case—monetary and different forms of use—were brought about by the arrival of consumer culture across France in the previous century, a phenomenon that must first be considered before turning to the particulars of the Talaru case.

Real Estate and Consumer Culture in Eighteenth-Century France

The director of the Paris Domain moved among different offices as the administration of which he was part changed form; among them was a wood-paneled office in the Hôtel d'Uzès, a mansion in the northwest of Paris near what is today the Opéra Garnier. Over the course of the eighteenth century, as the Old Regime administration expanded, numerous offices of state moved into exalted single-family homes around Paris.[1] During the Revolution, émigré homes in the capital were similarly repurposed. As the émigrés were excised from the new regime, their property was given a prominent place, quite literally becoming the face—or facade—of the new regime.

While the Parisian mansions of émigré aristocrats served the new regime, high-profile buildings associated with the nobility and the Church suffered a very different fate. In the early years of the Revolution, dozens of provincial châteaux were burned by peasants from the neighboring countryside; subsequently, a law passed at the height of the Terror called for châteaux that were not "useful" to be destroyed.[2] In Paris, many churches were destroyed or damaged: Saint-Jacques les Boucheries, in the center of the city, near the city hall, was dismantled for its stone; the church of Saint-Germain-des-Prés on the Left Bank, home to one of the wealthiest monastic orders in France, lost two bell towers and a wall, along with statues and artwork. The churches were targeted as symbols of the monarchy; the Gallic Church was a wing of the state and, as such, carried the same taint as the king and his ministers. In this sense, the fate of these buildings echoed that of the Bastille prison, which was attacked by a crowd of Parisians on July 14, 1789, and ultimately razed.

Mansions belonging to the émigrés were conspicuously spared from sale by the revolutionary government. Moreover, many traces of their former owners—including names of buildings, furnishings, and information about provenance—were also maintained by administrators working on behalf of the revolutionary state. In the Hôtel d'Uzès, which housed the Administration des Domaines Nationaux after it was vacated by the Paris bureau director, the furniture in the office of the head of archives included pieces gathered from the homes of victims of the guillotine, including "a round desk chair, with a cane seat and Moroccan leather cushion, the back decorated in the same way, sourced from la Roche du Maine, condemned." Another office contained "a large desk in Indian wood covered with black Moroccan leather, decorated with a large number of gilded bronzes and figures at the four feet, with three drawers, sourced from Durvey, condemned."[3] Records matter-of-factly note the sources of the furniture alongside other information about its appearance and quality that allowed it to be identified and evaluated.

Today, some of the most iconic addresses of the contemporary French state can also be traced back to émigré owners—though nearly all of these houses were transferred to private hands at some point before returning to state ownership. Especially spectacular examples are the Hôtel de Matignon, which serves as the prime minister's office and residence, and the former palace of the Princesse de Bourbon, now the seat of the National Assembly. The Ministry of Education, in the Hôtel de Rochechouart, and the Ministry of Defense, in the superb Hôtel de Brienne, share the same lineage. The French national furniture collection, the *Mobilier National,* which provides furnishings for public offices and state residences, still includes furnishings confiscated from royal and noble families during the Revolution. To this day, these furnishings bear a series of inventory marks that allow them to be traced to their original owners—even as they are stored together in warehouses and shuffled through ministries and official residences.[4]

In some cases, then, a connection was maintained between the émigré owner and their possessions even after the ownership claim had been dissolved. Yet as the houses and furniture became public property, they came to symbolize not the specific pasts of their noble owners but a more general, hazy past of cultural grandeur. A description of the Hôtel de Brienne on a now-defunct website of the Ministry of Defense demonstrates this sleight of hand. On the main floor, the office of the minister "is situated in the former apartments of Louise-Elisabeth de Bourbon-Condé, princesse de Conti, daughter of Mademoiselle de Nantes, grand-daughter of Louis XIV and Madame de Montespan."[5] Meanwhile, the first floor of the mansion includes the office occupied by General de Gaulle "for several days" in June 1940 and again for two years after the liberation of Paris. Also on the first floor, the boudoir of "Madame Mère," Laetizia Bonaparte, maintains all the original Empire furnishings placed there by Napoleon's mother. This description of the house elides distinct periods of French history: in the former home of an émigré, an Old Regime princess and a contemporary president of the republic are presented in the same breath.

A similar dynamic is apparent during National Patrimony Days, a weekend observed across European nations when public offices are opened for the public to visit. One of the most popular destinations in Paris is the Hôtel de Matignon, the French prime minister's office. Like 10 Downing Street or the White House, the name of the building is used to refer to the office of its occupant—though in the case of Matignon, the name is the same as that of an émigré family, the Goyon de Matignons, and the building itself was confiscated from the Grimaldi-Monaco family as émigré property (it has not been in continuous public ownership since the Revolution, however). Upon filing through the building, the awed visitor can take in a Louis XV furniture set covered in blue silk in the *"salon bleu."* As the Ministry of the Interior's website notes about the room, "After serving as office [*cabinet*] to the princes of Monaco, the salon today welcomes foreign personalities on official visits."[6] The yellow salon served as an office to a succession of French political luminaries including Léon Blum, Robert Schuman (one of the early advocates of what would become the European Union), Edgar Faure, and Pierre Mendès-France. The Ministry website notes that in this room, "one can admire under the alcove a tapestry from the *Gobelins* factory illustrating the birth of Diana and Apollo as part of the décors created by Pierre Mignard for the Château de Saint-Cloud (1692)." Much like the office of the Ministry of Defense, the prime minister's office integrates émigré property alongside the names of illustrious statesmen and art commissioned by the Sun King, Louis XIV; all are presented as parts of the French national patrimony.

Once symbols of Old Regime royal splendor, houses like the Hôtel de Brienne and the Hôtel de Matignon are now symbols of a shared, imaginary national heritage. Moreover, the state's public language elides the massive ruptures that transformed these buildings into emblems of national patrimony. To understand how this transformation was possible, we must consider what it meant to own an aristocratic mansion in Paris at the end of the eighteenth century.

The mansions of Paris were part of an expansion in consumer goods that took place over the course of the eighteenth century in Europe and America. Global trade and changing production techniques rapidly expanded the number of things available to buy and made many existing goods cheaper for people living in Europe.[7] The number of things the average person owned skyrocketed.[8] As things like china dishes and fashionable clothing came into the reach of a broader swath of society, they telegraphed specific meaning about the kind of person their owner was. In this way, the influx of consumer goods not only expanded the range of things a person could buy but also brought new significance to ownership.[9] Of course, the things a person owned had always provided information about what kind of person they were. But consumer goods radically expanded the range of information that things could provide and, as a result, the kind of persona their owner could project, to others or themselves.

The expansion of consumer goods was part of a broader transformation of the types of assets available over the course of the eighteenth century in France.[10] In addition to circulating new types of consumer goods, global trade brought new credit instruments into being. Overseas trading required vast amounts of capital, which were mobilized through the sale of shares to investors. In addition, the expanding sovereign debt provided opportunities for people to invest in public annuities, which they did across the social spectrum.[11] Before the Revolution, merchants sank their earnings into royal offices that could grant nobility—and then used the offices as security for loans. A market for private credit brokered by notaries thrived both in Paris and in the provinces at the end of the Old Regime.[12] Financial assets are generally treated separately from consumer goods, by everyone from tax authorities to historians, on the grounds that they are economically quite different. Consumer goods, as their name suggests, are meant to be consumed, whereas financial assets are intended to produce value by generating revenue. From the perspective of the owner, however, this distinction doesn't hold up all that well. Luxury goods can increase in value, while investments can contribute to the same kinds of consumption and identity building as consumer goods.[13]

Consumer goods fall into the category of movable or personal property in French law, but real estate could function in this way as well. The capital witnessed a massive building boom in the eighteenth century, which brought about a physical expansion of the city limits.

A number of the new neighborhoods were among the most fashionable in the city. In fact, over the course of the century, noble families largely decamped from mansions in the Marais, near the city center, to emerging neighborhoods in the west of the city. They were joined there by a relatively newly minted elite of financiers, who earned their fortunes investing in the growing commercial trade with East Asia and the East and West Indies—a trade driven, in no small part, by enslaved workers producing commodity crops—and earned their status by lending money to the monarchy.[14] A Paris townhome, then, was palpably different from a noble château, even if both were owned by the same family. A château connected its owner to a lineage reaching as far back into the past as possible (the older, the more elite). A newly built mansion in Paris, however, signaled that its owner was part of a new and rapidly changing world of fashionable elites.

The relative novelty of consumerism at the time of the Revolution is important because it introduced a new way of relating to things at a time when the relationship between people and things was taking on political significance. Modern European political theorists have described property as a realm in which humans exert dominion over nature.[15] The ability of a person to dominate the physical world became the basis for the modern liberal political model in which individuals are autonomous and equal. That is, our relationship to things, and specifically our ability to dominate and control the things around us, has defined our relationship to each other as citizens.[16] But our relationship to things is not a one-way street. We shape the physical world, but it also shapes us. Individuals, in this light, are not autonomous and powerful. Rather, they are enmeshed in webs of people and things that shape not only their identity but also their ability to act in the world. Consumer goods are a key part of this dynamic, because they allowed people to engage in self-fashioning to an extent that was not possible before. Consumer goods brought new ways of relating to self and others, as well as new ways of measuring value.[17] The late eighteenth century in Europe was a time when the appearance of new types of things intersected with new ways of theorizing humans' relationship to things, with consequences for political and economic life as well as culture.

The émigré laws, as we have seen, assumed a transparent relationship between people and things, such that things could be separated from their owners and then sold to someone else as a means of generating revenue for the state. This assumption was based on the idea that property can be taken from one person and transferred to another without fundamentally being altered by the operation. It is fungible and inert. Person and thing, however, were not so easily divided from each other. This was because people and things were interdependent in a variety of ways. People drew their identities from things, and things drew various forms of value (which will be explored in this chapter) from their owners. Depending on the human relationships into which property owners entered, their possessions might be used or altered by an array of other people as well. In some instances, such as the relationship between landlord and tenant, the thing itself brought the relationship into being. The boundaries between persons and things could not be clearly drawn. This dynamic was not limited to consumer goods, in the sense of personal property; it applied to real estate and investments as well as wine or art or mattresses. All of these types of property were created within a regime of consumption that shaped their monetary value and their usefulness. This meant that the Paris mansions of the émigrés could be repurposed in a way that churches and châteaux could not: the churches and châteaux were destroyed because they were so indelibly associated with the status hierarchies of the Old Regime. The mansions, in contrast, were part of the dynamic of consumerism: they were capable of inspiring desire and adaptable to the identity of a new owner.

The Talaru Dossier

The Talarus resembled many émigré families. Henriette Becdelièvre, the family member who stayed behind and with whom officials had to contend, came from nobility in Normandy. Her father owned a *seigneurie*—a feudal property with rights of justice attached to it—and her brother joined the Military Order of Malta. Her deceased husband, Louis-François de Talaru, came from a particularly high-ranking noble family.[18] A viscount, he had a position in the queen's household and served as a *Conseiller d'Etat;* these roles placed him at the highest levels of court nobility.

Louis-François's younger brother, Ange-François Talaru, bishop of Coutances, was elected to the Estates-General but fled to England after the passing of the Civil Constitution of the Clergy in June 1790, which required an oath of allegiance from all of France's priests. His flight made him a "voluntarily deported priest," a category that was rolled in with that of the émigrés.[19] Talaru's older brother César-Marie, a count, served in the Royal Army during the Seven Years' War and managed the domains of the queen. He was condemned by the Revolutionary Tribunal and guillotined on July 22, 1794, five days before the fall of Robespierre ended the Terror.[20] Like many noble military officers, Talaru and Becdelièvre's son, Louis-Justin, departed to the Austrian Empire, where he almost certainly joined the Prince de Condé's counterrevolutionary army. Their daughter Césarine stayed with Becdelièvre in Paris. In many ways, then, the Talarus embodied lawmakers' worst fears about the émigrés. Members of a retrograde social order, they actively resisted the Revolution: Ange-François refused to swear the oath of loyalty required of clergy, Louis-Justin left the country, and Becdelièvre actively contested the émigré laws meant to punish her family members.

During the Legislative Assembly debates over emigration, representatives frequently portrayed the émigrés as Old Regime relics, stuck in a bygone age. For example, one representative described them as "these ulcerated spirits, ashamed of outliving their prerogatives, who have carried their pride, who have interred their regrets and their despair in foreign lands."[21] When another representative noted how numerous the emigrations had become, a colleague interrupted him to shout, "All the better! All the better! They're aristocrats—so much rubbish carried out!"[22] Legislators' views reflected popular sentiment: cartoons that appeared in the Revolution portrayed the émigrés as desiccated figures in ragged frock coats—phantoms from the past, their fortunes literally in tatters.

There was nothing retrograde, however, about the Talarus' Paris-based assets, which telegraphed the latest fashions and savviest investment vehicles. Ange-François owned a Paris mansion in the Rue Saint-Fiacre, a fashionable address associated with the emergent financial elite of the capital. One of his brothers had purchased it for him in 1780, likely from the builder.[23] The contents of the house included a large wine collection, suggesting that Ange-François made the most of the booming wine industry of the eighteenth century. His brother César-Marie owned two other houses nearby in the Rue de Richelieu (known at the time as Rue de la Loi). The family also owned an interest in the Halle aux Vins, a wine warehouse in southeast Paris. As for liabilities, Becdelièvre and her late husband owed a *rente viagère* (a type of annuity) to Antoine Auget-Montyon in exchange for ownership of his estate after his death.[24] In this transaction, Becdelièvre and her husband had purchased the Auget-Montyon lands; selling patrimonial property against a life annuity was a relatively novel transaction.[25]

According to the dossier compiled by Domain officials in Paris, the Talaru confiscation took about eight years, from 1795 through December 1803. It may have taken longer; the date when the property was initially sequestered is not recorded, a fact common in the émigré dossiers. This amount of time was not particularly unusual for Paris dossiers, though the Talarus' was much thicker than most. This was in large part because Henriette Becdelièvre sparred with administrators for years as she sought to protect her daughter Césarine's inheritance. César-Marie left his estate to his brother Ange-François and his niece and nephew, Becdelièvre's children; they could inherit from him thanks to the law of 18 prairial III (June 6, 1795), which released the property of those condemned by the Revolutionary Tribunal to their heirs.[26] The children also stood to inherit from their uncle, Ange-François. Normally, as an émigré, Ange-François would have his assets seized and his heirs would receive nothing. However, the property of deported priests was allowed to be returned to heirs by the law of 20 fructidor IV (September 6, 1796).

The Talaru dossier resembles many other dossiers in that it reflects the efforts of a woman to preserve an interest in the assets of male relatives who left the country. The legal recourse of women in this position was limited, as married women only had a claim to assets as joint property held with their spouse; only widows could own property themselves. Even widows who could own property often only had claims to their husband's lineage assets in the form of life rights of occupancy. Women seeking to protect assets could seek a divorce, legal for the first time in 1792 as a result of the Revolution; this would protect a portion of marital assets.[27] Otherwise, a woman could occupy a threatened property, as laws made provision for the family members of émigrés to continue living in buildings under confiscation, and allowed certain types of goods deemed necessary—by lawmakers—for daily life to be excluded from sequester.[28]

For Becdelièvre, a widow who lived in her own home, neither option was available. Her approach, to act in the name of an underage heir, was rare. All the same, her relationship to the confiscated property echoes that of other women whose attempts to preserve their own property are documented in the dossiers. Like Becdelièvre, all of these women could only make claims indirectly, via their position as the widow or heir of a male property owner. In the face of formal barriers to women's property ownership, each woman mobilized her resources and knowledge of the law to make claims in other ways. During the Revolution, women repeatedly turned to existing legal means to respond to the novel threat of revolutionary confiscation. In the property seizure process, women operated as peripheral claimants—that is, people who were not formally the owners of a property, but made strategic use of the law to exert compelling ownership claims. Like other kinds of peripheral claimants represented in the dossiers, such as tenants in émigré properties, they often repurposed legal arguments and methods to respond to the unprecedented challenges of the confiscation process.

This chapter focuses especially on the ways in which the actions of Henriette Becdelièvre and the nature of the Talaru property thwarted Domain officials' attempts to separate one from the other. Owners and property were interconnected in many ways. The financial value of both personal property and real estate depended on the particular social position of their owner, even as owners used property to construct that identity. Moreover, relationships between property owners and other people made it difficult to separate assets. Henriette Becdelièvre's relationship with the Talaru property, for example, was frankly tenuous: she spent a great deal of time defending the assets of her brother-in-law, which she did not own nor would she ever own. But this did not reduce the significance of her role—even if her action was limited, it was action all the same.

You Are What You Drink

Sometime before 1795, the Domain bureau took steps to seize the houses that Ange-François and César-Marie owned on the Right Bank. It's not clear in the dossier when, exactly, the Talaru property was placed under sequester; this information was not systematically noted, perhaps because it was the municipality that placed seals on houses, but the

Domain that administered sequester once it was established. The furniture from the houses was removed to warehouses; Ange-François's household goods were taken to the former Capucin monastery, in the Rue Saint-Honoré, not far from his home. In August 1797, these things were moved to the former monastery of the Grands-Augustins, located on the Left Bank near Saint Germain-des-Prés.[29] Finally, in November 1798, they were moved again to the nearby seminary of Saint-Sulpice. To reach the Left Bank from the Rue Saint-Honoré, Ange-François's belongings would have made a long wagon journey across the Right Bank and over one of the bridges of the Seine. Administrators deemed the wine collection, however, too fragile and heavy to move. It remained in the Saint-Fiacre house, and a neighbor was hired to see that the seals on the doors and windows remained undisturbed. This guardian, a woman named in the Domain dossier as Citizen Aubertin, lived around the corner in the Rue Saint-Marc, about five minutes away.[30]

In eighteenth-century France, home to a growing luxury wine industry, a well-appointed Parisian home would have been expected to include a wine collection. No inventory of Ange-François's cellar has survived, but details of other émigré collections tell a tale of opulence. One émigré's collection contained 540 bottles of champagne. A lot of more than 200 bottles belonging to another émigré contained "60 bottles of Malvoisie, Constance; 60 bottles of Champagne; 60 bottles of Pacaret and Rivesaltes; 60 bottles of Hungarian wine, Tockay [sic] and Malaga."[31] The wine telegraphed both wealth and taste. Such a collection required the owner to invest in the services of dishes, beakers, and dining room furniture to show it off to advantage, not to mention servants to open and pour it. It also required, of course, a house large enough to store it.

Practically speaking, then, the house in the Rue Saint-Fiacre and its wine collection remained intact: one immovable, the other impractical to move. However, their inseparability reflects a deeper complementarity.

House and cellar together allowed Ange-François to construct his identity as a certain kind of wealthy elite. The neighborhoods of Paris situated their residents within a finely drawn, but shifting, social geography. Becdelièvre's home, for example, was located on the Left Bank in the Rue de Varennes, in a neighborhood associated with the court nobility, the most elite nobles who frequented Versailles. Both the Rue Saint-Fiacre and the Rue de Richelieu, meanwhile, were associated with high finance: investors, tax farmers, and other members of France's wealthiest elite. An address in the finance quarter, along with the elaborate parties for which the wine cellar was stocked, situated Ange-François among peers of a certain kind.[32] The house, recently bought, might easily be sold or rented out if tastes changed and Ange-François found it convenient to move elsewhere. Already in the eighteenth century, the axis of elite Paris had shifted from the Marais to Saint-Germain and the Faubourg Saint-Honoré. By the end of the eighteenth century, the Champs-Elysées was being developed, pushing the frontiers of the city westward.[33]

In the hands of the Domain, however, the wine quickly became an albatross as the costs of paying Aubertin to guard it mounted. It was supposed to be sold, like the rest of Ange-François's furnishings, but this failed to happen as years went by. The national directors of the Domain wrote to the Paris bureau director in July 1799 to scold him about the delay, noting that the costs of guarding the bottles had already eaten up their value. They wrote again in September with new urgency, reminding the director, "As you know, the wines that make up a part of this property are spoiling from one day to the next."[34] Finally, a week later, the sale was concluded.

Stacked in the cellar of Ange-François's house, the wine collection served as an avatar of its owner's elite status. The wine and the house complemented and reinforced Ange-François's position in French society: he both drew meaning from them as indicators of his place in society and realized their social value by using them properly to host lavish parties. But when the state assumed ownership of the house, the meaning of the bottles shifted. Gathering dust in the cellar, they became a simple repository of monetary value—and then, a financial encumbrance. This shift occurred because the Domain could not use the wine in the same way that Ange-François could. As a result, the bottles passed their peak of drinkability, which further altered their monetary value.

Since wine is a consumer good, Ange-François's collection might reasonably be assumed to be categorically different from his house—a piece of real property that could not be bought and consumed in the same way. But the house itself belies that distinction. Bought in 1780, it could not have been much older, as the neighborhood was not fashionable enough for such an expensive house to be built there much before then. Many such houses were built on speculation by an architect who did not have a specific client lined up.[35] To an extent, the dependence of the house on social context for monetary value reflects a transhistorical reality of property. But the Saint-Fiacre house was particularly dependent on fashionability, a product of the growth of consumerism and the expansion of the real estate market, two trends new to the eighteenth century. Real estate became an increasingly flexible asset over the course of the century, as a market for it grew.[36] Previously, it had overwhelmingly been something one inherited—so much so that in legal documents, *héritages* was a synonym for real property. At the same time, real estate began to take on a greater spectrum of meaning as it became more widely available and took on a wider variety of forms. Ultimately, both the house and the wine collection were brought into being by the logic of consumption, meant to be consumed and replaced.

The house and the wine collection had multiple sources of value for Talaru. Both had value in the sense that they were worth money—they could be sold, and they represented assets. They also had value to Talaru in their practical and social usefulness. The former could be expressed through consumption, in the sense that having a place to live or something to drink was useful to him. The latter could be expressed in the social currency they gave him: the house and the wine collection were valuable to him as social assets, one could say, that bolstered his social position. When the Domain seized these assets, it did so on the grounds of their monetary value. This was the stated purpose of the émigré property policy—to realize the monetary value of seized assets. But the state was not immune to the other sources of value émigré property possessed, even as it struggled to capture this value.

50,000 *Mattresses*

The meaning that Talaru's wine collection held for him, and the meaning that it helped him construct through its use, made it more useful to him than to the Domain, to which it was valuable only to the extent that it could raise cash. Or at least he was able to extract its value more successfully than Domain officials. This asymmetry was an aspect of property with which the émigré laws had not reckoned. The law assumed that émigré assets could be removed from their owners and sold in a modular way: the goods that belonged to the émigré would belong to the state, and in turn to a buyer, and the cash value would thus be transferred from émigré to state. But the cash value was not stable in this way. It depended on a number of variables, including the identity of the owner and the usefulness of the property to the owner, which were themselves highly contingent.

The hallmark of ownership is use. This is the logic behind the principle of *prescription* in French customary law, by which a piece of real property that lies unused or is notoriously in use by another party could cease to belong to its titular owner. The Domain struggled to assert ownership over émigré goods because it could not use them in the same way the émigré owners had. In the case of the wine collection, this led to a loss of value. But it was not only use that determined value: as

Talaru's expensive house and goods reflect, the recognition of owner-ship by others also contributes to the value. Ownership, in this light, is not something asserted at strategic moments, such as that of transfer; it has to be performed consistently over time.

As a steward of émigré property, the republic struggled to do this. Damage and theft constantly threatened goods under public adminis-tration. Sometimes, the threat came from within, as when the gardener at a house belonging to the former tax farmer Jean-Baptiste Tavernier de Boulogne sold off the grass in the garden.[37] Similarly, the buyer of the former Nesles mansion complained to the Domain that the out-going tenants, a group of *"artistes,"* had made off with "diverse objects such as doors, fireplace backings, locks, and built-in armoires."[38] Prob-lems also arose with clothing and furniture dealers contracted to handle sales, whose *"relations trop directes"* with buyers led to sweetheart deals at the expense of the state.[39] Scams and thefts could, of course, befall any owner, but private property under public administration seemed particularly attractive to people with nefarious intentions. The state, operating through officials at a distance, could not be as attentive as a flesh-and-blood owner overseeing the security of their assets.

Beyond the occasional unscrupulous gardener or rowdy tenants, the Domain had to contend with opportunists taking advantage of buildings known to be in limbo. A law passed by the Convention in October 1792 expressly banned the public from entering former royal palaces, reli-gious buildings, or émigré homes "to dispose of, by any manner, fur-nishings or effects from these buildings, unless they are the bearers of an express commission to this effect." It would not have been necessary to pass such a law unless people were already strolling into sequestered properties and carrying off their contents under various pretexts. The law asserted that guardians or concierges who let such people inside "will be held responsible for the disorders & damages that such people may cause there."[40] Problems persisted, as a 1796 report made in the Directory's lower house complained that "the prodigious quantity of émigré goods, that have not been sold, are degrading as an effect of poor management."[41]

Theft and spoilage were a threat because the state, as an owner, was essentially absent. The state had no use for most of the detritus of émigré life, and it made this clear by leaving the stuff under seal for months—at great cost in the wages paid to neighbors or building staff who served as caretakers.[42] The state's only interest in the flotsam of émigré households was the money that could be raised by selling it. For this reason, it languished in a transitional state until it could be sold to someone who would actually use it. The inability to exercise ownership apart from the act of selling a good undermined the state's very ability to own it.

That said, some émigré goods were set aside for use by various ministries of state. These different types of goods reflect multiple regimes of value, much as Talaru's house and wine collection offered their owner multiple sources of value. Many of the costliest goods were kept, suggesting that cash revenue was not the only criterion by which the value of goods was assessed. The ability to extract use from goods, and the ability to extract social value—or, in the case of the state, one might better say cultural value—was, in certain cases, worth the loss of the cash from a sale. A circular letter sent by the Domain to administrators across France detailed the different categories of émigré personal property and how they should be handled:

1. Furnishings and personal effects for use by wives, children, mothers and fathers of émigrés
2. Objects placed at the disposition of the Ministry of War
3. Gold and silver goods
4. Libraries and other scientific objects that should be reserved
5. Precious objects sent to safe deposit

6. Leads, coppers, tins, irons and steels, molds and metal from bells that should be put at the disposition of the Ministry of War

7. Finally, all the furnishing effects that were the object of separate inventories, or were held back from initial inventories, and not included in affidavits of sale for any reason[43]

Two different categories were explicitly reserved for the Ministry of War: the rather general "objects" and the various metals, including church bells. Previous laws and circular letters identified some of these "objects." In the fall of 1792, for example, the minister of the interior ordered the Departments to speed up their efforts to collect 50,000 mattresses from émigré homes so they could be sent to the troops fighting on the border.[44] The following autumn, sheets and blankets were requisitioned.[45] Another circular letter shortly thereafter asked for "horses, mules, wagons, mattresses, straw pallets, etc." The letter went on to explain, in the didactic tone of revolutionary officialdom, "By assigning this purpose to goods belonging to the émigrés, so that the nation may procure, as promptly as necessary, the resources that it needs, the legislators have not lost from view the means of assuring the faithful use and the exactitude of the recovery of these goods, or of their value."[46] The point of this addendum seems to have been to justify why requisitioning the goods did not violate the spirit of the law, which directed that émigré goods should be sold and their revenue taken as an indemnity. Specifically, the requisitioning measures followed the imperative of indemnifying the nation by securing resources that it needed for the war.

The heterogeneity of the listed items, however, shows that if requisitioning was a reasonable way to extract value from seized goods, such value itself was unstable and contingent. Furnishings and personal effects were, in terms of cash value, the least valuable objects taken out of the houses: used cooking implements and clothing could not command the kind of prices that real estate or furniture could. And yet, to family members living in a sequestered house, these everyday essentials were incredibly valuable, in the sense that they were useful. The list also distinguished between metals of use to the military (copper, lead, etc.) and gold and silver goods. For a nation at war, there might be few substances as precious as iron and lead, but they were classified differently, quite naturally, from gold or other "precious objects" that required safe deposit.

The situation or condition of the person or institution using the goods was not, of course, the only factor that determined the regime of value ascribed to them. The uniqueness of the goods in question was a factor as well. Inventories of books or artworks prepared by specialists discerned high-quality objects suitable for accessioning into public collections.[47] The regimes of value governing mattresses destined for the troops and leather-bound books set aside for public collections are rather different. Goods for the military were interchangeable commodities: one mattress did not differ from another. Fifty thousand mattresses could be assembled and disbursed on the assumption that they were all more or less the same; the books and artworks, meanwhile, had value in their specificity, in the sense that a particular edition of a particular title, set in a particular binding, was worth more money than another, physically similar book. The value of this specificity to the state did not lie solely in the books' resale value—if it had, they would have been sold. There was a value to the state in building a library of rare and special volumes, a value that resembled the social value Ange-François Talaru drew from his house and wine collection.

At the end of the Revolution, the transitional Directory regime staked great importance on its role in promoting culture and education. Numerous institutions, from a national natural history museum, to an art museum in the Louvre, to a national library, were founded in this period. The national library contained many books from the previous, royal library. Other libraries in Paris, such as the Sainte-Geneviève, absorbed important ecclesiastical collections. But émigré books and artwork also contributed to these institutions and others, allowing books to be distributed across several collections around the capital. Even as the state struggled to assert ownership over seized goods, it did extract value from them. This value, much like that of Talaru's wine collection, was not only monetary; it included usefulness and, within usefulness, the less easily quantifiable currency of reputation.

"A Large and Beautiful House"

The house and wine collection helped Ange-François Talaru present himself as a certain kind of person. At the same time, however, the kind of person he was—a bishop from a noble family living in a fashionable quarter of Paris and keeping up an expensive train of life—influenced the meaning associated with his things. This meaning gave his belongings particular desirability. The appeal of émigré property is especially striking in the case of their Paris mansions, such as the Hôtel d'Uzès. When a public office or agency needed office space, the architects, who had an unparalleled knowledge of seized real estate, would be consulted about which confiscated properties might suit. This task meant matching the particular needs of an administration to a building of the right size and in the right location. It also meant mediating the demands of officials, some of whom shopped the émigré collection more aggressively than others. In February 1800, the official printer for the legislature, Baudouin, needed to be moved to new quarters. He mentioned to the architect that he would like to be on the Quai Voltaire or the Rue de Lille, two of the best addresses—the most socially rarefied—in town. The Domain architect, Bourla, reported that Baudouin had subsequently asked for a house on the Quai Voltaire "serving as the *chief of staff* [*état major*] of the 17th division." Without any comment on the absurdity of the request besides what was implied in his choice of underlining (shown in italic text here), he noted that he had instead offered buildings in several other streets, "but [Baudouin] finds these properties to be too far from his business."[48] Another architect who had been set to work on the same task reported that nothing seemed to suit Baudouin in his area either. He tried to palm the task off on Bourla, telling the director, "I think that in the area managed by Citizen Bourla there is a better chance of finding something than in mine." As it began to look like nothing but the house on the Quai Voltaire would satisfy the printer, the régisseurs expressed concern that the house was rather larger than they had envisioned for Baudouin, and instructed "it's necessary to determine what portion of the house is strictly necessary for his printing."[49] Baudouin got his way, sort of—he was granted the carriage house of the property he wanted for his print shop.

The minister of war engaged in some maneuvering of his own. Writing to the Commission of Expenses (*Commission des Dépenses*) in the winter of 1797, he recalled the restraint that his ministry had exercised in its demands, noting that "only what was indispensible was kept." His offices were scheduled to be moved to a former convent, but, he observed hopefully, "if this arrangement should suffer any difficulties, one could exchange it for a large and beautiful house that I just returned to the Domain in the rue de l'Université, at the corner of the Rue du Bac." The letter essentially suggests that the state might find it more convenient to assign the ministry a valuable mansion instead of an unsellable convent with minimal decoration and a warren of nun's cells. He concluded the letter by recalling once again his record of modest demands and forbearance, observing that while it was true that the ministry had occupied many buildings in the past, "the reforms that have successively been put in place have freed up 8 superb houses that are currently either sold or rented to different citizens by the Domain, such as the houses of d'Orsay and de Broglie in the Rue de Varennes, the Monaco house in the rue Dominique, the houses of d'Avray, de Périgord, and de Montmorency in the rue de Lille, [and] a part of the Bourbon Palace."[50]

The purpose of the letter seems to have been to capitalize on the administrative holdup that had delayed the ministry's move to a drab convent, using it as an excuse to remain in a "large and beautiful house" on one of the most expensive corners in Paris. Clearly loathe to relinquish his office in this mansion, the minister appears to have made a last-ditch effort to derail the planned relocation.

The naked machinations of administrators from the state printer to the minister of war clearly show that former émigré homes carried a special cachet even for state officials. In this sense, the cultural status of émigré properties echoed their former significance as a reflection of their owners' fortunes and status. In fact, the names of those owners added a sheen to the properties themselves: the Maison Monaco and the Maison d'Orsay carried a cachet that extended even beyond their desirable addresses. The phenomenon of officials pressing their noses against the glass to gawk at the opulent lifestyles of Old Regime elites reflects a paradox in their attitudes toward émigré property. On the one hand, these objects were supposed to be inventoried and sold for the benefit of the Treasury. This was easily done for items like the mattresses, which were all essentially interchangeable. Yet on the other hand, the émigrés also owned many unique objects with an aesthetic value that could be judged—or, more directly, felt—in the emotional response they inspired. Officials often did not simply inventory and sell these objects, but rather admired and appropriated them for their use. A round desk chair with a red leather cushion was plucked from a warehouse, placed in an office, and carefully described in an inventory. Every step of the way, it was distinguished from any other desk chair. The people who chose, placed, and sat in that chair related to it not only as impersonal officers of the state but also as consumers. The administrator was an interpreter of the law, but always also a human being with emotions that could be stirred by the objects they confiscated: desire and admiration.

An Unfaithful Account

Even after officials had identified all the Talaru property, they continued to discover that the family's assets were not exactly as they seemed.[51] Henriette's sparring with the Domain brought to light a different source of instability in the cash value of the Talaru assets. As she sought to have the property, and notably the Saint-Fiacre house, released, various revelations and changes to the status of the assets created roadblocks for her and the officials managing the case. This was in part due to Becdelièvre's attempts to get the property released from sequester, which led officials to look into the assets more closely.

The Saint-Fiacre house was eligible to be released to Césarine after the law of 13 ventôse III (March 3, 1795) released the property of those condemned by the Revolutionary Tribunal. Before this could happen, however, Henriette Becdelièvre had to pay a guarantee, because half the house belonged to her émigré son Louis-Justin; when his interest was liquidated, the guarantee would be released. The sum was furnished by a man named Denis, with an address in the Rue Saint-Fiacre—a tantalizing tidbit that suggests he may have been a neighbor of Ange-François's, like Aubertin, the guardian of the wine collection. The house was finally released to Becdelièvre in April 1797, only to be placed under sequester once again in May 1797.

The house in the Rue Saint-Fiacre was placed under renewed sequester because the value of the guarantee that Becdelièvre provided lost value. Denis, the neighbor who provided the money, had mortgaged a public debt certificate, but its value plummeted when the state wrote down its debt in August 1795.[52] Becdelièvre's own ability to raise funds was limited by another turn of revolutionary law. In December 1794, the Convention required the parents of émigrés to prepare a division of their assets so that their children's inheritance could be separated out, something Becdelièvre had not done. As a result, Becdelièvre's own home, a house in the Rue de Varennes that had belonged to her husband, was also sequestered. The order detailing the reasons for the sequester of her house noted that Becdelièvre's "linens and personal effects" would be left out for her use, on the condition that she "makes herself guardian and liable and obliges herself to present them in kind to any requisition."

After the guarantee failed and the Domain delayed the release of Cesarine's inheritance, Henriette Becdelièvre undertook a campaign of direct influence at the Saint-Fiacre house. Having attempted legal measures to get the house released, she leaned on the tenants the Domain had placed in the building to recognize her as their landlord. In September 1800, she had a bailiff serve the two tenants in the Saint-Fiacre house with papers ordering them not to pay any rent to the Domain while she was contesting the confiscation.[53] The Domain learned of this when the tenants wrote to the local receiver, complaining about conflicting instructions. The receiver, ruffled by the incident, assured the Domain director, "These oppositions and denunciations, pure and simple, do not seem to me sufficient to stop the recovery of the rents in question, given that they have been under national sequester for many years, and that Citizen Talaru has not obtained their release."[54] The receiver suggested a dark reading of the tenants' decision to report Becdelièvre's action to his office. "I observe to you," he penned at the bottom of the letter, "that Citizen Berthon owes two terms of rent, amounting to 625 livres 10 sols. With regard to Citizen Massieu, he presented a petition to the Prefect, which I responded to in a letter dated the 19th of this month, number 1353. He will once again owe 618 livres 15 sols on 1 messidor." By including this information about what the tenants owed, the receiver may have wanted to imply that the tenants were taking advantage of the dispute between Becdelièvre and the Domain to avoid paying rent. He does not make this explicit, but rather simply gives the information and allows the director to draw the conclusion himself. This kind of explanatory shorthand points to the working intimacy of these officials, who clearly wrote to each other frequently enough that the receiver knew his boss would understand his point without extra explanation.

The receiver's description of the house as having been "under national sequester for many years" suggests that the case was long settled, presenting public administration of the property as a continuous state extending over time. The tenants' complaint, however, indicates that the state struggled to maintain its hold over the property. After the state took legal ownership of the Talaru property, it struggled to maintain ownership in practice. Ange-François's wine collection had to be guarded by a neighbor; the tenants in the Rue Saint-Fiacre were not paying their rent. The state had a variety of powerful tools at its disposal to control the Talaru property, including orders from the prefect, laws, decrees, and the actions of bailiffs. But its ability to hold on to the property still depended on the recognition of tenants, neighbors, and the relatives of émigré owners. From this perspective, ownership may have been a continuous state from a legal perspective, but practically speaking, it had to be performed continuously in the face of repeated challenges. Put another way, the legal category of ownership was joined to a social one, which had to be constantly renewed by the recognition of other parties.

In fact, the clerks' description of the Saint-Fiacre house was not technically accurate. It had not been under continuous administration, but rather released and then sequestered again. The house was not overseen by stable, continuous administration, but rather modeled profound instability as ownership of it shifted between Ange-François, Louis-Justin and Césarine, and the state. In 1795, the state had released the house to Ange-François's estate, to be transferred to his heirs. Louis-Justin's status as an émigré then caused Becdelièvre's own property to be sequestered and caused the episode of the failed guarantee. One might also consider Becdelièvre's challenge to the collection of rents, and the tenants' withholding of their payments, as an interruption in the smooth administration of the house.

Contrary to the clerk's account, then, the administration of the Saint-Fiacre house shifted repeatedly over time. Furthermore, the state continuously recognized the house as belonging to different pools of assets. The house was initially sequestered as the property of Ange-François, then in 1795 it became the property of Louis-Justin and his sister because Ange-François was no longer considered an émigré, thanks to the new law releasing property of deported priests. It was released to Becdelièvre on behalf of her daughter, only to be sequestered again along with a package of property in Becdelièvre's possession. Over the course of the confiscation process, then, it belonged to three different members of the family: Ange-François, Louis-Justin, and Césarine, through her mother, Henriette Becdelièvre.

The tenant challenges that arose in the case of the Rue Saint-Fiacre house were relatively straightforward, as compared with other cases recorded in the dossiers. The tenants were behind on their rent, but the Domain at least knew who they were, how much they owed, and when payment was due. Obtaining information about tenants and getting them to recognize the Domain as a new landlord could pose significant challenges to administrators tasked with assuming ownership of a property. It was not enough, in these cases, for the Domain to identify the property and obtain its title, or to place seals on the building (it could not, in any event, if the building was occupied). The Domain needed to collect rent from the tenants and, importantly, stop them from continuing to pay their rent to an émigré landlord, which meant identifying the tenants and informing them of the change. In such cases, a bailiff was dispatched to the property in question. He might speak to a lead tenant, who collected rent from the other tenants on behalf of the landlord, or to a building concierge who lived on the premises, in order to obtain a list of current occupants.

Building staff could provide crucial information, but as employees of the émigré owners their allegiance was dubious. In the Marché Boulainvilliers, an enormous building with hundreds of tenants, the concierge kept track of comings and goings and collected rent. The régisseurs, at the national level, were skeptical about relying on this individual for information about the building. They wrote to the director that "it seems abusive to us to keep Citizen Petitpierre in the job and salary that were given to him by Citizen Boulainvilliers."[55] Still, they acknowledged that "the nature of this property and its revenues may require that someone be appointed for the policing and surveillance of the tenants in these buildings." Petitpierre provided the bailiff, Sapinault, with a list of 200 tenants—which, Sapinault complained to the director, turned out to be "infidèle." Sapinault went back to the concierge's quarters inside the Marché and, finding Petitpierre's wife there, demanded that she hand over the concierge's personal account books. She finally complied, and Sapinault discovered that the original list was correct after all. He had been the victim of "fallacious reports." One of the reasons for the confusion was the "considerable number of subletters," who did not appear in the master register and, occasionally, did not know the name of the leaseholder but only the name of the tenant to whom they gave their rent money.[56]

For all the trouble with Petitpierre, the Domain was lucky to obtain a full list of the tenants with such relative ease. The house belonging to the émigré Bonneval was much smaller but had a mixture of tenants, each of whom had a different arrangement. Two tenants had leases, one tenant did not have a lease, another tenant had moved in only a few months earlier, and one tenant was one of Bonneval's servants. The arrangements for paying rent were equally byzantine. An official from the Paris rental bureau explained, "The sirs Goubert and Teray have until now always paid Mr. de Bonneval, who sends them receipts—they are both in the countryside—it wasn't possible to get any further information; the sir Favre collected the rents due through October 1st for the apartment of Mr Mars and those due September 11th for the one occupied by Mme de Neuchèze, these last two rents were used to pay the wages of the doorman . . . and the bill from a roofer . . . the surplus Mr Favre retained as an advance on his wages."[57] The arrival of the Domain, which had to determine the legal status of every tenant before either evicting them or collecting rent from them, threatened to destroy the delicate ecosystems of Paris rental buildings. It also reflected the practical qualities of ownership. It was one thing to place a building on a list or to take possession of its title documents. But ownership of a property also meant collecting the revenue it produced, which required knowledge of the property and its circumstances. The Domain knew this well, as its primary mandate in confiscating émigré property was to create revenue for the state. Ownership of a building rang hollow if someone else was pocketing the rental income.

Identifying the tenants was only the beginning of what could be a long period of public administration of a property. Domain officials spent a great deal of time chasing after tenants for rent and responding to their incessant requests and reclamations.[58] At the height of the Terror, a group of musicians wrote to ask that the escutcheon be removed from over the door of the Marquis de Bouthillier's stately home near the Place des Victoires, because it was preventing them from hanging a sign.[59] The group had been given use of the house by the Committee of Public Safety, "considering the necessity of assuring the rapid production of patriotic songs."[60] At the same time, in the same house, the régisseurs responsible for Paris—one of whom was Dr. Guillotin—sought advice from the director about a dispute between a tenant and a leaseholder. After being freed from prison, the Breton nobleman Jean-Pierre Poulain, count of Tramain, had been authorized by the building's guardian to collect his belongings from his old apartment, but the leaseholder, a man named Sarette, demanded that he pay a term of rent before taking away the furniture.[61] The director took Sarette's side, advising local officials to reject Poulain's request to empty the apartment.[62] It behooved the Domain to make concessions to leaseholders, because the rental market had collapsed and the bureau was having trouble signing new leases.[63]

In theory, confiscated property became a public asset, to be used by the state or sold for the profit of the Treasury. The practice was not so clear cut. Many of the tenants in such buildings had signed leases with the émigré owner, which the state chose to honor. Their presence, alongside the émigré family members who continued to occupy their homes, complicates the idea of émigré owners as "absent." Many of these properties were far from abandoned, and many émigré landlords, while not physically present, continued to collect revenue from their tenants. While the republic stockpiled its confiscated goods in darkened warehouses, unaware of thefts until months after the fact, émigré owners exercised possession of their properties from afar. To the tenants who diligently paid rent on a fixed date, they were eminently present.

Turning back to the house in the Rue Saint-Fiacre, Henriette Becdelièvre went in for one more round with the Domain after the scuffle over the house's tenants. The settled nature of the state's administration was further undermined in January 1802, when new revelations challenged the monetary value of the Saint-Fiacre house and revealed new ownership claims on it. Becdelièvre sought to have Ange-François's estate liquidated, a move that would separate Césarine's portion from her brother's and thus eliminate the need for a guarantee.[64] As the Domain prepared this arrangement, officials examined the documents behind the assets. The house in the Rue Saint-Fiacre turned out to be situated on land partially owned by the City of Paris.[65] Becdelièvre's husband had bought out the bond on the land, creating a mortgage backed by the City, but there was a balance on the payments—meaning the house didn't entirely belong to the family. The Domain official charged with investigating the case concluded that the property should not be released to Césarine until the mortgage was paid off.

The mortgage meant that the house was not worth what it had initially been assessed for; a lien on its title was, literally, a liability. It also connected the property to its owner by entwining its financial solidity with his own—or rather, that of his brother Louis-François, who had purchased the house. House and owner could be physically separated by legal action: the placing of seals on the doors, the removal of furniture, and the identification and confiscation of the deed. But the two remained connected all the same, through the tie of credit. The mortgage on the land created a tie between Talaru and the house in the Rue Saint-Fiacre that was, really, a relationship between borrower and creditor that had consequences for the house. Talaru and the City of Paris, as an institution, had made an agreement that influenced the ownership of the house and its value by creating a lien. The house was not worth what the Domain initially calculated, and there was another ownership claim—through the lien—to be contended with.

In a final chapter of intrigue, the Domain turned around and claimed a debt against Becdelièvre. The bureau alleged that she and her husband owed the state money on a credit contract it had seized from a different émigré; as a result, her husband's heirs—Césarine and her brother—owed this money. This came out as the prefecture of Paris and officials in the national Domain sought to close the Talaru dossier and release the assets in it to the family. Becdelièvre and her husband had bought a piece of land from one Auget-Monthyon, furnishing a lifetime annuity in payment. The state seized Auget-Monthyon's property, taking over collection on the annuity. The director of the Paris Domain bureau, at this point a man named Eparvier, calculated that 1,900 francs 48 centimes was still owed as a result of back payments on the contract. Since Césarine and her brother were heirs to their father's estate as well as that of their uncle, the Domain director considered them responsible for the payments and wanted to hold up the liquidation of their claims until the payments were made. The liquidation had already been authorized by the national government, however, and it was unsympathetic to his point of view. A member of the Conseil d'Etat under the Napoleonic Consulate wrote to Eparvier in March 1810, finally putting an end to the matter. Eparvier's calculations were based on equivalencies between the revolutionary assignat, the Old Regime livre, and the new currency the franc. The councillor of state found that, in fact, the Talaru children did not owe anything further.

This final claim against the Talaru estate highlights the extent to which the Talaru assets and the Talaru family members formed a bloc. Césarine's inheritance from her uncle was imperiled one final time by a claim against an asset that belonged to her father. The assets of the family members were interconnected by the claims of inheritance, which linked them together as a single pool of resources. In addition, the cash value of the assets was once again made unstable, this time by the exchanges among different revolutionary-era currencies.

Conclusion

A circular from the Ministry of Finances, issued in September 1793, urged local officials to scrupulously track the provenance of all the metals being requisitioned from émigré estates. The specific owner's identity should be tracked, the minister warned, so that an account of the value could be made to émigré creditors. The instruction to note the provenance of copper and lead before it was melted down starkly embodies the paradox of émigré confiscation. On the one hand, it reflected the urgency and confusion of large-scale requisitioning: the materials were destined to serve the war effort, recalling the underlying logic of the first émigré confiscation law, which called for émigré property to be held as an indemnity for the expenses of the war. On the other hand, it reflected an awareness of the careful accounting that was necessary to satisfy a debt and cancel a contract: émigré assets were often enmeshed in existing credit networks, and there was no guarantee that the requisitioned metals belonged to the émigré owner alone.

The metals are a fitting counterpoint to émigré houses, which could not easily be separated from their owners or transformed into a different form of value, whether cash or use. To calculate the value of Talaru's assets in financial terms (how much they could be sold for) required extracting them from relationships of ownership that paradoxically gave them value—whether this value was reflected in monetary terms or in the social currency of desirability. These relationships unfolded in time, as did the life of the assets themselves. The wine collection and the annuity tied to the Auget-Monthyon estate changed in value over time and in relation to other parties. Presumably, if Auget-Monthyon suffered an illness, the value of Talaru's assets would increase; the wine collection, meanwhile, declined in value over time. The value of the goods not only depends on what price they will fetch but also depends on the relationship of the owner to the asset—their ability to exercise ownership in relation to other people, over time.

Property law is full of dichotomies: persons and things, movable and immovable, public and private. These dichotomies suggest that property divides, delineates, or separates categories. These neat divisions, however, conceal the ways that property stitches things together: people use property to connect themselves with other people, to contain various forms of value, and to construct meaning.[66] The connection that property forged between citizen and state was the basis for the émigré confiscation laws in the first place. But émigré property already reflected an array of connections between people and ideas, which had been forged under the Old Regime. Officials not only had to confront and untangle these existing connections but also added new ones created by their very involvement, such as issues with tenants or the attempts by officials in other departments to get properties assigned for their use.

Tracing the process by which Domain officials separated émigrés from their belongings shows that the relationship between persons and things, though a legal category, did not depend on law alone. In fact, a significant reason why the law could not unwind these relationships was because the relationship between owner and property constructed value, which was measured in terms that ranged from the economic—cash value—to the other forms we have seen in this chapter: social status, desirability, and cultural relevance. Breaking the legal tie between owner and property could compromise the monetary worth of the property to the extent that the asset almost ceased to exist—such was the case with the wine collection. Property belonged to a realm of social relations in which various types of value were constructed, and the law could not act upon this process in a definitive way.

It is telling that the property of Ange-François Talaru was handled within a dossier that had the name Becdelièvre on the cover. His house and wine collection were handled alongside his brother's assets. His property was considered in the context of his family and tenants, not merely in relation to himself as an individual. Furthermore, while the pieces of his property were technically discrete objects—a house, bottles of wine—they too were bound together by a web of interdependence. Chapters 5 and 6 will look more deeply into the social relations that played such a crucial role in shaping property. Chapter 5 will examine family control of property, and Chapter 6 will turn to economic relationships outside the family.

Property, Family, and Patrimony

MADAME BLONDEL D'AZINCOURT WAS NOT DEAD, and this posed a conundrum for the director of the Domain bureau in Paris. After four of her five children emigrated, the bureau confiscated her house in the Rue Notre-Dame-de-Nazareth. Even though d'Azincourt still lived there, the Domain sold four-fifths of the ownership of the house in June 1797, leaving her life occupancy. Like many Parisian mansions, the house was decorated throughout with gilded mirrors, worth a substantial sum.[1] After the sale was completed, Domain officials took steps to move four-fifths of the mirrors to a public warehouse, corresponding to the four-fifths ownership of her émigré heirs. Upon doing so, they learned that the mirrors could not be removed because Madame d'Azincourt had not completed the legal formalities necessary to divide her estate. The Paris bureau director's superior in the Ministry of Finances pressured him to get the job done, reminding him, "The interest of the Public Treasury and the circumstances of the decoration of the Château of Saint-Cloud, make this operation that much more urgent."[2] The mirrors were needed to redecorate Napoleon's country retreat at Saint-Cloud, so officials did not want to wait. But as long as d'Azincourt lived, the mirrors belonged to her and could not be taken away. As one employee in the bureau pointed out, "The Republic has no interest in undertaking this division, because Madame d'Azincourt is very old, and her death will make the Domain the owner of all but 1 / 5 of the mirrors which are, after all, not likely to spoil in the meantime."[3] Bringing out "the interest of the Republic" to justify his position and, perhaps, casually trump the interest of the Treasury, the official resisted taking any precipitous action. In spite of the official's implication that it would be small-minded to strip an elderly widow of her possessions, however, officials in other departments already had plans for the mirrors—specifically, for the decoration of Napoleon's country house. To them it seemed a trifling obstacle that the owner was still alive.

The officials who wanted to seize the mirrors considered them as good as belonging to the republic already, given d'Azincourt's advanced age and her heirs' status as émigrés. This view reflected a practical reality of how assets were held within families. Property moved between generations by formal or informal promises before a parent died; this meant there could be a long period when an asset belonged to parent and child simultaneously, because it had been promised to an heir but the parent was still alive. When an older relative died, multiple heirs might share fractional ownership of the estate, as the d'Azincourt children would share their mother's house and mirrors among themselves. The republic could extract the shares of the émigré heirs because even though family assets were held in common, the rights of each member remained discrete. One-fifth of a set of mirrors may be a difficult quantity to physically apportion out, but its value is calculable.

Madame d'Azincourt's situation was the direct product of revolutionary policy.[4] Under Old Regime law, she could have easily disinherited her émigré heirs, preserving the integrity of her property. But because of inheritance reforms passed in 1791–1792, children were guaranteed equal shares of their parents' estates. The logic by which emigration became a crime, and which justified property seizure, focused on the individual citizen's duty to the polity as established in the social contract. In practice, however, lawmakers recognized bonds between people that translated into property claims. A child had a claim on their parents' property, a domestic servant had a claim to their wages, and a creditor had a claim to the borrower's assets. These claims were not, in the view of lawmakers, purely contractual. Even in the absence of a formal contract, they were backed by a kind of moral weight that lawmakers recognized. In this way, property was not only an individual right; it connected people through interdependence based in moral claims.

The d'Azincourt case highlights the central but ambiguous place of the family in the émigré seizure process. Families had to be contended with, because the interconnection of family claims meant that to separate property from an individual, the claims of other family members had to be unwound. Ostensibly, this posed a challenge to the individualism implicit in émigré policy and in property rights as they were shaped by revolutionary reform. Reforms to family law undertaken in the Revolution tended to break apart the legal dependence of family members on each other, freeing children from paternal authority and giving spouses greater liberty to separate from unhappy marriages. Overall, one could look at revolutionary law and find it in opposition to the kind of intertwined claims presented in the d'Azincourt family, favoring instead individual autonomy grounded in property rights.

And yet, revolutionary policy toward émigrés and toward inheritance did not favor individualism. After all, d'Azincourt's property was only under threat because her children were émigrés. She was being held responsible for the behavior of her children, and to such an extent that, in her old age, officials were preparing to burst into her home and pry the mirrors out of their plaster mountings on the walls. Alongside the rhetoric of individualism that informed property reform ran another current. Lawmakers applied a moralistic logic to émigré relationships, holding parents accountable for the emigration of their children. Revolutionary family law paradoxically supported such an approach, in spite of its overall tendency toward autonomy. Reforms to inheritance law actually bound the generations together more tightly so that parents could not disinherit a wayward child.

Family life played an important role in lawmakers' vision for a revolutionized society before emigration became an issue. Reforms to family law were intended to transform familial relationships so that families would be populated by equals and held together by bonds of affection.[5] This vision intentionally contrasted with the Old Regime family model, which was understood to be hierarchical and oriented around paternal authority. Ideas about how families should behave had changed in France over the course of the eighteenth century, as cultural shifts in attitudes and changes to ideals around marriage, child rearing, and family life in the home evolved. Rousseau's blockbuster novel, La nouvelle Héloïse, and his treatise on education, Emile, exemplify the emerging sentimental values of this period. The two works emphasize romantic love, greater equality between spouses, and parental engagement in child rearing. Literary representations, however, reflect only a fraction of the broad social changes that took place within the realm of family life, encompassing relations between spouses and between parents and children.[6] By the 1790s, when revolutionary lawmakers took up the issue of reforming family law, new attitudes toward family relations had firmly taken root.[7]

Revolutionary lawmakers took a series of concrete steps to shift the legal basis of family relations, inspired by the new ideas about family life that had emerged in the eighteenth century. In particular, they sought to encourage bonds of affection rooted in equality. First, in April 1791, the Constituent Assembly decreed that estates should be divided equally between all heirs, male and female, when there was no will. Then, in September 1792, the Convention legalized divorce, a move intended to improve married life by allowing unhappy couples to legally dissolve ties. In March 1793, the Convention went a step further in its policy and abolished wills.[8] This meant that individuals could not disinherit their children and could no longer freely dispose of their estates. Instead, all children, male and female, legitimate and illegitimate, would receive equal shares of inheritance.

The émigré confiscation process, however, was not well adapted to the way that property flowed through families. In rhetoric and legislation relating to the émigrés, revolutionary lawmakers approached property ownership as inherently static in nature, but in fact, property continually changed hands within families through the flow of patrimony. No sooner did property transfer to one family member than it was already reaching forward toward the next heir. Rarely did it stay in the possession of a single individual even in life, as multiple family members inherited from the same ascendant, receiving fractions of the whole. When the inheritance was a house or other real estate, this division depended on a legal fiction that sliced up a property into infinitely small fractions. A family's ability to share assets in various ways made it possible to stretch family patrimony so that it could support multiple generations or multiple branches simultaneously. The flexibility of property, in the sense of its ability to be divided, shared, and leveraged, crucially enabled families to achieve a broad array of goals, from settling children in marriages, to launching them in careers, to caring for relatives in old age, to sharing an inheritance among many heirs in the most financially advantageous way for all.

Dealing with families meant addressing the issue of creditors, and vice versa. Revolutionary leaders took advantage of family-based credit networks to identify émigrés and extract wealth from them, but they struggled to square the consequences of credit with their political goals: they envisioned property attached to an individual owner, but credit linked assets to multiple claimants. The operations of credit and debt within families bothered many legislators and jurists, who tended to frame issues in moral terms. In the émigré context, this dynamic played out in debate around the creditors of émigrés, who were pitted against the coheirs of émigrés when the state seized a portion of a parent's estate and, in so doing, compromised its solvency. The jurists who framed the Civil Code showed similar discomfort with the idea of families leveraging assets when they debated whether future inheritances could be mortgaged.

We think of the Revolution as a moment where family hierarchies and relationships based on obligation were broken down in favor of links of affection between autonomous individuals. However, the émigré confiscation process reveals the way that the Revolution gave family a new, moralizing valence. By emphasizing mutual obligation, revolutionary rhetoric around the family may seem to touch on themes similar to those of duty and obligation that characterized family relations in the Old Regime. However, the revolutionary rhetoric was inspired by the new, sentimentalizing tones of the eighteenth century, and in this it represented a departure from the past.[9]

This moralizing view of the family is particularly paradoxical because, in fact, émigré families structured their assets in sophisticated ways. The practice of distributing assets was not new, but some of the assets themselves were, such as lifetime annuities and investment in public debt. Assets were deployed in a way that reflected strategy more than sentiment. Families used shared assets as capital that could support the projects of many different family members. This disconnect between rhetoric and practice is significant, because the aggressive use of financial strategies by families points to their continued influence as an institution in economic life.[10]

This chapter will first examine the flow of property between generations and the struggle, as a consequence, of the Domain to attribute assets to a single individual. Next, it will look closely at how émigré families structured assets to benefit many members simultaneously. A third section will turn to lawmakers, examining how émigré confiscation and revolutionary inheritance laws bound family members together in moral obligation. Finally, we will look ahead to see how the debates around the Civil Code of 1804 echoed similar concerns; the views implicit in the émigré laws did not represent an isolated or fleeting moment in this regard.

Genealogies of Title

Administrators faced several practical challenges in their attempts to separate individuals from their families for punishment under the émigré laws. These difficulties began with the émigré lists themselves, the starting point for the seizure process. As described in Chapter 3, lists of émigrés were produced by the Ministry of the Interior, which received information about individuals "in a state of emigration" from communities. This seemingly simple task posed problems, however. Administrators complained that the émigré lists were riddled with errors, making it impossible to follow through with sequestration. The same individual could be listed multiple times; in many cases, surnames or given names were listed alone, making it impossible to tell if the same person had been put on the list multiple times by different communities or if, in fact, the entries referred to different people with the same last name. In a letter to the regional officials responsible for compiling draft lists, the minister of the interior complained that "these lists are insufficient, in that out of twenty individuals designated, barely five are identified with their surnames [noms patronimiques]." He was repeating a complaint he had received from the minister of the marine, who worried that "this lack of specific designation creates the situation that, by sending these incomplete lists to the Colonies, or by sequestering all the property of everyone with the same name, there could be a real injustice [une véritable injustice]; or, to only apply the law inconsistently, which would inevitably compromise the interests of the nation."[11] In many cases, imprecision in the émigré lists led to property confiscations from the wrong people. By the spring of 1796, the problems were so well known that Pardoux Bordas, a representative to the Council of Five Hundred reporting on the state of émigré liquidations, referred to "the poor composition [*rédaction*] of the émigré lists." It was so bad that "it would barely be possible to bring together more errors and inexactitudes."[12] Attempts to connect a given property to its owner only introduced more problems, as administrators confronted the fact that many properties did not neatly belong to a single family member. The émigré lists were transferred to the regional Domain bureaus within the Ministry of Finances, which handled the confiscation of property from individuals on the lists. Each Domain bureau made a master list of all the properties belonging to émigrés within their region and the name of the owner. The overlapping names and identities in the lists are evidence of more than clerical error. The property registers, maintained over a period of years, tracked property that was itself in motion through generations of heirs. Reading the register for the city of Paris, it is impossible to tell whether a group of properties belonged to a single person or to multiple members of the same family. Take the example of Jean-Baptiste-Robert Auget de Monthion and his son, Antoine-Jean-Baptiste-Robert Auget de Monthion. In the register of seized properties, the name Auget de Monthion, without any given names, appeared three times. Which properties belonged to the father and which to the son? Or did all belong to the son, Antoine-Jean-Baptiste-Robert? The same ambiguity is present in the case of Marthe-Antoinette Aubery de Vastan, widow of Jean-Louis Portail de Conflans, and her daughter-in-law, Antoinette-Magdeleine-Jeanne Portail, widow of Louis-Gabriel Conflans. When the Domain clerk noted "Widow Conflans" in the property register, did he mean the mother or the daughter-in-law?

Just as multiple family members could be listed under the same name, a single estate could be listed under the names of its owner and heirs. In addition to determining who was who, the Domain officials needed to figure out which generation was which, and then to whom a property belonged. When property was linked between two generations, this was not an easy task. For example, the La Trémoille family owned seven properties in Paris that were seized after the emigration of the Duc de la Trémoille and his three sons (a fourth son was condemned by the Revolutionary Tribunal and guillotined). In the master list maintained by the Domain, two of the properties are listed under the names of two of the brothers, Antoine-Philippe and Charles-Bretagne. The other five properties are listed simply under the family name or under the note "La Trémoille heirs." All seven properties were part of the same estate, but in different states of transfer toward the younger generation—some already passed down to the heir, others still in the hands of their parents. From the perspective of the Domain bureau, the existence of the property itself was more important than the precise identity of the owner. It was still eligible for sequester, no matter which generation of the La Trémoille family owned it. But the inability to differentiate highlighted the problem of shared ownership.

Family connections made it harder for administrators to trace property ownership, but paradoxically, they also provided the only means by which to do so. Throughout France, direct inheritances flowed untaxed and unregistered from one generation to the next. Other property sales were often formalized by notaries, but they did not have to be. Establishing ownership of assets was especially difficult in Paris because Parisian notaries did not have to submit their records for state audits. In other parts of France, these audits made it easier to find relevant acts within a notary's voluminous files. And yet, even as inheritance made property ownership difficult to pinpoint, family transactions such as estate settlements and marriage contracts provided administrators with the only means of tracing assets. Marriage contracts were particularly useful, because families used the occasion of a marriage to lay out assets and declare intentions.[13]

Genealogy became a thread that led administrators through the forests of paper to the documents that really mattered. The papers seized from the la Cour de Balleroy family provide a typical chain of titles documenting the family's ownership of a house in the Rue Saint-Honoré, near the Tuileries gardens.[14] The property had initially belonged to the Montmorency-Luxembourg family but was inherited by members of the Crozat family. Two women who had married into the family and then been widowed, Marie-Marguerite-Legendre and Marie-Thérèse-Catherine Gouffier, later traded it to François Castanier, director of the powerful Compagnie des Indes, in exchange for another property. Castanier's nephew Guillaume Castanier d'Auriac inherited the property from him in 1757 and subsequently sold it to Antoinette-Marie de la Roche in 1763. When de la Roche died without heirs, the property ended up in the hands of Marie-Elisabeth de Matignon, wife of Philippe-Auguste-Jacques de la Cour de Balleroy and mother of two émigré sons. The Balleroys had kept the documentation of all these prior transfers because in order to prove that they owned their property, they had to prove that it had been transferred to them by the previous owner. To make sense of these papers, administrators had to understand the networks of family ties along which the property moved.

In situations where the Domain bureau lacked original titles, it benefited from reliance on contracts and notarial records that documented the transfer of property titles among family members. Catherine Seulse, the mother of an émigré named Brisson, had promised her son property in his marriage contract, of which the Domain had a copy. The titles themselves, however, were the subject of some concern as they seemed to have disappeared. The régisseurs, to whom the director of the Domain reported, advised him, "Presumably no other titles exist for these annuities except the ones mentioned in the marriage contract . . . and these titles, along with all the others belonging to this émigré, were included under the seals that should have been placed after his emigration, and then were inventoried and placed in a public warehouse."[15] They suggested that the director consult Brisson's notary to find out which depository it could have been. But it seems they did not have much faith in the possibility of finding the titles, because they concluded by suggesting, "These same titles are described in the marriage contract, you could if necessary go back to the notarial minutes and get a copy of the extract." In lieu of paper titles, proof of the relationship between the current and former owners via contracts and notarial records was enough to prove a property claim. Even without the titles themselves, Domain officials could use the marriage contract to prove what Brisson owned, and confiscate it.

The difficulty that administrators faced in determining émigré property ownership reflected an important characteristic of property: it could belong to multiple people at the same time. The identities of Auget de Monthion father and son were particularly difficult to distinguish because of their similar names. Yet even if their names were different, they still would have been more or less indistinguishable as owners of the family property. Property often moved between generations multiple times—in promise and in fact—and at various moments before and after the death of the owner. The seizure process naturally implicated an émigré's family members through the ties of property that bound their interests together. Revolutionary reforms had changed the nature of citizenship and reimagined the role of the individual in the family, changing legal arrangements around marriage and patrimony. Nevertheless, legal arrangements concluded by émigrés before the Revolution remained intact. Moreover, administrators in the Domain took advantage of the relationship between genealogy and property to facilitate the task of confiscation.

Lawmakers did not originally intend for the confiscation of émigré property to involve families. On the contrary, the initial laws sequestering émigré property envisioned emigration as a crime committed by individuals in their function as members of the social contract—that is to say, as citizens. As the seizure process unfolded, however, administrators faced the interlocking ownership arrangements common in families. Entanglements across generations made it difficult to determine who owned what, and the simultaneous claims of owners and heirs made it difficult to isolate a single owner's share. Paradoxically, however, records of property inheritance facilitated administrators' work, as family genealogy could be used to trace property titles. On the one hand, it was not possible to separate émigré owners from property without implicating their families. On the other hand, the inextricability of family and property facilitated the confiscation process, which would have been nearly impossible had property really been rigorously individual.

Inheritance Practices at the End of the Old Regime

Links between generations made it difficult for administrators to distinguish who, among the members of a family, really owned something. To ask who "really" owned it, in fact, is clumsy. The Duc de la Trémoille and his son both owned their property. They simply had different claims to the same assets. The legal arrangements used to share assets among family members, based in customary law and unchanged in the Revolution, were actually quite clear on what each member of a family owned. A single asset could be shared by dividing different claims— such as use versus underlying ownership—or by creating fractional shares. Property "belonged" to several people at once, and yet each share was rigorously individual. In this sense, distinguishing between a regime of individual property and a communal approach to assets— as lawmakers sought to do—did not truly reflect the nature of family holdings either before or after the Revolution: property was both individual and shared at the same time. Families did not necessarily share resources out of sentimentality or a desire to help each other. Rather, managing family assets made it possible for a family's patrimony to support multiple households and multiple generations. This point further highlights how inadequately the idea of sharing captures the way families acted. Carefully delimiting the rights of each member allowed the family to maximize its assets.

The practices of the la Cour de Balleroy family exemplify the ways in which families shared property strategically across time.[16] The family was targeted by the émigré laws after Charles-Auguste de la Cour, Marquis de Balleroy, was guillotined and his wife, Sophie l'Epineau, emigrated. The marriage contract of Charles-Auguste's son, Philippe-Auguste, shows parental assets apportioned carefully to benefit both young and old simultaneously. Philippe Auguste, an only son, married Elisabeth-Jacqueline Maignard de la Vaupalière in April 1784.[17] Like many couples, they signed a marriage contract that enumerated the financial settlement arranged by their parents.[18] In the contract, the groom's parents each settled annuities on their son, drawn on various funds. The military commission previously purchased for the groom by his father was also listed as part of the settlement. The bride received a dowry of 300,000 livres, to be paid in part to her husband in cash on the wedding day, and the rest to be delivered in installments of no less than 50,000 livres at will by her father. She was also guaranteed her inheritance portion in the future. A key element of the marriage contract was the way it allowed the parents to continue benefiting from their property while still supporting the young couple. This was made possible by offering many different forms of property, including cash, annuities, and assets in kind such as the military commission. One particular ownership claim is worth highlighting: the bride's family promised to lodge the newlyweds in their home, rent-free, for three years.[19] Essentially the gift was a three-year lease, which represented a form of ownership claim on the parents' home. Significantly, however, promises of cash in this contract were secured against the parents' land. The promise of payment was not enough; the contract enumerated where the money would come from. In this case, the bride's parents took care to maintain the ability to sell property that had been used to secure their daughter's dowry. One clause of the contract stated that the parents could still sell, but also specified the new security they would provide to ensure their daughter still received her contractual payments.

Each spouse's and child's claims were clearly articulated, even as the decision to attribute property to different family members reflected a strategy to benefit the family as a whole. The bride and the groom each received gifts from their mother and father separately. The burden of specific expenses, such as who would pay the bride's chambermaids (the bride), and the resolution of various eventualities, such as what would happen to the bride's dowry if she should die before her husband and without any children (it would be returned to her parents), were carefully outlined. Even though husband and wife were joined in marriage and merged certain assets, the origin of property still mattered. The groom's inheritance from his maternal grandmother, Marie-Élisabeth Goyon de Matignon, exemplifies this point. The contract specified that de la Cour de Balleroy *père* would pay his son 10,000 livres annually out of an annuity worth 200,000 livres that the son had inherited from his maternal grandmother five years before. The chain of ownership was traced back two generations in the marriage contract—even though the inheritance was cash, not real property that would require a title. The bride's portion further highlighted the individuality of marital assets, as it was divided between money the bride could access without her husband's permission and payments to be made directly to the groom.

These distinctions between different members' claims protected the interests of the family as a whole. Keeping the spouses' wealth separate meant that each family lineage could preserve its wealth, and allowed for family assets to be kept within the bloodline. This distinction preserved family assets intact across generations, as when Balleroy's grandmother's wealth passed to him without being merged into his parents' assets. Even when the bride and groom became a family of their own, they continued to belong to separate family lines with separate patrimonies. The fate of Elisabeth-Jacqueline's dowry further highlights the careful flow of wealth, as the contract provided that it would flow either to her children or back to her parents, but never to her husband should she predecease him. It was all, essentially, cash, but its relationship to Vaupalière's parents, herself, and her other family members distinguished one sum from another.

When a family member died, wealth that had been shared across generations could revert back to the deceased, and in some cases, it was lost entirely to the next generation. This was the case when Marie-Élisabeth Goyon de Matignon's husband, Jacques-Claude-Augustin de la Cour, Marquis de Balleroy died: his children chose to renounce their claims to his estate so that they would not be held responsible for his debts. This was surely a financial blow to all of them, who might have expected to inherit at least some property. His daughter Élisabeth-Louise was especially impacted, however, as she lost her dowry when her father died.[20] The promise he had made to her in her marriage contract put a lien on his estate, meaning that after his death she could make a claim for it as a creditor, but other creditors had prior claims. A memorandum prepared by her notary formally recognized that of the 202,385 livres 8 sols 4 deniers of her dowry, she had received only 105,164l 12s 2d. For the remaining 97,220l 16s 2d, she became a creditor of her father's estate, "without any hope of recovery [of the money]."[21] Although property belonging simultaneously to parents and children could serve the needs of multiple generations at once, the death of one family member could upend those arrangements to the financial devastation of the rest.

In bankruptcy, property became exceptionally individual, as family members who might have continued the flow of property within the lineage renounced their claims. Elisabeth-Louise's husband, Anne Simon Piarron de Chamousset, died in debt. His heir, Claude Landais, accepted the estate only *sous bénéfice d'inventaire,* which protected her from its debts.[22] Normally, to accept the benefits of an estate also meant assuming its debts. The strategy followed by Chamousset's heir allowed her to determine the assets and liabilities of the estate before deciding whether to accept it. If she did not accept it, his creditors would be satisfied only up to the value of the estate, but would have no recourse when its resources had been exhausted. By rejecting the status of heir, she stopped the flow of property. Wealth flowed from one generation to the next, but this could mean that liability did, too. Interestingly, Chamousset's heir, Claude Landais, was his grandmother. As the provision in Elisabeth-Louise's parents' marriage contract concerning her mother's dowry had made clear, inheritance could flow upward toward ascendants, as well as downward toward descendants. Her father had inherited from his grandmother, and her husband's grandmother was inheriting from her grandson.[23]

In addition to stretching vertically over generations, property was also shared laterally among living family members. Fractional ownership split a property across generations and among siblings as it passed through the family. This was the situation in Madame d'Azincourt's family, as her children each had a claim to one-fifth of her house and mirrors. As such arrangements extended over generations, the fractions became smaller. The Talaru family's interest in the Halle aux Vins, a wine warehouse in southeast Paris, exemplifies this: the family held an interest of 7 / 16 in the business, which Césarine and Louis-Justin inherited together. This meant that each sibling individually had a claim to 7 / 32 of the total asset. The émigré dossiers are filled with such situations. For example, two houses at numbers 35 and 36 Rue Saint-Paul, in the Marais, were shared fractionally among several generations of family. The properties belonged to the paternal line of Henriette Desmaretes de Vanbourg. After her death, a two-thirds share of the houses went to Guillaume-Louis de Broglie, and from him to his sister, Marie-Françoise de Broglie. The other third devolved to Maximillienne de Béthune de Sully and Marie Baylens de Poyanne. The two women had left their one-third share undivided, which meant in practice that they would have collected one-third of the rents on the properties and divided the money between them.

Lateral sharing also occurred between spouses, through communal marital assets. Assets accumulated during the marriage were treated differently than those brought to the marriage by each spouse, depending on the region in which the marriage took place and the birthplaces of the spouses. The various legal regimes that operated in Old Regime France handled such assets differently; in Paris, they were considered shared spousal property and reverted to the surviving spouse.[24] During a marriage, the assets of both spouses would be under the management of the husband, with limitations placed on his ability to sell or otherwise alienate his wife's assets. At the death of one spouse, individual assets had to be separated. Widows could also have access to life rights in a portion of their husband's real assets.[25]

Emigration made visible the entwinement of a couple's assets. Layers of claims to different forms of ownership of a single property meant that it was not always clear what, exactly, was being seized. It also meant that ownership came loaded with contingencies that made it impossible to sell the property immediately. Such was the case for Elisabeth-Eleanore-Angelique Beauterne, whose husband, Charles-Paul-Jean-Baptiste Bourgevin Vialart Saint Moriz, emigrated with the couple's adult son, Charles-Etienne. Beauterne and her husband shared the usufruct of a house they had inherited from Paul-Etienne Boucher, located in the Rue Vivienne near the Palais-Royal and its gardens (and near what is today the Opéra Garnier). Boucher had left the ownership of the property to Charles-Etienne, with the stipulation that whichever of the spouses survived would get the full use of the property until his or her own death, when both portions of usufruct would pass to their son to be reunited with the right of real ownership. The emigration of Charles-Etienne meant that the state could seize the real ownership of the house, and the emigration of Charles-Paul allowed the state to claim half of the usufruct as well. They could not, however, seize the half of the usufruct that Elisabeth owned.

The case came to the attention of the Domain bureau in 1799, when the man who had purchased the real property of the house from the state, one Monsieur Baraumont, stopped making his rental payments.

He argued that since he had bought the house in December 1797 and acquitted his debt on it, he should no longer have to pay anything. This prompted an elaborate study of the situation by Cornebize, the receiver responsible for the arrondissement, to determine what Baraumont had actually bought when he purchased the house. Under normal circumstances, the usufruct belonging to Charles-Paul would have been seized and sold along with the real proprietorship. The problem was that if Beauterne survived her husband, the full usufruct would revert to her. So even though the state had seized the property, it only owned the usufruct conditionally—because that was how Charles-Paul had owned it. In trying to reason out the situation to his superior, Cornebize posed a counterfactual "let's consider the case that neither the father, nor the son should have ever emigrated," before concluding tentatively, "it seems to me, based on this, that the department could not have sold to Citizen Baraumont, the 1 / 2 usufruct in question" because even though it belonged to an émigré, if Beauterne survived her husband, it would transfer to her by right. "In effect, this would have meant very probably to sell a thing, that didn't at all belong to the nation, since it should or could belong to Citizen Beauterne."[26] It could belong to her in a year if her husband died that soon, or it could revert to her after fifty years if there was no news of him, according to the law governing émigré inheritances. If she died before her husband or before fifty years, it could revert to the state along with the rest of the ownership.

The property interest shared between Bourgevin Vialart and Beauterne was never meant to be split in half. When the couple could no longer share the usufruct in life, one of the two would own it entirely in death. This was the source of the Domain bureau's difficulties, as officials sought to differentiate Bourgevin Vialart's claims from those of his wife. Assets acquired during a marriage were owned jointly from the beginning and were never divided. In this sense, they differed from assets inherited by a group of family members. When multiple relatives inherited a single asset, they could either own it jointly or sell it and share the proceeds—division of some kind was assumed. This fact highlights the basic absurdity of the state's attempt to confiscate spousal property. It was one thing for the republic to take the place of an émigré's heir—this resembled the procedure for estates without an heir, another type of case the Domain handled alongside émigré matters—but to take the place of an émigré's spouse was not a legal operation with any kind of precedent. Ostensibly, in the Bourgevin Vialart case, the Domain bureau was acting on behalf of the son. And yet, the details of the case placed it in the situation of acting in the place of the husband.

Moral Obligation and Émigré Families

Lawmakers took advantage of the interconnection between property and lineage to identify the assets of individual émigrés. They were able to do this because, as much as families shared property, the rights of any one person were recorded in a contract and could be separated out. This might result in clumsy fractions, like one-fifth of Madame d'Azincourt's mirrors, but in any case the division could be made. Although the original émigré laws did not consider family connections, lawmakers increasingly recognized these ties and used them to strengthen the moral claims they contained. As early as September, 1792 parents of émigrés were required to pay to supply two troops; in December 1793 new legislation sequestered their property.[27] These measures not only took advantage of family connections to identify assets but also held parents responsible for the moral dereliction of their émigré children. In contrast to Old Regime family property settlements, which carefully outlined the claims of each person, revolutionary legislation emphasized the broad, amorphous moral bonds that connected family members.

The family reforms of 1791–1792 were intended to make family members more autonomous, and yet policy toward émigré families did just the opposite, tying parents to the crimes of their children. On September 17, 1793, Philippe-Antoine Merlin de Douai proposed a new measure that would categorize the immediate family of émigrés as suspects, a legal category that exposed them to punitive measures of the Terror. This included spouses, parents, and children. Of these categories, only one, spouses, could dissolve the tie that connected them to an émigré. The wives of émigrés, notably, made use of revolutionary divorce laws to separate themselves from their husbands. The Convention officially recognized the legitimacy of this move, voting on 7 Brumaire II (October 28, 1793) that the divorced wives of émigrés would not be classified as suspects. The law specified wives, instead of using the neutral term "spouses," recognizing that when one-half of a couple emigrated, it was most frequently the husband who did so.

The parents of émigrés could not dissolve their ties so easily. Inheritance reform paradoxically attributed a great deal of power to lineage, making it illegal to disinherit a child. The 1792 law outlawing wills dictated what a child could expect, making their inheritance a legal fact.[28] In this sense, inheritance reform was meant to free individuals from being blackmailed by their parents or from seeing their own interests sacrificed in the name of dynastic strategies. But guaranteeing a child a fixed portion of their parents' estates glossed over the possibility that parents might actually use up their estates. A division in life assumed that a parent would not leverage bequests in the meantime, creating liens that could swallow up an inheritance.

Thus, the reform to testamentary law had the unintentional effect of strengthening the flow of patrimony. The Convention made explicit use of this link rather than seeking to give émigré parents a way to separate themselves from their children. In December 1793, the Convention ordered that the property of the ascendants of émigrés—parents and grandparents, anyone from whom the émigré might inherit directly—be placed under sequester unless "the fathers & mothers prove that they acted actively & with all their power to prevent the emigration."[29]

Parents could not simply liquidate their estates to prevent émigré children from inheriting anything, as legislation in March 1793 had nullified property transfers by parents or grandparents of émigrés made since the child's emigration or since February 1, 1793.[30]

Numerous beleaguered parents wrote letters of protest to the Convention, pointing out the absurdity of holding parents responsible for the behavior of adult children. As one mother put it, "To act with all one's power, one must have power." She could not prevent her children from emigrating, because "our laws, our customs, don't give a mother any power over daughters who have been married for fourteen or twenty years."[31] A father could not claim any more influence over children who were "beyond his authority, one being forty, the other thirty-four, neither living at home, the eldest married for thirteen years."[32] The same was true for grandparents, who "only rarely have, in fact or in law, any authority over their grandson."[33] Age had nothing to do with the Breslons' inability to influence their son who, "if he has emigrated, has followed the tendencies of a vicious character, which it has been impossible for them to correct."[34] These avowals of powerlessness highlight how bizarre it was for the Convention to assume that parents had such influence to begin with. The law did not set an expiration date on parental influence, holding the parents of adult children responsible for their offspring's behavior as though they were legal minors.

In April 1795, the Directory released émigré parents' assets from sequester and new rules were issued. These rules proved even more restrictive, as they demanded that administrators divide up émigré parents' estates and confiscate the émigré heir's portion before releasing the rest of the property back to them.[35] The republic would take the place of émigré children in the division, inheriting their portions. Measures for estate division in life already existed in customary law, through the procedure known as pre-succession. This allowed parents to settle their estates while still alive, making clear exactly how their property would be divided after their death. The émigré laws effectively required the parents of émigrés to make use of pre-succession. Once the property of an émigré's parents had been divided, its original owner could no longer sell or transfer it. In the eyes of the law, what belonged to the parents already belonged to their children.

Holding parents responsible for their adult children's behavior suggested that there was a moral bond that endured within the family. The bond of property seemed to justify an ongoing relationship between parent and child. This is striking because it suggests a rather different approach to the family than the one outlined elsewhere in revolutionary law. In other contexts, legal reforms consistently recognized the independence of family members, allowing unhappy spouses to go their own way and freeing children from the despotic influence of a parent. At the same time, they stressed the centrality of affinity and sentiment: family members would not be bound by the Old Regime values of duty and obligation, but rather financially independent individuals would be brought together by affection. Yet the case of émigré inheritance reveals that bonds of duty and obligation remained enshrined in revolutionary law. Parents and children clearly were tied together not only by sentiment but also by moral bonds that required parents to take responsibility for their children's actions. Paradoxically, these bonds were cemented by the very reforms to inheritance intended to give children greater autonomy. Seemingly, the move to give family members greater legal liberty did not mean dissolving their moral bonds; the émigré laws suggest that these remained as strong as ever, and even enhanced to a certain degree.

These moral bonds functioned beyond immediate family ties. Officials recognized the legitimacy of some property claims that were based solely on relationships, with no formal contract at all, such as verbal promises made by émigrés to their tenants or employees. At a variety of levels in national and municipal government, officials expressed concern for the people who could be unfairly injured when émigré

property was sequestered. At particular risk were the servants of émigrés who, after their employer's property had been sequestered, would
lose the wages and pensions they had earned. The minister of the interior wrote to the president of the Convention in August 1793 with concern for elderly servants who "are now reduced to frightful poverty.
Many claimed they were due pensions after receiving their back wages
[from the state], but no law accords these."[36] Similarly, the Committee of Legislation wrote to the Bureau for the Execution of the Laws,
an organ of the Terror, with concern for servants left without recourse
after their employers had promised them benefits.[37] In April 1795, the
Convention made an exception to its previous, retroactive nullification
of émigré property transfers to allow servants, nurses, and teachers
to collect benefits that had been promised to them.[38] Officials recognized the legitimacy of property claims based on the claim of a dependent to a beneficiary, as these types of work were performed in
the household, with such legacies paid out in recognition of long and
faithful service.[39]

Tenants farming land owned by émigrés could also be untowardly
affected by punishments intended for their landlords. A circular from
the Régie in May 1793 warned the local bureaus that farmers on national
lands "and particularly tenants of the émigrés, whose leases have expired, cannot, under any pretext, be deprived of the year's harvest,
regardless of when their farm is sold."[40] The following month, the
Convention decreed that even tenants on émigré lands who had planted
without a valid lease would be allowed to remain in possession of their
lands until the harvest.[41] Of course, this concession may have been
linked to fears of food riots should locals learn that harvests were being taken away. But in doing this, the government acquiesced to the
popular understanding that the people who planted the land had the
right to harvest it. Tenants and servants formed legitimate claims to
the property of their landlords or masters, based on their service or occupancy. These claims did not depend on the assent of the owner;

they endured well after the owner's own claim had been dissolved. This concern, however, did not extend to urban tenants or to employees in émigré buildings under state administration, who frequently sent multiple imprecations for the Domain to pay their wages.[42] The treatment of urban tenants and employees may reflect the political clout of the peasantry, or could be due to lawmakers' lack of recognition for the context of urban apartment-dwelling—they may not have considered building staff and apartment tenants to have the same dependency on property owners as rural tenants and servants.

Rival Credit Claims to Émigré Property

Lawmakers weighed duty when they assessed property claims, identifying the moral obligations of parents and employers that allowed children and servants to make claims. This approach, however, became difficult to maintain given how property ownership functioned at the end of the eighteenth century. Families had long shared resources among individual members, operating according to dynastic concerns for centuries. The variety of assets available, however, changed over the course of the eighteenth century.[43] In particular, much more credit circulated in France at the end of the eighteenth century than previously. Credit took shape in a variety of instruments, ranging from shares of public debt, to annuities, to various types of consumer and commercial obligations. Émigrés tended to be quite heavily leveraged, and the events of the Revolution devastated many of their credit-based assets without damaging the claims of creditors against them. As this fact became apparent to legislators, they had to decide which set of moral obligations to honor: Should property be awarded to creditors seeking their due, or to family members who had claims on it? In the summer of 1797, a debate broke out over the respective claims of family members and creditors who stood to lose money when the state seized an émigré's assets. The debate burned hot for over a year. Later, the framers of the Civil Code of 1804 became embroiled in a similar debate over the right to leverage an inheritance that had not yet been received. Both debates handled the intersection of family patrimony and credit, reflecting real ambivalence on the part of lawmakers and jurists toward families' tendency to leverage dynastic assets. In the view of many lawmakers, patrimony was something to be maintained and then passed on, not wagered.

The issue initially arose in situations where an émigré inherited from a parent along with other heirs, as in the case of Madame Blondel d' Azincourt's children. Four of her children had emigrated, but one had stayed in France, such that the state had to divide the inheritance with this one remaining heir. Inevitably, this arrangement meant that the property would be sold and the remaining heir would receive money instead of a share in the house. It also meant that the state would take a share in any debts left by Blondel d'Azincourt. Normally, when faced with a group of heirs responsible for a single debt, creditors had recourse to a principle known as solidarity. A creditor could pursue a single individual out of the group of heirs for the entire sum of the debt; the understanding was that the obligation fell on that borrower to sue the cosigners for their shares of the money. Solidarity, however, assumed that the creditor's target could turn to coheirs to be reimbursed. When the state was the coheir, this wasn't possible. The unlucky target of the creditor's action had to pay the entire debt, without hope of redistributing the burden.

Adding to the difficulty posed by credit claims against émigrés was the heterogeneity of the creditors themselves, who often included the émigré's own family members in addition to commercial contacts. In a report to the legislature outlining the expertise required to parse all the credit claims, Pardoux Bordas enumerated the various categories of creditors: "Here, there are workers and suppliers who demand payment, and against whom the statute of limitations must be invoked if applicable. There, the execution of contractual rights requires an understanding of the principles controlling bequests. On one side, there is the spouse of an émigré demanding the return of her patrimonial property and settlement of debts; on the other side, there is a divorcée who has the right to the indemnity guaranteed by the law of 20 September 1792."[44] The claims shaded seamlessly from business expenses to family credit arrangements. Though they depended on different types of contracts, all fell into the same category as liabilities. At the same time, private and commercial claims were secured by different types of instruments, and a business partner enjoyed different types of rights than a spouse or widow.

Though it was technically legal for creditors to go after coheirs when disappointed by the republic, it struck lawmakers as unfair. The burden of debt was supposed to be shared equally by heirs, but when the state stepped in for an émigré, relatives were left with no recourse. In one of the earliest discussions of the issue, Jean-Baptiste Crenière imagined an apocalyptic situation where an heir found himself pursued for more than his share was worth. Laden with more debt than he could handle, this imaginary heir "would abandon his patrimony to the creditors; his goods would be put under judicial administration; that is to say, he would undergo a new sequester, a civil sequester in truth, but just as disastrous as a revolutionary sequester." The creditors, in spite of all this, wouldn't see their loans repaid: "All the creditors, without exception, would be sent away, with regret and shame to have stripped and reduced to poverty and despair the unhappy owners, without any advantage for themselves."[45] Crenière felt particular sympathy for heirs affected by the émigré laws because he considered them to be in a fundamentally different moral position than other borrowers who might also find themselves unable to repay a debt. He noted that his colleagues approached the issue "as one would if this were a question of an ordinary borrower." But heirs were different: "One is confusing the unfortunate who obeys necessity, with the debtor in bad faith who impudently provokes injustice."

In June 1797 another representative, Alexandre de Bonnières, proposed that solidarity be eliminated for the coheirs of émigrés in a report delivered to the Directory's lower house.[46] He pointed out that when the state took the place of an émigré coheir but refused to honor debts belonging to borrowers deemed to be insolvent, it disrupted the basis of solidarity. Given that solidarity could not function as intended under these circumstances, it was already in effect suspended. His proposal sparked an immediate response. In spite of any perceived injustice, creditors had a right of property in a borrower's assets. As one lawmaker put it, "A right is property just like a movable or real asset," which meant that "these loans are thus a sacred debt that the heir must acquit & before the payment of which no inheritance exists."[47] Another representative asserted that the principle by which liens were secured against a person's entire estate "is a truth as obvious as two plus two is four."[48] It seemed clear to these representatives, and to those who agreed with them, that whatever unfortunate consequences might result, the law was the law. Moreover, changing the law would mean attacking a right of property.

All the same, legislators reasoned that they were in a position to take action. Several representatives pointed out that they should not be bound by existing law: "I respect the decisions of jurists, when their objective falls within judicial routine; but it is precisely because one is a jurist, that one is not in a position to decide questions that fall outside ordinary jurisprudence." Siméon Bonnesoeur, another representative, echoed this sentiment, pointing out to his colleagues, "You take a position, not as a tribunal that sees nothing but particular interests, but as legislators who want to foil the projects of evil, confound royalism, and firm up the current constitution by facilitating the sale of national properties."[49] This was almost the same reasoning that he had offered years earlier when, during the trial of Louis XVI, he reminded his colleagues in the Convention, "In my opinion, we pronounce on this important question as legislators and not as judges."[50]

For all this debate, no change was made to the law. However, in the fall of 1796—amid the ongoing debate in the legislature—a court in the Seine-Inférieure department ruled in favor of a coheir of an émigré, Mr. Duval-Bonnetier, when he sued the creditors of his father's estate to prevent them from claiming the entire value of his share. The court found that since solidarity assumed the ability of individuals to have recourse to other heirs, the fact that the complainant could not go to the republic for solidarity meant that the principle of solidarity itself was nullified. Ultimately, the verdict was overthrown. We know about it mostly because the jurist and revolutionary legislator Merlin de Douai wrote it up, in the 1820s, in his influential legal encyclopedia.[51] He was scathing in his critique of the court's decision, pointing out that the ability to sue coheirs was a consequence of solidarity, but not something on which the legal principle itself depended.

Rights protected the ability of an individual to dispose of one's property at will, but they depended on a fiction of individualism that did not carry through in practice. In debates leading up to the Civil Code of 1804, legislators addressed this tension in their approach to mortgage reform. The Civil Code forbid mortgages on future assets, such as an expected inheritance. At the time it was created, however, some jurists rejected outright the idea of limiting mortgages to current assets only. They argued that such a limitation was an attack on property rights. The rights of multiple family members to the same piece of property were interlocking, such that failing to recognize the right of heirs to mortgage their future inheritance would "limit the right of property." Those who argued otherwise "have misunderstood the nature of obligations."[52] According to François-Denis Tronchet, a particularly influential jurist and Civil Code author, ending mortgages for future assets "destroys the essence of all contracts."[53] The view that future assets could be mortgaged by an expectant heir before the previous owner had died echoed the principle that underlay the law against the ascendants of émigrés. In both cases, the line between the generations was blurred so much as to functionally disappear. Both the émigré laws and Civil Code mortgage reform, separately but in parallel, reflect a tension within revolutionary law. Legal reforms purportedly intended to assign property to the individual, but the nature of property made such divisions impossible to uphold in practice.

The Civil Code authors who defended the existing mortgage law did not see a contradiction between property rights and interlocking, even overlapping, ownership across generations. For these jurists, recognizing future property offered an economic benefit by allowing individuals to use more credit. In these situations, however, lawmakers recognized that the transfer of property between generations involved a period when assets "belonged" to multiple people at once. A report presented during the work on the Civil Code laid out the argument in favor of mortgaging future assets.[54] It addressed the objection that recognizing future property could "lead to speculation on successions that have not yet occurred, and to their being consumed in advance." On the contrary, the report pointed out, measures were already in place to protect against dealing on such successions and to restore inheritances to minors if they were mishandled. The law "could not go further without attacking the freedom to dispose, which is the essential attribute of the right of property." The report understood the interest of an heir in a living relative's estate to be a right of property. This distinction, that inheritance could be mortgaged but could not be "negotiated on" (*traiter*), points to the complexity of how such relationships could be recognized legally and play out in the scheme of rights.

The worry of some jurists, that inheritances might be "consumed" in advance, boiled down to a fear that people would make poor choices with their property. As their opponents pointed out, legitimate financial interests might inspire a person to act in such a way. The jurists' fear was similar, though not explicitly connected, to the one that had motivated the émigré laws—that citizens might choose to withdraw their property from France, with negative consequences for society.

The right to use and abuse was an ancient attribute of property, one that contemporaries traced back to Roman law. The potential for people to misuse property was not new; what was new was the fear that such behavior would have grave consequences for society as a whole. The reforms of the Revolution depended on the idea that property owners would behave patriotically, and the authors of the Civil Code similarly envisioned a society in which property owners behaved in what the authors deemed to be the right way.

Conclusion

Tracing the property seizure process inevitably leads the historian, on the heels of the officials in the Domain, into the intricacies of émigré family trees. Many of the struggles that officials faced reflect the long-standing truth that property flows through families, making any attempt to establish the boundaries of individual ownership—a revolutionary ideal—ultimately artificial. In the eighteenth century, however, the entwinement of family and property took on a new aspect as credit became more widespread. The family was well suited to the expanding economy of credit, as families naturally pooled capital and contracted relationships based on trust among their members. If the family formed a natural credit institution, however, it did not enter the calculations of lawmakers as such. The result was an emphasis, on the part of lawmakers, on moral bonds as the primary connection of family members, as opposed to the kind of interdependent mobilization of capital that characterized the strategies of families at the end of the Old Regime.

The ability of families to layer claims to a single asset meshed seamlessly with the nature of credit arrangements, which proliferated in the eighteenth century and continued to serve as the bedrock of market economies. As Chapter 4 showed, the Revolution took place at the end of a century of European commercial expansion defined by increased consumption of manufactured goods, as well as new capital-intensive production methods and coordinated markets. Families were particularly well adapted to take advantage of credit arrangements, leverage assets, and pool capital, as reflected by the fact that émigré wealth was enmeshed in webs of family claimants and external creditors.

As lawmakers ran up against the entanglement of property claims with family networks, they came to understand how gravely these networks threatened the state's ability to extract revenue from the émigrés. Still, many lawmakers preferred to view family relationships in moralistic terms. This was true of the legislative response to competition between émigré creditors and the coheirs of émigrés, and it was true in debates during the framing of the Civil Code: in both cases, lawmakers were aware of the importance that credit relations played, and yet they did not legislate with an eye to the realities of their impact.

It is perhaps not surprising that so many lawmakers took this view; a similarly moralistic logic informed the émigré laws themselves, which relied on an understanding of the émigrés' behavior as morally derelict. In other situations, however, revolutionary leaders did not take such a view. Such was the case when peasants and the urban poor made moral claims to demand that prices for bread and other essentials match what people could pay, something that happened throughout the Revolution.[55] Leaders asserted that markets should set prices, with only a short-lived exception in 1793, when the Convention put in place a maximum price on grain. Clashes around the moral economy—that is, the claim by the poor that prices for essentials should be fair—are generally framed by historians in terms of lawmakers' modern approach to property, asserted against the archaic claims of peasants.[56] In the context of family law, however, lawmakers very much still subscribed to the idea that moral obligations governed property claims.

The example of émigré property challenges the artificial separation that casts the family outside the market. The postrevolutionary era of the nineteenth century is portrayed as a time when markets became more impersonal as the family endured as an archaic institution, grounded in moral bonds of dependence and obligation.[57] On the contrary, the family adapted quite naturally to credit relationships: it was already an economic institution, in the sense that families engaged in economic life as units, and a natural reservoir of capital. It was revolutionary reform that framed the family in moralizing terms that were essentially new: portraying members as linked together by primarily moral bonds is the novelty.

The arrangements discussed in this chapter show property in motion among family members. In these aristocratic émigré families, owning certain types of property—and owning a significant quantity of total assets—reflected and cemented social status. And yet, these assets also connected family members to one another through interdependent claims. The motion of property through families knitted members together even as the assets themselves empowered individuals to act in the world.

The economic practices of families were, of course, just one aspect of economic life. Property was similarly in motion in the marketplace, where it was exchanged, divided, and leveraged through debt. Chapter 6 will turn to the space of the market and the various types of actors who populated it. Émigré property created opportunities for exchange and investment that extended beyond the owners themselves. Tenants, creditors, and lessees who signed contracts with the state for émigré properties all looked to turn a profit, and they were aided in their pursuits by a range of financial instruments. The motion of property was not limited to buying and selling; in fact, property did not even necessarily circulate in the marketplace whole. Real estate could be broken apart in various ways—either financially, through debt, or physically, by breaking it into component pieces. Property, even real estate, was a flexible financial tool, and émigré property was no exception.

By Iron or Nail

W HILE PROPERTY WAS ENTIRELY REIMAGINED through the abo- lition of feudalism in 1789 and the establishment of a new con- stitution in 1791, it remained a symbol of social and political stability and authority. This was true for the Legislative Assembly and the Con- vention, as well as for the Thermidorean and Directory regimes that succeeded the Convention and brought the Revolution to a close. When lawmakers discussed assets throughout the Revolution, they focused on land, and farms in particular. The small farm, owned by a single producer and worked by his family and perhaps some hired hands, lent itself to a political model based on individual, rights-bearing citizens.[1] This model depended on the assumption that property owners could be relied on to secure the social order. It also depended on the as- sumption that property owners favored real estate over other types of property.

These assumptions persisted as the Revolution came to a close. Lead- ers across the revolutionary regimes defended property rights, but those in the Directory and Empire, faced with putting an end to the social conflict unleashed by the Revolution, put particular faith in the ability of physical property to secure social and political order.[2] Echoing the previous regimes, the Constitution of 1795 placed property qualifications on political rights. One of its framers, François-Antoine de Boissy d' Anglas, explained, "We must be governed by the best; the best are the most educated and the most interested in maintaining the law."[3] He clarified that "with few exceptions, you will not find such men except among those who, possessing a property, are attached to the country in which it is located, to the laws that protect it, to the tranquility that preserves it." This faith in land ownership as a source of social stability underpinned the social vision pursued by the Directory broadly.[4] Similar convictions characterized the Napoleonic regime, which depended on the "masses of granite" of land-owning notability for stability.[5] Beyond simply defending property rights, these regimes wanted to empower landowners as stewards of the legitimacy and stability of the political order.

There is a conflict over property distribution in the Revolution that is highlighted by historians, and it is the one between revolutionary leaders, on the one hand, and the peasantry and the Parisian workers, or sansculottes, on the other.[6] As lawmakers created property rights, these disenfranchised groups called for the opposite: the redistribution of property for the benefit of those who had none. The particularly strong assertion of the sanctity of property rights by the Directory is often read as a response to such demands.[7] In this confrontation, revolutionary leaders represent a kind of vanguard, bringing modern property rights to a resistant populace. The émigré dossiers, however, offer a glimpse into a different confrontation, where the dynamic is reversed. In this other confrontation, lawmakers clung to the idea of a polity of reliable landowners in the face of a population that, in contrast, treated property as a source of capital and credit. This was the situation in Paris, where real estate represented one financial tool among many. In relation to a population that viewed real estate in this way, it is the lawmakers who seem archaic or traditionalist in their quaint attachment to the land.

The émigré dossiers show that in Paris, real estate rarely worked in the ways that lawmakers theorized it should, and property owners rarely behaved as expected. Real estate was an unstable bargaining chip in a freewheeling culture of negotiation, not a privileged asset that ensured its owner's financial solidity. It was used as a financial tool that could be broken apart, exchanged, or leveraged. Sometimes, land ownership was itself the object of a person's desire, but just as often it was only a stepping-stone to a more distant goal, such as developing an art collection or growing a business or even—as in one of the cases examined here—fattening a goat. What emerges from the dossiers is a disconnect between the government's belief that landowners would hold on to their real estate in perpetuity and the realities of marketplace negotiation at the turn of the century. This disconnect was so strong that the government itself, through its administrators, sought to treat real estate primarily as an asset that could be physically broken up and converted into cash. In actuality, landowners did not treat real estate as a privileged form of asset; instead, they sold or leveraged it in favor of other things, notably cash. Land was so far from being a unitary, unmoving asset that even people who didn't own real estate could get a piece of it through credit arrangements, not because they hoped to own it but because it offered a convenient means of turning a profit.

At the time of the Revolution, this market-oriented approach to real estate was still relatively new. Consumer goods came to France in the eighteenth century, as we have seen, with significant consequences for how people used their property. The arrival of consumer goods, however, was just one aspect of the emergence of a global, capital-driven market that took place in this period.[8] Important changes to economic behavior inside France were part of this broader trend; notably, these changes included the development of a real estate market and the expansion of credit networks.[9] By the end of the eighteenth century, real estate was a financial tool that, through credit, could be leveraged to generate revenue or liquidated for its capital. This was the situation when lawmakers in the revolutionary legislatures began to reimagine property rights and reshape French society. The Revolution came at a time when broad, significant economic changes, with consequences for how people used property, were already underway.

The freewheeling investments of urban property owners reveal a high level of engagement with the market.[10] The Revolution brought a variety of new opportunities for these people, but it did not fundamentally change a basic comfort with risk that already characterized transactions before the Revolution. Certainly, property owners represented a minority, both within the city itself and to an even greater degree when compared with France as a whole. But they were a minority that lawmakers could not ignore, because the Revolution was committed to defending their property rights—even as they used those rights in unorthodox ways. Lawmakers worked enthusiastically to regenerate property rights in the Revolution; less clear is whether property owners themselves could be revolutionized.

This chapter uses cases from the émigré dossiers to explore the ways in which real property was divided and its boundaries—legal and physical—blurred through the action of owners or, just as likely, tenants, creditors, or buyers.[11] Property could be divided in a financial sense, through leveraging and borrowing; it could also be physically broken apart into pieces that could be sold individually. Multiple people could make use of a single property, or a single person could buy, sell, and mortgage a variety of properties. Property was not a stable asset, in the sense that it anchored its owner to one place and represented a unitary, reliable monetary value. Similarly, ownership was not a stable state, in the sense that it was constantly shifting among various stakeholders. While previous chapters have primarily observed how owners made use of their property, this chapter will examine the broad range of interested parties who could use real estate to their benefit—whether they owned it or not. These interested parties included tenants in seized properties leased by the state, creditors of owners, and officials in the Domain who also participated in dividing up property for sale.

Three pairs of cases are followed by a longer, final case. The first case shows how use, ownership, and revenue from a single property could be divided among multiple people simultaneously, while in the second case, the multiple roles of tenant, landlord, and creditor could be exercised by the same person. The third and fourth cases move beyond questions of ownership to trace the challenges associated with dividing up physical property, as the Domain authority tried to sell real estate in separate pieces or, relatedly, as the monetary value of property fluctuated in relation to other assets or even assessments about the person holding the property. The fifth and sixth cases show how landowners fit real estate into portfolios of personal wealth that they managed opportunistically. In both cases, owners converted land into financial assets and showed a preference for other types of assets over land. A final case draws together the problems of layered claims, unstable physical boundaries, the contingency of value, and the relationship between real estate and other assets in the startling example of a man who wanted to cut a door in the wall on his property line. Together, these seven cases, drawn from the émigré dossiers and supplemented with information from notarial records, collectively show the range of ways in which property was used as a financial asset, as opposed to a reliable, long-lived source of wealth.

These cases, for the most part, only involve émigrés indirectly. The people in the foreground here all were seeking some benefit from an émigré property and may be considered peripheral figures to the drama of the émigrés. Even so, their names, in many cases, figure on the cover of the dossier they appear in. The Domain dossiers document administrative correspondence, so any person who generated a good deal of official attention could become the subject of a dossier. Some of them leased émigré property from the state; others were tenants in émigré buildings. All are joined together by their attempts to turn a profit from a piece of property, whether they owned it or not. As a group, then, they present a portrait of property ownership that contrasts with the one envisioned by lawmakers.

Each of these individual cases drew ample attention from Domain officials. This was because the individuals involved undertook operations that were complicated or unusual in the eyes of the administrators handling the cases. As a result, these cases are rather unusual, in the sense that they both received extra attention from officials and clearly involved practices that were, in the estimation of officials familiar with the practices of the time, surprising. In each case, the relevant parties were involved in complicated real estate transactions that made it hard to isolate the single owner of a property or the revenue stream of an asset for the benefit of the state. Yet these outliers are in fact perhaps the most useful cases for understanding common, widespread practices among property owners and investors. The people who figure in these cases differ from anyone else who may have bought, sold, or leased property in Paris only in the scale of their transactions, not in their substance. The people who drew the attention of the Domain were making use of widely available contracts and perfectly legal business maneuvers.

These cases did not pose a legal dilemma so much as an administrative one for officials attempting to confiscate property on behalf of the state. In this sense, the people involved—most of whom were not themselves émigrés—may be unusual in the scale of their wealth or in their boldness, but there is no reason to believe they were fundamentally different from anyone else in the strategies they employed and the attitudes that motivated them. They acknowledged their motivations frankly, in preambles to contracts drawn up by notaries and in letters to Domain bureau officials. An examination of their cases shows that those who held real property, or held an interest in it, put it to a far greater range of purposes than revolutionary law, and the policies of postrevolutionary regimes, assumed.

Berthaud's Goat

Julien Berthaud needed a place to graze his goat. As it happened, Jean
Brousse, a locksmith, had leased a piece of land abutting the Luxembourg Garden from the Domain, which had been confiscated from
the brother of Louis XVI.[12] In the spring of 1795, Brousse sublet the land
to Berthaud, a clockmaker, who conveniently lived nearby in the Rue
Notre-Dame-des-Champs. Berthaud installed a fence with a gate that
locked and set his little goat to roam about in the grass. The Luxembourg Garden lease, however, was not the only one that Brousse had
signed with the Domain. He also held properties in the Palais-Royal
and the Marais, and things weren't going well. He had been embroiled
in a dispute with the Domain over the Palais-Royal property, which he
claimed he was unable to sublet because it was in such poor repair. He
also owed back rent on the property in the Marais, a mansion that had
belonged to the Périgord-Chalais family.

Brousse's affairs took another turn for the worse when a man named
Branthomme materialized, claiming to have purchased the Luxembourg property from the king's brother (known as Monsieur) in 1790,
before it was seized—a fact that, if true, would mean it should never
have been seized from Monsieur.[13] The Domain director wrote to
Brousse in the early autumn of 1793 to inform him of the problem and
cancel his lease. Brousse told Berthaud he could no longer rent the property, then responded to the Domain by claiming that since he had never
been able to take possession of the property, he would not be paying
any of the rent that was due on it.[14] The case worked its way up through
the territorial administration, reaching the prefect's desk in 1800.
No one could find the director's letter canceling Brousse's lease, and
both the Domain and the prefect assumed it didn't exist.[15] Meanwhile,
Berthaud continued living in the neighborhood. He noticed the grass
on the land was getting long. Realizing that nothing was happening

with the land, he put his goat back out to graze. Brousse went bankrupt, and in the summer of 1795 his furniture was sold by the state to pay his debts. Meanwhile, Berthaud's goat milled about, cropping the grass.

The goat pen highlights three different types of claims to the use of the land. Berthaud possessed the property by using it to the exclusion of others. The claims of Brousse and the Domain were based on contracts, raising the questions of whether the Domain could legally enter a lease on property it didn't own, and whether Brousse had taken possession of it. As for Branthomme and Monsieur, their claims depended on the question of whether a transfer of ownership had taken place, and whether Monsieur could legally own property, given his émigré status. Four layers of claims—by possession, lease, purchase, or confiscation—existed simultaneously.

One could argue that Berthaud had no legal claim to the property, as even he recognized. After admitting how he had used the property, he assured the director, "I have no title to show you that could prevent the sale of this land, or its rental."[16] But his situation did not differ very much from that of the Domain. Berthaud's claim to the property had ended when Brousse terminated his lease, but he continued to use the property in the interim. Similarly, the Domain tried to continue extracting rent from Brousse even after Branthomme materialized and challenged the republic's claim to it. As for Branthomme, his title predated all the others, but that did not matter as long as the republic could find no record of his claim. The relationship of these actors to the little plot of land was profoundly unstable. Berthaud, whose claim was the most dubious, proved to be the only one getting any benefit from it.

The chaos that unfolded around Berthaud's goat points to the complex arrangements by which property was held and used at the end of the eighteenth century. The legal structures around property were well equipped to mediate among the various layers of ownership being exercised, as Chapter 1 has shown. Creative investments did not pose a legal challenge so much as a political one. Revolutionary reforms sought to impose some order on economic life, emphasizing the values of individualism and transparency.[17] These values motivated, for example, a ceiling of ninety-nine years on leases and the establishment of a public registry of mortgages.[18] The same asset could not be leveraged repeatedly at the expense of creditors who did not know it already had liens. A person's assets were, at least to some extent, public knowledge, so that others could decide whether to enter into a contract with them. Individualism and transparency of ownership also connected owners to the state: first, because the state took on new oversight roles by maintaining the registries and policing their accuracy; and second because the extent of a citizen's political rights depended on their status as the owner of a certain quantity of assets.

The reforms of the Revolution changed the structures within which business was done, but they did not impede the flexible environment of negotiation that characterized the end of the Old Regime. This context allowed for a diverse array of assets to be leveraged in creative ways.[19] For Berthaud and the others, the overlapping claims that their various ownership arrangements made possible were a boon, allowing multiple people to drain revenue from the same piece of land. Brousse, of course, ultimately fell victim to a system that had allowed him to speculate in leases, signing more than his capital would allow him to maintain.

While revolutionary legal reforms sought to make the lines of ownership clearer and more definite, these actors walked a fine line between owning and not owning. Their arrangements shifted constantly between a harmonious layering of shared claims and confrontation: a finding in favor of Branthomme, for example, would displace Berthaud and Brousse. The instability of claims based on these complex lease agreements meant that a person's status could also swing rapidly, from landlord to bankrupt, or from tenant to squatter.

The Widow's Lease

In the case of Berthaud's goat, the claims to use, revenue, and ownership were divided among multiple people. In this next case, however, the roles of tenant, landlord, and creditor joined together in the same individual, the Widow Planoy. Planoy's story destabilizes the boundaries of what it meant to own property, because she generated an ownership claim in the building where she was a tenant, and as a result, she became a landlord to her fellow tenants. The lawmakers who framed the émigré laws were troubled by the idea of émigré property owners behaving badly, and administrators tasked with carrying out the laws labored to identify the émigré owners of the properties they received information about. But in addition to contending with unexpected coheirs and surprise mortgages, they were also faced with unrelated people making use of property without actually owning it.

The Widow Planoy rented an apartment from the late Bochard, Marquis de Champigny.[20] She also held a promissory note for a small sum that she had loaned him, which placed her among a "crowd" of creditors owed money by his estate. The dead man's affairs were in disarray: his two sisters had renounced their shares of the inheritance, and a third heir would only accept his portion *sous bénéfice d'inventaire,* which meant he feared the estate was in deficit and did not want to be held responsible for its debts. Planoy and the other creditors were unlikely to see any money, as anything that could be scrounged up would go to larger, more privileged creditors. Even worse for Planoy, who had lived in the house "for 42 years,"[21] and the other tenants, the death of their landlord meant that they faced eviction in six months.

At the point that Planoy's situation came to the attention of the Domain, in December 1793, Bochard-Champigny's estate had already been in disarray for some time. Planoy, "seeing the business drag on lengthily," approached the heir and proposed that she sign a lease as lead tenant on the building, which sat in the Rue du Cloître Notre-Dame, facing the Cathedral. She planned to sublet the place so that she "could accelerate [her] payments, in the interest of creditors equally as legitimate as [her]." The creditors in question "seemed very happy with this arrangement and wanted to be paid." She claimed to the Domain that the executor of the estate had signed documents giving his blessing to the arrangement.

Planoy presented these explanations in a letter sent to a local administrator to justify her situation. She knew that her arrangement would be considered irregular and wanted to win over the decision makers. Flattering her correspondent, she announced in the first line, "I learn with great satisfaction, Citizen, that you are responsible for making a decision about the affairs relative to the lease I hold from the creditors of Citizen Bochard de Champigny." The rest of the letter deftly presented a series of arguments. First, she mentioned that she had been living in the house for forty-two years. By mentioning her status as a loyal resident of the building, she implied that she had a right to stay there and that she was operating in good faith. She moved on to highlight that Bochard's creditors were "all working people" from the neighborhood, with "incontestable rights." Such a deserving population, at risk of ruin, could not have been better chosen to appeal to a revolutionary official. She also emphasized the legality of her contract. It had been signed privately, without a notary, which weakened it, but she noted that Bochard's heir "signed many before a notary on the same date" (Planoy and Bochard probably signed the lease on June 20, 1791, the same day that Bochard signed four acts in the family notary's office).[22] The arrangement was also "accepted by the executor of his estate by an official affidavit [*acte*] before a notary."[23] The existence of notarized contracts from the same date could perhaps lend some legitimacy to Planoy's private contract. The executor's blessing further strengthened her contract with the heir.

Planoy may have felt at ease negotiating with Bochard de Champigny's heir and addressing the Domain officials because she had married a noble and came from a family of royal administrators. Her husband, Charles-Louis Aubin de Planoy, had been a counselor in the Parlement de Paris, just like her father, Anne-Jean-Baptiste Goislard. Ironically, her maternal uncle had held a charge as inspector in the royal Domain office. Being the wife and daughter of magistrates could explain her familiarity with the language of persuasion. Her background does not make her maneuver any less impressive, though. As she set her plan in motion, Planoy moved through multiple types of relations toward the house. It was her home, but it was also, as part of the Bochard estate, collateral against her and other debts. Perhaps most importantly, it was an asset that could produce cash. When she signed the new lease with Bochard's heir, the house became an investment for her. The property represented a home, security, and income stream, all at the same time.

The widow moved quickly. She sent her explanatory letter to the Domain in December 1793, before the director even knew the house belonged to an émigré. Five months later, in March 1794, the administrator of the Department of the Seine wrote to the director of the Domain, Gentil, to alert him that Bochard would be on the next émigré list and that he owned a house in the Cloître Notre-Dame. In December 1795, the Domain finally took action on the property, sending their bailiff, Sapinault, to inform the tenants that they would have to leave in six months because a new lease was going to be auctioned off for the building. Planoy shot back in early July, serving the Domain with an opposition to a new lease on the grounds that she held a valid lease. Confusion ensued in the Domain. The director scribbled a note on some scrap paper: "Citoyen Barbié said in his summary that it was a tenant without a lease in the building: get the facts from him and if he doesn't know anything about this so-called lease send an order to the lady Planoy to prove it."[24] Apparently Barbié could not shed any light on the alleged lease, because two days after receiving Planoy's papers, the director wrote to Sapinault asking him to serve Planoy with a summons to prove her claim. The next day, Sapinault knocked on her door.

Finally, the national Domain bureau recognized Planoy's claim, allowing the Paris office to take action. The Domain receiver for the Ile de la Cité, where the house was located, received a letter noting that even though "Citizen Planoy only had the place in truth by a lease under private signature that she concluded with the émigré Bochard de Champigny," still "as this business has by its nature raised various issues" the lease should be honored until "Citizen Planoy should see her expenses covered."[25] Clearly, the administration found the situation unorthodox. From their point of view, Planoy's lease, having been signed by an émigré, should not be honored. The widow had showed herself to be legally savvy by formally opposing the cancellation of her lease, so it is possible that the Domain wanted to avoid becoming embroiled in a lengthy legal dispute with her. But they never recognized her legal claim to the house, only her fiscal one. The letter emphasized that her lease was dubious: she "only had the place in truth by a lease under private signature." Once Planoy had been reimbursed for her expenses, the lease would be canceled.

In allowing Planoy's lease to stand provisionally, the Domain shared her understanding of the building as an investment. She wanted to be able to stay in her home, but by her account she signed the lease in order to get her debt reimbursed and to resolve the estate's financial problems. She had approached the arrangement as a means of generating cash, and it was as such that the Domain honored it. In their decision, officials made no mention of the patriotic workers whom Planoy had invoked in her letter, or of her vulnerable status as a widow. The argument that she had been in the house for forty-two years apparently left the decision makers unmoved, as they were still prepared to force her out at the end of the lease.[26] Similarly, officials accorded no legal standing to the document that she and Bochard had signed. The money she had sunk in the place was her only source of reprieve, the only factor that seemed relevant to Domain officials. Of course, they may have felt hostility toward her because she was the wife of a noble, but in this case they could simply have evicted her immediately—they had, after all, deemed her lease invalid.

To what extent, though, is Planoy's story a revolutionary one? She made the agreement with Bochard's heir well before the fall of the Bastille. Her attitude toward property, so far as it is reflected in her dealings, was not a product of the émigré laws. Really, it is a story in two parts that reveals a distinction between a legal arrangement made in the Old Regime and the response of various actors to a revolutionary situation. On the one hand, the original lease arrangement provides certain information about what was legally possible and economically desirable in the waning years of the Old Regime—specifically, signing a lease privately (as opposed to in a notary's office) and lending money from tenant to landlord, both moves that suggest a certain level of trust and informality. On the other hand, the response of the Domain to Planoy's arrangement illuminates the priorities that shaped how the Domain and, through it, the revolutionary state made decisions about property: they were not prepared to make exceptions to the letter of the law, except to the extent that they found a financial arrangement expedient. For Planoy, the executor, and the patriotic workers, drawing revenue from the house in the Cloître Notre-Dame became a collaborative effort. The actual ownership of the house was only one factor among many that shaped the ability of concerned parties to make the building pay. Bochard himself behaved in the same way when, before his death, he took a loan from his tenant. For all these people, the interdependent nature of their claims on the house granted each of them more security. The executor was more likely to keep the estate from default if Planoy was able to reimburse herself and the workers; similarly, the other creditors apparently helped Planoy negotiate with the executor, as the pressure of so many claims pushed him to make a deal.

The prerevolutionary context helps explain the Domain's response to the case. Officials rejected Planoy's legal claim as a tenant by deeming her contracts with Bochard's estate invalid. Nor did Planoy's status as a widow and a longtime tenant give her a moral claim to stay. The decision to let her stay provisionally seems, from these decisions, incongruous. If they were prepared to evict a widow on the grounds that her contract had not been formalized, surely they would have no scruples about invalidating her dubious financial scheme. But the officials, like everyone else in this story, recognized capital as a legitimate claim, even in the absence of any other kind. Planoy's story, seemingly a tale about the vicissitudes of Old Regime law, is a revolutionary one in the sense that the state—through its administrators—applied the same set of assumptions about property that she did, even though they were operating in a new legal and social context.

Like Henriette Becdelièvre, Planoy was a noble widow seeking to preserve assets—in this case, to see her landlord's debt to her reimbursed. It is no coincidence that widows populate the émigré dossiers so thickly: men were more likely to be guillotined, and as a result many women found themselves in the position of making the case for their assets.[27] Planoy was not a revolutionary widow, and although she pursued her case in a moment when it was more common for women to negotiate over property, it is also true that she was not entirely successful in achieving her goals. Even so, the Revolution put Planoy in a situation that required her to advocate for her property to the state. Her situation highlights that the tools of the law could be wielded by someone who knew how to use them, even though she, as a woman, was not meant to be able to. Like Berthaud with his goat, Planoy could engage strategies at the fringes of the law, achieving ends that were not intended by the law, but not excluded by it.

Planoy's case, like Berthaud's, reveals a single piece of property with a variety of claims being made on it. This is perhaps not so different from the ways families shared assets, in the sense that claims could be layered. What is different in these cases is the instability of simultaneous claims. Each participant in the case approached the property in question with their own purposes and not necessarily in collaboration, and as a result it was not always clear to whom ownership should be attributed. In families, property created stability, drawing together different generations or branches of a family and providing everyone with the resources they needed (assuming a bankruptcy didn't intervene). In the situations faced by Berthaud and Planoy, property provided a kind of stability in the immediate—a place to graze a goat, an apartment to live in—but it also became a source of instability as competing claims intervened. In Planoy's case, this instability played out in the form of her multiple, simultaneous relationships to the building and the Bochard estate—tenant, creditor, and landlord. In addition to these roles, she was a woman wielding the law. If property in the correct hands creates stability, and if the law creates order, then everything about her situation flew in the face of these principles.

The Stone Doghouse

The Domain may have been sensitive to Planoy's investment because administrators were no strangers to maximizing revenue. Extracting a profit from émigré property was one of the mandates of the Domain, and officials took a fine-grained approach to their task. This meant dividing a property into as many salable objects as possible. Administrators themselves made real estate a flexible and unstable asset; as owners and tenants separated real assets into pieces in order to leverage them or use them in various ways, administrators literally dismantled them. In both cases, there was nothing solid about property: as an asset, it did not represent a stable lump of capital, and even in its physicality it did not represent a unitary whole, because even something as seemingly stable as a house could be stripped into pieces. When a merchant from Hamburg named Berckmeyer won a house in the desirable Rue de Varennes in the National Lottery, the Domain bureau swung into action assessing the building for architectural features it could bill him for.[28] The régisseurs at the national level wrote to the director to reproach him for several objects that had been omitted from the list of furnishings that Berckmeyer would be given the opportunity to buy. These included two wood-burning stoves "built in place" and a stone doghouse. Delassaux, the agent who had made the list, had counted them as built-in elements of the house and did not estimate prices for them. He had, however, counted as furniture a pair of wooden buffets, a wood stove sheathed in marble, and a swinging door upholstered in toile fabric.

The apparent difference of opinion between the Domain agent and his superior, the régisseur, over whether the stone doghouse should be counted as part of the property or as a piece of furniture touched on a poorly settled point of administration and, underlying it, of law. The question was where the category of real estate ended and that of personal property began; there was no clean line. Delassaux, in spite of having missed the doghouse, had made a careful distinction between a wood stove covered in marble and a wood stove built in place. According to Domain practice, he was absolutely right, as anything bound to the property by metal fastenings, "by iron and by nail," counted as part of the real estate.[29] This definition was respected enough that in another case the director, upon learning of some objects whose nature appeared dubious, warned the local receiver that "it is . . . essential to verify the installation of these objects."[30] The claim of the Domain to a wood stove or a mirror could turn entirely on the presence of a couple of iron nails.

But the régisseur was also right to challenge Delassaux's cataloging, as legal tradition recognized the stickiness of the question. In his landmark treatise on property, the legal expert Robert-Joseph Pothier meditated on whether a mirror inside a home should be considered real estate (*biens immeubles*) or personal property (*biens meubles*). To determine the category of a mirror installed over a hearth, a variety of factors must be taken into consideration:

If the place where [the mirror] is attached is decorated with carvings, or with a plaster detail that matches the rest of the hearth, it must be determined to be personal property: for it is only placed there as additional decoration. . . . On the contrary, if the part of the hearth where the mirror has been attached is plain, or if, to protect the mirror, the wall is covered with planks that do not match the rest of the hearth, in this case it must be determined that the mirror is part of the house, for it is placed *ad integrandam dominum;* it serves to complete the hearth which, without it, would not be *numeris omnibus absolutus,* and would require something more.[31]

The particular qualities of the mirror and the wall to which it is attached, in other words, determine their relationship to each other. This relationship is essential, because both the qualities of the mirror and the qualities of the wall have a bearing on the former's legal status. Mirror and wall are not absolute categories: their status can only be ascertained in a given situation, and one mirror may have a different status than another, based on its particular relationship to a given wall.

Ultimately, the opinion of the régisseur, who maintained that the doghouse was a piece of furniture, prevailed. His letter instructed Delassaux to bill Berckmeyer for it, along with the other pieces deemed to be furniture. He did not mention Pothier or express any doubt as to the status of the doghouse based on how it was attached to the wall. One can imagine that his priority was to maximize the revenue the Domain could collect on the property. He was not concerned with the difference between real property and furniture or the implications that blurring this line might have for the political foundations of the republic. The interest of the case, however, lies exactly in the point that the instability of real estate was not limited to financial arrangements that could compromise its value. Even the physical boundaries of real estate were unstable.

The Missing Mirrors

The way that a mirror was attached to the wall had financial implications as well as legal ones. The absence of a mirror subtracted more from the value of a house than just the mirror's own price. Just as the legal status of a mirror depended on the wall, so did the value of a property depend on a variety of circumstantial factors. After signing a lease on the sumptuous Hôtel des Deux-Ponts, near Saint Sulpice, a man named Bouvrain complained that since the Domain had removed the house's mirrors, he had been unable to find a tenant for the first-floor apartment.[32] The prefect expressed doubt that the removal of the mirrors should have caused such a loss, but Daubigny, the receiver, determined that the apartment in question had indeed been empty for a significant amount of time. As a result, he argued, "it is just to reimburse this tenant for the damage that may have been caused by the removal of the mirrors decorating his house."[33] Determining the amount of the indemnity proved complicated, however. Initially, the architect had calculated the indemnity according to the rent that Bouvrain might have gotten on the apartment. The prefect took issue with this approach, instructing Daubigny that the indemnity should be based "not, as the Domain's architect pretends, on the rate at which they could be rented, but on the cost that their disappearance must have occasioned him."[34]

To calculate the new indemnity, the architect looked up what it would cost to rent the same quantity of mirrors for the period in question. Upholsterers sold and installed mirrors, which they got from factories in the Faubourg Saint-Antoine, the major hub of furniture production in Paris. Bouvrain would not make a particularly enticing client for them, though: he had already twice been the target of bankruptcy proceedings. Given his background, Daubigny pointed out, "What tradesman would consent to place mirrors for such a short time, in the home of a tenant such as Mr. Bouvrain."[35] The removal of the mirrors proved catastrophic for Bouvrain in a way that it might not have for another lessee, because his credit was not good enough to replace them. All of this had to be considered in addition to the damage to the walls "that the removal of the mirrors inevitably caused."[36] This damage was particularly serious because Bouvrain had been trying to rent the place furnished. Daubigny recommended indemnifying Bouvrain for half of one term of rent. He acknowledged, however, that the indemnification would do Bouvrain little good. He was already significantly behind on the rent, and officials were preparing to seize his furniture. The man was on the brink of bankruptcy.

Everyone seemed to accept that the mirrors were part of both the property and the furnishings. On the one hand, their absence posed a problem primarily because Bouvrain was trying to rent the place furnished. On the other hand, their removal had seriously damaged the wall. The sticking point was how much their removal lowered the rental value of the property.[37] Here, three variables came into play: the cost of the mirrors; the cost of the rent on the apartment as a whole; and the cost of replacing the mirrors, which included hidden costs associated with renting new ones. Their value had to be calculated with respect to Bouvrain specifically, based on his particular ability to obtain replacements.

The uncertain boundary between real estate and other forms of property created instability in the value of all the property in question. A house's worth—in the sense of what it could be rented for—depended on a triangulation of the physical object of the building itself, the use that was being made of it, and the ability of a given person to use it. Based on these variables, three different officials offered three different means of calculating the monetary value of Bouvrain's loss. The architect, whose area of expertise was buildings and their contents, focused on the rental value of the house and the cost of the mirrors. The prefect dealt in the administrative terms of liability and indemnification. Daubigny, at the local level, paid attention to the situation of the particular man in question. In this case, it was not only the specificity of wall and mirror that affected the rental value of a property. For Bouvrain, the value of the house he rented also depended on his own status as a person with bad credit. In this sense, an asset couldn't be considered as a fixed thing with a stable value, because its value depended on the qualifications of the person renting it.

Plowshares into Paintbrushes

What about the classic image of the property owner, comfortable on his lands, preparing to pass on his estate and title to his descendants? Many of the individuals featured in this chapter were on the brink of bankruptcy or, like Bouvrain, had actually gone over the edge. People with more to lose were perhaps more circumspect in the way they handled their property. High-flying émigrés with seigniorial lands avoided verbal battles with Domain architects, but they sought to maximize their income just as craftily as anyone else. The émigré Guillaume Baillet possessed that most coveted object, a piece of land that granted a name: he called himself Baron Saint-Julien after the barony he owned in Burgundy. His townhouse in Dijon, the Hôtel Baillet, also bore his name, even though he had moved to a rented apartment in Paris. An art collector and critic, he filled his home with books and curiosities.[38] His collection included drawings by Rubens, Brueghel, and Coypel, along with thousands of other paintings and drawings, jewelry, and fine furniture. An inventory of his belongings reveals that he kept his books scattered all over his apartment; the notaries who drew up the inventory chose to highlight one particular painting from his collection, depicting "—donnant leçons d'amour accompagnée de Vénus sa mère" (—giving lessons in love accompanied by her mother, Venus).

As Baillet grew older, he began to wish he could give up the burden of managing his estate and secure more disposable income. He considered selling his lands outside Paris but felt that the property "naturally should never leave the family."[39] In order to both keep the lands and get the cash he wanted, he struck a deal in March 1783 with his two cousins once removed.[40] He used a gift-in-life to transfer the Saint-Julien lands and the Dijon townhouse to Madeleine and Marguerite Fyot de la Marche, known by their married names as de Barberie de Courteilles and de Voyer de Paulmy d'Argenson.[41] In exchange, they agreed to pay him a lifetime annuity of 12,000 livres per year, in installments of 1,000 livres per month.[42] The arrangement was ideal, because it meant that Baillet could leverage his real estate into a convenient fixed income without actually selling it.

Baillet wasn't the only one who found the Saint-Julien property cumbersome. Less than a year after the transfer, Courteilles and Paulmy turned around and sold the lands. The buyer, Jean Perard, paid 300,000 francs. Given that the franc and the livre were roughly equal in value, this represented a tidy profit for the women. In January 1784, Paulmy's husband decided that Perard's payment schedule was too slow for his liking. He explained to a notary that he "wanted to place the 190,000 francs belonging to his spouse in a more advantageous manner, without having to wait for the payments due by Perard." Courteilles agreed to buy her sister's share in Perard's debt. She would pay Paulmy the 190,000 francs in the form of an annuity of 9,500 francs, with the option to reimburse it in three lump sums.[43] At the end of these transactions, Perard owned the Saint-Julien lands and owed their price to Courteilles, who in turn owed money to Paulmy. Meanwhile, Courteilles had kept the house in Dijon, which was rented out.[44]

Again and again, members of the Baillet-Fyot family picked other investments over real estate. The Saint-Julien property was not an unattractive proposition—when Baillet gave it to his cousins, it was providing 7,500 livres annually in revenue. It was not the property itself that motivated its sellers, however, but the appeal of other prospects. Each of the sellers had their own reasons for giving it up: for Baillet, peace of mind; for the cousins, a profit; for d'Argenson and her husband, who sold their share of the sale price, it was to make a better investment elsewhere. For each one, ownership of land was appealing only insofar as it could lead to another kind of benefit. Land ownership, in other words, was not a position they sought for its own sake. Baillet's family nostalgia couldn't make him keep the barony, and it couldn't keep it in the family either.

Much of the revolutionary rhetoric around property was based on the assumption that land was something desirable. After all, it was at one point meant to be a reward to deserving patriots. But Baillet and his family members each individually made the decision that they would prefer cash. Baillet wanted to buy art, but Paulmy's husband just wanted the cash so he could invest it more profitably. One might consider that the family already owned other land, such that they found this property superfluous. But none of them seemed to be selling it off just to get rid of it—they had other projects in mind for the capital. Land did not hold particular cachet for them, and in fact they considered other forms of property to be more attractive.

Living off the Land

Pierre-Elisabeth Fontanieu chose to hold on to his property, letting his cousins inherit it after he died. Unfortunately for his heirs, Antoine-Louis Belzunce and Anne-Marguerite Doublet de Bandeville, he died with significant debts in 1784. The inheritance consisted of a marquisate called the Terre de Fiennes, located in the Pas-de-Calais region. The pair quickly sold the property in exchange for an annuity that could be directed toward the estate's creditors when they presented themselves. Belzunce, who would later emigrate, was the picture of a late Old Regime *bon vivant*. He and his wife lived in the Rue du Faubourg

Saint-Honoré, one of the most coveted addresses in Paris. His wife, Marie-Madeleine Verger, was born in the French colony of Saint-Domingue, a point that places her among the many French families who owned property in the Caribbean and brought profits of enslavement back to Europe.[45] The couple had indulged in that luxury of noble life, a separation of fortunes, which meant that the marquis could no longer manage his wife's wealth. This was a legal arrangement that was difficult to obtain and only undertaken by the very wealthy; it did not necessarily mean the Belzunces didn't get along, and they continued to live together.[46]

Bandeville and Belzunce were hardly parting with an ancient family seat. The Terre de Fiennes had only been in the family since Fontanieu's father bought it in 1730. When Fontanieu's mother died, in 1752, his father transferred the property to him and his older brother as part of the estate settlement. The property that each spouse brought to a marriage was kept separate from anything accumulated during the marriage, and after the death of either spouse, the heirs reclaimed this original property from the surviving spouse. The boys collected their mother's original property but renounced her share of marital property. As a result, their father found himself responsible for the couple's debts and also for the value of his wife's property. Fontanieu *père* arranged to transfer all his marital property, including Fiennes, to his sons on the condition that they accept their mother's share of marital debts along with her personal wealth. This worked out so that the sons collected the full value of their mother's estate and the father wiped out all of the debts contracted during his marriage.[47]

The sale concluded between Belzunce and Bandeville and their buyer, Gallini, in July 1791 had some similarities to the previous transfer of property by Fontanieu's father. The property was sold for 700,000 livres which broke down to 600,000 for the land and 100,000 for the mineral rights to coal deposits under the earth. In the notarial act, the cousins stated that "the present sale is necessary to acquit the debts on the estate of Mr. Fontanieu."[48] As in the previous generation, debt was forcing the transfer of property. Fontanieu's estate owed sixteen different annuities totaling 25,500 livres. No money, however, changed hands at the time of the sale. Instead, Gallini, an Italian opera producer living in London, agreed to pay 510,000 livres of the sale price in lifetime annuities at 5 percent interest.[49] The remaining 190,000 livres could not be paid until eighteen months had elapsed, after which date it would accrue interest at 5 percent as well. This second chunk was to be delivered directly to the executor of the Fontanieu estate in order to discharge any debts.

It is interesting that Fontanieu's debts were cited as the reason for the sale, given that such a relatively small portion of the price was designated to discharge them. The sellers' choice to be paid in lifetime annuities, rather than a *rente foncière,* a type of annuity intended to finance real estate purchases, seems to cast doubt on the statement in the notary's office. Because a lifetime annuity would be extinguished when its beneficiary died, it's possible that Gallini agreed to a higher sale price than he would have if he had been paying with a *rente foncière.* Belzunce and Bandeville would get more money in the short term, but if either of them died prematurely, their estates could be left exposed to Fontanieu's debts. According to Domain officials researching the case, Gallini paid only 98,804 livres and 3 sous to Fontanieu's creditors—though this could be because he ran out of money or simply stopped paying, and not because the creditors had been satisfied.

A possible motivation for the sale of the Fiennes property emerges when we consider that Belzunce had already sold a similar piece of land five years earlier. He inherited the Barony of Gavaudun from his father when he was still a minor. In March 1786, more than forty years after his father's death, he and his wife sold it for a package of cash and annuities. To satisfy the 180,000 livre price, the buyer, Philibert de Fumel, transferred two annuities valued at a little under 35,000 livres, of which he was the beneficiary, to Belzunce.[50] In addition, he paid a little over

15,000 livres in cash and agreed to pay the balance of 130,000 livres in annual installments of not less than 20,000 livres. One year after the deal was formalized, Belzunce delegated 52,500 livres of the sale price to satisfy a clutch of tradesmen to whom he owed money. The debts included 5,000 livres to a saddle maker, 8,000 livres to an upholsterer, and 12,000 livres to Rose Bertin, stylist to Marie-Antoinette (who became an émigré herself, and had her property confiscated).

By the time the Domain became involved, Rose Bertin had sold her share of Fumel's debt to Jean François Coypel. Fumel, however, had been placed on the émigré list and apparently stopped making payments on the land. Coypel approached the Domain in hopes of collecting Fumel's debt from the state, which, as the owner of Fumel's assets, he was now responsible for his debt as well. The prefect alerted the director that Fumel had sold Gavaudun before emigrating and that Coypel was trying to get the property seized from the buyer for the debt.[51] Two years later, the director reported to the prefect that, in fact, Fumel had never sold the land. The fate of Coypel's debt remained uncertain.

The Fiennes property shared a similar fate, but not at the hands of Belzunce or anyone connected to him. In July 1802, posters went up announcing that *"la Ferme de Fiennes"* would be sold at auction to pay Gallini's debts. The proceedings had been initiated on behalf of a woman named Marie-Louise-Elisabeth Venant. Gallini owed her an annuity of 4,000 livres per year, and he was behind on it by 34,361.35 francs. Where the Fontanieu family and Belzunce had found ways to stay ahead of their debts, Gallini had come up short.

Over and over, the owners of the Marquisate of Fiennes and the Barony of Gavaudun transferred the properties in ways that made them almost indistinguishable from other forms of assets. These noble terrains were sold against annuities or transferred as payment for debts. Their value was carved up among multiple owners and claimants such that a sum of money paid to a dressmaker could later be leveraged to have the entire property seized for debt (though, it appears, unsuccessfully). Returning to Baillet Saint-Julien's preference for annuities over the hassle of real estate, though, it seems that land was distinguishable from other types of assets: it was less desirable.

What's striking in the Belzunce case is not only that land was not particularly desirable but also that it involved numerous, complex transactions. The reason land was unstable was not simply that it could be sold. It was unstable because buyers and sellers multiplied transactions. Land was traded against debt and converted into annuities in spider webs of transactions that linked together a string of buyers and sellers. These transactions make it clear why a mortgage registry, where buyers and sellers could get accurate information about each other, was so essential. But one might also wonder what transparency meant in the face of multiple, complex transactions. It might take a forensic accountant, and not just a land transfer register, to determine the financial solidity of Gallini, Fumel, Fontanieu, or Belzunce at any given point in time.

The Door in the Wall

A firewood dealer named Claude-François Cagnion did not want to part with the house and the piece of land he owned on the Left Bank. The government planned to join Cagnion's property in the Boulevard de l' Hôpital, near the banks of the Seine, with land it already owned to create the Museum of Natural History and Jardin des Plantes. Cagnion didn't have a choice in the matter. The Convention passed a law declaring that a swath of land that included his house and garden would be *"réuni"* (joined) with the Jardin des Plantes.[52] He was, however, allowed to choose publicly owned property in exchange for his own, and he was given an indemnity payment on top of the value of his property for his trouble. Cagnion selected portions of the grounds of the royal châteaux at Marly and Saint-Cloud. The government denied this request, then denied his second choice of a piece of Church property on the Left Bank.

He finally got his third choice, a package of farmland also in Marly. The estimate came in well below that of the property in the Boulevard de l' Hôpital, which, including an indemnity, was valued at 237,500 livres. The republic still owed Cagnion over 100,000 livres, to be paid off in additional properties that Cagnion would identify. He chose a house in the Rue Neuve-Laurent (also called Rue Neuve-Saint-Laurent, near what is now the Gare de l'Est), another in the Rue du Temple in the Marais, and a third in the Rue de Vaugirard. The value of the three houses exceeded what was owed to him by 3,516.90 francs, which Cagnion was supposed to pay before taking possession.

Cagnion had a business selling firewood. His original property was well situated to receive the shipments of timber that came on barges up the Seine, and was large enough for him to stock inventory. The property in the Rue de Vaugirard, to which he moved his business, proved not to be suited to his purposes. It had been the site of excavation by the city, leaving the surface fragile and prone to collapse. The Department sent its inspector of quarries to view the site after one such incident, and Cagnion was told he could no longer stack wood on the compromised areas. Three weeks later Cagnion called the inspector back to complain that he had a new shipment at the port and nowhere to put it. The inspector returned and determined that if Cagnion cut a door in a wall abutting a projected extension of the Rue Cassette, he could bring the wood in and store it along the wall.[53] Cagnion was prepared to undertake additional work to consolidate the endangered areas, which further reassured the bureaucrat. He reported back to his superiors, "I don't see any other drawbacks to letting him have use of it for his business."[54] The administrators were inclined to agree, given the nature of Cagnion's business. As they noted to the Domain, "The interest of commerce for provisioning Paris, obliges us to take this circumstance into consideration, when the proposed measure seems to reconcile with public security."[55] Cagnion was selling his firewood to the bakers of Paris to fire their ovens. Any interruption in his supply chain could compromise the bakers' ability to meet demand. Officials were painfully aware of the consequences of bread shortages—they had already inspired, spectacularly, the women's march to Versailles in October 1789 and numerous disturbances since then. For the administrators, it was worth bending the rules a bit to allow Cagnion to use public land if it meant keeping the city under control.

Cagnion began lining up his inventory of wood on the strip of land designated for the street extension. Instead of opening a door in the wall that separated his property from the public land, as the Administration had directed, he tore down the entire wall. The strip in question had belonged to his neighbor, Christophe-Charles Bailly, who bought it from the Domain and subsequently traded it to the city in exchange for another plot. The terms of the sale granted him the new property "with the charge to leave the necessary space for opening projected streets."[56] While Cagnion moved in loads of wood, Bailly continued using his former land as well. The gears of administration engaged, producing a punitive opinion from the prefect. Though he had permission to use the land, Cagnion, "by an abuse of this permission has taken over the totality of the projected street and has mixed up this street with his property by taking down his wall, by closing off the projected street at the end of the Rue de Fleurus and also by reserving himself private entry on the side by the Rue de Vaugirard. . . . In this way he has drawn an illegitimate profit from a property that belongs to the Republic." Cagnion had been authorized to use the land, but he had taken over too much space and, crucially, closed off the public land for his exclusive use. He had been given use of the space for "his business," but he had gone too far, taking "an illegitimate profit." The prefect ordered that Cagnion and Bailly "will be held to restrain themselves within the terms of their respective titles." The pair had physically overstepped their property lines in taking over the projected road and, in the prefect's evocative language, had also legally overstepped the boundaries of their property titles.

The decision to allow Cagnion to use the land, in view of the public good, and the countervailing move to punish him for his illegitimate profit, reveal the delicate balance of priorities within the administration. In many respects, Cagnion's behavior recalls Planoy's, in that both stepped into dubious legal territory in order to turn a profit. Both could make a claim to a larger benefit: Planoy was reimbursing worthy workers, while Cagnion was ensuring that the ovens of Paris stayed hot. The difference was that Cagnion hit the tipping point of the bureaucracy's tolerance and was censured. The key was his illegitimate financial profit. Cagnion, by tearing down the wall, crossed over from using public land for the public good to taking over the land for his own personal use. In both cases, the interested parties were only allowed to use public property within certain parameters of profit. Planoy was only allowed to be "reimbursed for the sum of her advances." Similarly, Cagnion was only allowed to stack wood on the street provisionally. The controlling factor was profit, not public interest.

The prefect ordered Cagnion to pay rent for the period that he had illegally occupied the land. The local receiver notified Cagnion that he should appoint an architect of his own to work with the Domain's architect, Bourla, on establishing the rental value of the land. Cagnion began dragging his feet immediately. He filed an opposition to the prefect's decision and asked for an extra ten days to clear the land.[57] Then he asked for another ten days. More than two weeks later, and for the third time, he asked for another ten days. Finally, he refused to name an architect of his own, adding a new layer of paperwork before the estimation could be done.

In June 1801, four months after the prefect's decision, Bourla and Pierre Giraud, an architect he had found to represent Cagnion, trooped onto Cagnion's land at eleven in the morning to do the estimation.[58] They had already been put off once by Cagnion, a week earlier. This time, he met them on his land and immediately launched into a tirade. As Bourla reported it, "[Cagnion] observed to us that he believed to be even more founded in refusing payment for the rental of the street, which was the purpose of our mission; that he had only obtained it by virtue of an authorization from the central bureau following the report by Citizen Guillaumot, to serve him as a sort of indemnity for the collapses that took place on his land." Cagnion further "invited" the architects to append to their report the series of letters from the Departmental administration and from the inspector of quarries that had originally granted him use of the land—and brandished copies of them. The architects took the materials and went on with their estimation, ignoring Cagnion's "diverse observations and pretensions" as they worked. From the architects' report, the Domain determined that Cagnion owed 1,383.33 francs in rent.

The sums produced by the Domain officials are rigorously precise: 1,383.33 francs for the strip of land, 3,516.90 francs for the property swap. These figures reflect what each property was worth, and yet more than property changed hands in each of these transactions. When Cagnion gave up his property in the Boulevard de l'Hôpital, he was exchanging property with the republic, but he was also exchanging an inconvenience for an indemnity. The architects could only assess what the property should be sold for, not what it was worth to Cagnion to give it up. Similarly, the rental value assigned to the strip of land abutting the Vaugirard property did not adequately reflect the transaction between Cagnion and the Domain. Each party had a different idea of what was being exchanged, but they could agree that it was not rent. Cagnion believed that he had been given use of the land in exchange for his lost business when the quarry collapsed. From the prefect's perspective, Cagnion was being fined an indemnity because he had improperly used the land. Cash and property moved back and forth between Cagnion and the government as compensation for other things.

Even the architects' calculations reflected an understanding of value that extended beyond the amount of money for which each property could be sold. Elaborate reports made on the three properties that

Cagnion received in exchange for his home in the Boulevard de l'Hôpital reflect the range of circumstantial considerations that influenced the architects' calculations.[59] In the Rue de Vaugirard, there was the collapse from the old quarry that became the source of so much trouble. At the time the exchange was made formal, the collapse had already happened, and Cagnion had already been forced to move his stock, "which caused him transport costs, a pure loss for his business." He was also planning to expand the existing buildings and would have to pay for extensive foundation work given the unstable land. Taking this into account, the architects reduced the value of the property from 38,700 francs to 34,000.

Similar considerations influenced the assessed values of the other Paris properties Cagnion had selected in the swap with the state. The house in the Rue du Temple had benefited from several arrangements with neighbors that would no longer be possible. Previously the house "suffered from water leaks from the neighboring house."[60] Cagnion would be required to build a new wall and paved courtyard that would redirect the flow of rainwater into the street. Before the Revolution, there had also been a convent next door filled with pensioners. The architects noted that at the time of the last evaluation, in 1786, "this house would have been valued higher, due to the existence of a convent that attracted pensioners who enjoyed a certain revenue and the freedom to go out as they pleased." The closing of the convent, by their estimation, had a negative impact on the value of the neighboring house. One almost detects a note of nostalgia, as the report went on wistfully, "things having changed their face, the value is no longer the same."

In the Rue Neuve Saint-Laurent, a reorientation of the street would require significant demolition and rebuilding. An expert assessment noted that the work exposed Cagnion "to considerable expenses."[61] Even when this construction was done, the architects noted the "poor state of the buildings" and that "their inconvenient distribution is not very suitable for normal habitation." The neighborhood posed challenges as well; the prison of Madelonnettes abutted the property, and the architects noted the rumbling of conveyances serving a nearby granary, "rendering the neighboring lodgings very incommodious." Given these concerns, the architects assessed the house at a value of only 19,000 francs, compared with 34,000 for the Rue de Vaugirard house and 60,000 for the one in the Rue du Temple.

It was only years later that the Domain discovered that as Cagnion paced around in his yard, haranguing the two officials, he was concealing a stunning secret. Three days before the prefect's opinion was registered, he had sold the land. This bombshell only came to light for the Domain after Cagnion's buyer defaulted and the property was resold at public auction. A representative for the new buyer wrote to the director to request a receipt for the payment Cagnion had owed as part of his land exchange with the republic. The new buyer, André-Daniel Laffon-Ladebat, assumed the payment had been made, "because in fact he was put in possession of [the property]."[62] Indeed, the deal had required that Cagnion "be given possession and use of the property after the payment of the sum." These terms were quoted in Laffon-Ladebat's own contract with Cagnion, so he knew them well.[63] Oddly, though, the contract with Laffon-Ladebat also noted that "the sellers promise to justify this payment very soon." This promise by the seller to pay the remaining balance directly contradicted the idea that taking possession was conditional on having already paid. Why, if the sale depended on the payment, had the buyers been given possession of the land before the republic received the payment? The local receiver began scrambling to find out what had happened to the money, which he had already spent years trying to collect without success. No one could find any record of it. The director replied to Laffon-Ladebat's agent that he couldn't issue him the receipt, because the payment hadn't been made.

The money he owed to the government was not, however, foremost in Cagnion's mind when he signed the sale contract with Laffon-Ladebat. As with Belzunce's case, the sale of the property allowed him to accomplish a variety of goals at once. First, the property had a lien on it from a loan he had taken out from a man named François Blanchet. It was a lifetime annuity, so Cagnion was required to make payments annually throughout Blanchet's life. Laffon-Ladebat agreed to take responsibility for this debt as part of the sale. But that wasn't all. When Laffon-Ladebat paid for the property, he gave the money not to Cagnion but to one Joseph André. Cagnion owed André 59,000 francs, and this deal was the last step in paying him back. Already Cagnion and his wife had sold the farm in Marly (to yet another person, one Lecouteux) and paid 480.25 francs in cash to André.

With the appearance of the buyer, a new possibility dawned for the Domain. Debellavoine, the new receiver for the 11th and 12th arrondissements, wrote to the director asking for the address of Laffon-Ladebat's business agent so that he could go after him for the money Cagnion owed. He learned, after following through on the issue, that Laffon-Ladebat had indeed bought Cagnion's property near the Rue de Vaugirard, but that Cagnion's debt had been transferred to another man, who had bought a house in the Rue du Temple that had also been part of the deal. Cagnion had put a stipulation in the contract that the buyer would be responsible for the debt if it hadn't been discharged within four months of the sale. Cagnion, as the Domain was painfully aware, never did make the payment. But the buyer, François Lebaigné, did. In the end, then, Cagnion never paid either the debt on the property exchange or the assessment for the Vaugirard property. This is an important detail, because Cagnion's interactions with the republic were shaped entirely by coercion, beginning the moment Cagnion learned that he would be parting with his home in the Boulevard de l'Hôpital. He had little recourse, and in fact avoided paying one of his debts by having someone else do it for him. The value of his property came into question again and again, but each time administrators were able to impose their interpretation on the basis of perceived public interest.

Throughout the lengthy relationship between Cagnion and the republic, physical property served as a means for both parties to obtain another desired outcome. For the republic, the desired outcome was the Natural History Museum and its gardens. The deal was not about acquiring real estate so much as it was about pursuing the ideal of an enlightened government advancing human knowledge. Similarly, the walls of Cagnion's title were relaxed, in the prefect's words, in order to obtain public tranquility. The desired outcome for Cagnion was more worldly, but real estate still served as a means to obtaining it. He wanted to advance his business and turn a profit. He used real estate as a bargaining chip, leveraging it to obtain cash and then trading it against debts. The contracts that he signed were laced with contingencies on both sides: he would pay off the money he owed the republic, but the buyer would take over the back payments on an annuity; he would get the house in the Rue du Temple, but he would rebuild the facade in accordance with the modified trajectory of the street.

Clearly, Cagnion was something of an operator. He became embroiled in a set of transactions that were much more elaborate than those in the other cases in this chapter, and in this sense, it is reasonable to believe that he is not particularly representative of the way most people managed their property. Significantly, however, Cagnion did not act in isolation. Every one of his machinations required another contracting party. Each deal on its own is unremarkable in the context of the range of property transactions possible at the time. Furthermore, the Domain itself contributed to Cagnion's feverish activity. It was the Domain that first approached him about his house in the Boulevard de l'Hôpital. It was the Domain that gave him two properties in exchange for his one (and the elusive 3,516.90 francs).

Cagnion's story connects to a number of themes that emerged in the previous cases in this chapter. First, he approached land as capital that could be used strategically. When the state demanded that he part with his original property, he worked to turn the situation in his favor. This meant leveraging his new properties in order to raise the cash he needed to close the deal. He recognized that a property could produce the revenue to pay for itself, just as the Widow Planoy did when she used the lease on the Bochard de Champigny house to bail out the entire estate. The swaps of property that occurred between Cagnion and the state recall those undertaken by Baillet, Belzunce, and the other parties to their land sales. Cagnion and the state exchanged plots of land with a view to other goals—constructing a museum and advancing business interests. Cagnion's initial choice of property outside Paris in exchange for the plot in the Boulevard de l'Hôpital suggests he may have seen the exchange as an opportunity to reorient his business in a new direction.

Cagnion's machinations in the Rue de Vaugirard recall issues around the boundaries of property raised by the stone doghouse and Bouvrain's trouble with the mirrors in his rented property. The physical boundaries of his property shifted several times, starting with the collapse caused by the compromised land inside his parcel, and culminating in his removal of the boundary wall on the Rue Cassette. There was a difference between the parcel he was legally entitled to, based on his property title, and the surface area he could de facto make use of. The legality of his use was a matter of discretion: he was allowed to stack his wood outside the walls of his property, but he was not allowed to obstruct the entire space that had been reserved to cut a new street. For this reason, the envelope of his property was not limited to the boundaries named in any title he may have held; instead, the boundaries of his property were set by officials with an eye to what he was deemed to need for his business, a determination that was shaped by the understanding that his business served the public interest. The shape of his property, then, varied according to a variety of administrative and political considerations beyond the legal terms of his title.

The assessed value of the properties depended on their social context in addition to their physical qualities. The republic's interest in Cagnion's property for the Jardin des Plantes and his own interest in the lands around the royal châteaux at Marly and Saint-Cloud recall the social value of property, based in desirability, that we first saw in the

Talaru dossier in Chapter 4. The republic wanted Cagnion's property—officials would say they needed Cagnion's property—to complete an aesthetic vision of a cultural institution, gardens and a museum, that they imagined for the beauty of the capital and the edification of the nation. Cagnion was first drawn to properties that bore a glittering royal past. The value of these properties to the interested parties, in the sense of their attractiveness, was shaped by a social context in which particular artifacts of the Old Regime, repurposed, offered new opportunities for constructing social position. Of course, the nation did not really construct social position, but by trading in a kind of cultural currency, it constructed an identity based in part on promoting the arts and sciences, as well as on a reworking of the past that transformed trappings of monarchy into a new form of dignity.

Overall, Cagnion's dossier reflects an understanding of property as a financial tool that was flexible and contingent both in its monetary value and in its physical shape—a view held by both Cagnion and the officials he interacted with. This understanding manifested itself in a variety of ways. These included exchanging and leveraging various pieces of land, as well as precise valuations, down to the centime, that took into account not only the physical qualities of the property but also the context of their neighborhood. Property could be broken apart into component pieces, and its boundaries were determined not only on a physical plane but also contingently on the basis of who the owner was: they included considerations such as how the owner planned to use the land (the nature of Cagnion's business allowed for a door in the wall at the Rue de Vaugirard).

Conclusion

In all of these transactions, property was used as a financial tool that could be broken apart, exchanged, or leveraged. Ownership was a potentially temporary position that depended on a variety of factors, such as the other investment opportunities available and the suitability of the property in question to the owner's larger financial goals. The negotiations that surrounded these transactions were freewheeling, often drawing many exchanges into a single contract. In many cases, the lack of a shared approach to value further complicated matters. The state could, ultimately, impose its own valuations when its interests were at stake, but individual citizens also had access to a variety of strategies, from negotiation to subterfuge, to represent their own interests. In many of these operations, the state and the private parties involved were far from citizens meeting each other frankly in the public square. The actors in these cases instead approached property almost as a game, with maneuvers and countermaneuvers on either side. For some, like Bouvrain and Brousse, the stakes were quite high.[64]

The way that property deals were structured reveals quite a bit about the intentions of the contracting parties. Rarely was a property simply bought or sold without other conditions being placed on the transaction. Cagnion, for example, was expected to rebuild the facade of the house in the Rue Neuve Laurent; Gallini had to keep making payments to Belzunce and Bandeville until they died. Furthermore, the contingency of ownership extended beyond the terms of the sale. The republic's ownership of the land in the Luxembourg garden depended not only on its claim that Monsieur was an émigré but also on the solidity of Monsieur's own title. The ability of buyers of émigré property to obtain architectural elements as part of their purchases depended on how those elements were affixed to the wall. These factors meant that even after a transaction had been concluded, an owner could discover that they did not actually own what they thought they did.

The decision to buy, sell, or lease a piece of property in nearly all of these cases was driven by the desire to obtain a goal other than the ownership of real estate: Planoy wanted to stay in her home; Baillet wanted to spend more money on art; Cagnion was trying to stay ahead of his creditors. Property served these people as a means to an end rather than an end in itself. The way that a given person valued a piece of property depended on how they calculated these external goals. The case of Bouvrain showed this particularly clearly, as members of the administration approached the valuation of Bouvrain's rental differently depending on the factors that they deemed most salient.

Neither the monetary value of property nor the boundaries of ownership are absolute. Both depend on all manner of contingencies, considerations, and preexisting arrangements. The contingency of property claims and the fluidity of property transfers were products of long-standing Old Regime customary law, which remained largely untouched by revolutionary policy. French law was well equipped to deal with issues raised by property: after all, the section of the Civil Code titled *"biens"* ("goods" or "property") is twice as long as any of the others. Everything the people in this chapter undertook was perfectly legal, with the possible exception of some of Cagnion's subterfuges.

The challenge posed by the fluidity of property—by its financialization—was not a legal one but a political and administrative one. Further, the issues raised by the émigré confiscation process were not only problematic within the scope of administering and selling seized assets. They also point up a deeper disconnect at work in revolutionary property reform. Emergent and ongoing economic practices around property took on new meaning in the new context created by the Revolution, because property reform undertaken in the Revolution changed aspects of property law and, most significantly, changed the political significance attributed to property ownership. The émigré confiscation process makes these dynamics visible to the historian; in addition, however, the émigré confiscation process accelerated them, to the extent that it put new assets into the market.

Conclusion

T HE LEGAL AMBITIONS FOR PROPERTY at the outset of the Revolution were broad. Lawmakers undertook to transform property
in ways that would give shape to a new society. Notably, they sought
to distribute property rights equally among individuals regardless of
social status, as the basis for a society of equals. They also sought to
link property to its owner transparently, so that owners could meet
each other frankly and openly. This transparency, they believed, would
facilitate property exchanges. It would also strengthen the link between property and citizenship, since the amount of property that a
citizen owned also determined access to political leadership such as
serving as an elector or standing for office. There was already a tension in this approach to property, between the private nature of business dealings and the public nature of citizenship.

The new relationship between property and citizenship established
by the early legal reforms of the Revolution made emigration a problem in the eyes of lawmakers. It also offered the means for a solution.
Given the centrality of property to the new regime, property owners
behaving badly—leaving the country to join an enemy army—posed
an existential threat to the nascent republic. The émigré laws limited

freedom of movement on the basis that the émigrés owned property: they were capable of paying an indemnity, and their departure was perceived as a threat to the republic. Legislation against emigration provided an opportunity for lawmakers to develop a nascent moralistic link between property ownership and citizenship: lawmakers described the émigrés as derelict citizens and considered giving their property to patriotic, deserving citizens who would use it properly. The laws against the émigrés also revealed a gap between lawmakers' ideas and actual patterns of property ownership. The émigré laws equated property with land, despite the fact that property also included consumer goods and assets. Ironically, they did so even as they fretted about the "emigration of things," recognizing that émigrés might carry these other forms of property with them as they fled France.

The tensions within revolutionary property policy, and within the émigré laws specifically, highlight the limitations of law when it came to redefining property and establishing a protocol for its distribution. The administration of the émigré laws clarifies these legal limitations still further. Administrators were meant to follow the law, and they did so as they attempted to confiscate émigré property. Following the law, however, also required the application of judgment: administrators used their expertise to determine the correct course of action as they navigated situations where the lines of ownership were not clear. Their work operationalized a tension within revolutionary politics around property: while property empowered citizens as members of the sovereign, it was the state—and in particular, administrators—that determined what a person owned.

Yet separating owners from their assets was difficult, owing to the nature of property in a market economy oriented around consumerism. Consumer goods were adapted to create meaning for their owners in a particular social context, such that the monetary value of these goods might depend on their ability to be used in a particular setting. This meant that when the state confiscated property, from houses to furniture to wine, it could not always realize the same value that the original owner could. The value of a property—the money it was worth—depended on social relations, either through the marketplace or through the social recognition that an asset inspired. By destroying a tie between owner and property through the confiscation process, administrators could functionally destroy the asset, nullifying its sale value.

The social ties in which property was enmeshed included, notably, family relations. The circulation of property within the family created utility and financial stability for its members. Lineage assets passed from one generation to the next over time, placing them in a long period of limbo between the birth of an heir and the death of an ascendant relative. Formal promises made in marriage contracts placed real legal limits on an owner's ability to dispose of their property: the terms of spousal property created claims that endured after the death of one party to the marriage. Family control of assets was long established in Old Regime law and society, and it did not go away in the Revolution. In fact, revolutionary reforms to family law only strengthened the claims of lineage by making it impossible to disinherit a child. Even as revolutionary legislators aspired to make property rights more individualistic, they also recognized the moral claims of family. In the case of the émigrés, lawmakers strengthened moral claims within the family at its broadest, recognizing the claims of servants and other dependents on moral grounds. In this way, émigré law pushed legislators to articulate more clearly certain types of commitments relating to property. These commitments added further complexity to the legal definition of property by recognizing that it performed additional functions beyond those relating to the individual citizen.

Of course, property also circulated in the marketplace, beyond family ties. Marketplace circulation occurred in a freewheeling setting that did not privilege certain types of assets—such as land—over others. Notably, property did not circulate in the marketplace as a unitary whole;

instead, assets were broken apart in various ways to suit the purposes of buyers and sellers. The means to divide and leverage property by owners and nonowners alike blurred the terms of ownership. In the case of the émigrés, the confiscation process was meant to separate assets from owners. Yet assets themselves could be separated into pieces, either physically, by breaking a house apart into various pieces of movable property, or financially, by creating liens of various types. The use of property in the market posed a further challenge to revolutionary property policy because it highlighted the gap between lawmakers' aspiration to a republic of property owners and the economic reality that land did not provide the kind of financial stability lawmakers imagined. Land could be leveraged in a variety of ways, such that the owner of the land did not retain the capital of its value. Landowners were not so different from anyone else operating in the market, in that all parties sought to leverage credit and debt to achieve their purposes.

Ultimately, property law was based on a vision of society that did not line up with the reality of property ownership and usage. Revolutionary reform of property law was meant to bring about a new society of property owners, in which land exercised a financially and politically stabilizing effect on owners, inspiring them to behave in ways that supported national economic well-being and tying them to the state patriotically. Property, however, circulated in a variety of ways, both within the marketplace and outside or adjacent to it, where it served both as a form of social currency and as family patrimony. Property remained entwined with the private realm of family and personal affairs, even as it also operated in the public space of the market and in relation to the politics of citizenship.

As property owners, émigré women exemplify these two key features of revolutionary property: first, that it was poorly contained by law; and second, that it existed in both the public and private realms of social life. Legally, women's ability to own property was limited. Yet as the cases of Henriette Becdelièvre and the Widow Planoy show, some women exercised claims on and circulated property. They could, for example, act through family ties to male relatives. Alternatively, they could participate in the marketplace, where other buyers, sellers, borrowers, or lenders entered into contracts with them.

This does not mean that revolutionary lawmakers "failed" to redefine property or that property law was somehow incomplete. Property was far more flexible than those in charge of legislating it realized. The purposes that revolutionary law attributed to property were simply added on to a variety of other purposes, long-standing and emergent. As a result, the nature of property ownership and the uses of property it allowed were more complex than the political vision of it that undergirded revolutionary property laws.

The Return of the Émigrés

Much of the revolutionary program was dismantled or revised under the Thermidorean regime, which began after the fall of Robespierre in 1794, as well as by the Civil Code of 1804. Some authority over family life was returned to fathers, and in 1803 divorce became more difficult to obtain; in 1816, it was once again banned by the restored Bourbon monarchy. Prohibitions on lending at interest were lifted, changing the array of financial instruments available and greatly expanding opportunities for investment and leverage.

However, some of the core assumptions informing property policy remained stable through the nineteenth century. What I have called the moral valence of property expanded, as private philanthropy and public assistance took on a larger role in the secular society of the new regime, filling in where the Church had previously operated. The Napoleonic land survey of 1812, which resulted in the creation of a cadastre recording property lines and information about owners, further tightened the grip of administrators on property.

The issues raised by émigré property did not disappear at the end of the Revolution or with the arrival of the Civil Code. After the fall of Robespierre in 1794, the émigrés began to return to France, encouraged by the end of the Terror; this trend only continued into the establishment of Napoleon's Consulate in 1799. Their return created a potentially explosive situation for confiscated properties that had been sold to new owners. In April 1802, the Consulate passed a decree offering a general amnesty to the émigrés. Crucially, this did not restore their property to them. A long period of limbo ensued, during which time the émigrés lobbied for the return of their assets, and the market for seized property cratered. Finally, Charles X established an indemnity fund under the Bourbon Restoration in 1825.[1] The indemnities, however, paid émigrés or their heirs only a fraction of the value of what had been confiscated. Moreover, by indemnifying rather than restoring property, the Bourbon regime acknowledged the revolutionary confiscations as legitimate.

In Paris, the majority of seized property was eventually restored to its owners. Restorations began as early as 1795, with laws that gave the parents of émigrés access to some of their property, and laws that returned property to the families of those condemned by the Revolutionary Tribunal.[2] The proportion of émigré properties in Paris that were sold seems to be lower than elsewhere in France, perhaps due to the higher total number of properties and, perhaps, a preference for empty land on the part of buyers. However, only property that the state had not already sold was returned. In addition, the location of various properties within the city informed the state's decisions about which to sell and which to return to the émigrés. The vast majority of unsold, restored property was situated in the eastern regions of the city, which contained poorer neighborhoods of artisans and working people. Many of the more expensive properties in the west remained in the hands of the state. Some state-held properties in the west—particularly those on the Left Bank, in what is now the 7th arrondissement—were instead designated for public use. This disparity reflects the fact that property's meaning—and accordingly, its social value—is always informed by social context. Location, size, and beauty all shaped the desirability of these properties, their financial value, their ability to be sold, and the cultural relevance accorded to them. Many of the western and Left Bank properties were seen as assets that could lend gravitas to the new regime, which may have been reluctant to let them go for this reason.

Henriette Becdelièvre won the restitution of the Saint-Fiacre house in June 1802, shortly after recovering the houses in the Rue Richelieu. The family's interest in the Halle aux Vins was also restored, though this would prove temporary: Napoleon ultimately took over the complex and converted it to state management. Louis-Justin, Becdelièvre's son, claimed an indemnity in November 1825 for other assets that had been sold.[3] The Becdelièvre-Talaru family emerged from the Revolution remarkably intact, but their good fortune was not enduring. Becdelièvre's children, Louis-Justin and Césarine, died without heirs; Louis-Justin's death in 1850 ended the Marquisat of Talaru.

The goal of the émigré laws was to erase the émigrés themselves from the nation, "like so much rubbish carried out."[4] They represented a way of life that no longer existed: feudal hierarchies had been dissolved, and society legally reorganized on the basis of civic equality. For this reason, noble property—including feudal dues—was dissolved at the same time that feudalism was abolished on August 4, 1789. The Paris dossier on the Talaru family does not mention loss of noble property: any such property would have been located in the provinces, outside the scope of the Paris Domain bureau. But given their lineage from families of the old nobility, the Talaru family likely did own and lose property outside the city. Noble property was not transferred—it was destroyed. It could not be returned to its owners after the Revolution, nor did the 1802 indemnity funds include any financial compensation for the loss of such property.

And yet, the value of noble property was not entirely demolished. In Paris, assets that had belonged to nobles were laundered into the public-facing offices of the new regime. In some regard, it was their value as the assets of former nobles that was conferred on the Domain offices in the Hôtel d'Uzès or the minister of war's desired address in the Hôtel d'Orsay. These were not technically noble properties, in the sense of the assets that were dissolved on the night of August 4. And yet, they were properties that belonged to nobles and that reflected the status of their owners in their luxury and beauty. The desirability they held was in some ways a reflection of their former owners.

The relatively small imprint of the issue of émigré property in the history of the Revolution may reflect the declining political fortunes of émigrés, many of whom were, like the Talarus, Old Regime aristocrats. Their property didn't go away; it simply became something different—its meaning was changed. The reason, perhaps, the episode left such a minor mark, to the extent this is true, is that the property was so effectively laundered into something new. Unlike the families of émigrés, who lost their social and political prominence with the end of the Old Regime, the properties themselves didn't go anywhere. Paris today is thick with former émigré mansions. The Ministry of Defense is housed in the elegant and sumptuous Hôtel de Brienne, while the Assemblée Nationale deliberates in the palace of the Princesse de Bourbon. The roofline of the Bourbon palace is distinctive enough that the outline of its facade is used as an emblem of the French legislature. Similarly, the prime minister's office is referred to simply by the name of an aristocrat who owned it before the Revolution, Matignon. The purpose and the meaning of these émigré homes have transformed radically since the time of the Revolution. Yet curiously, they still transmit information about their former owners: the names of the émigré owners are still attached to the properties, even though in many cases the émigré was not the last owner before the property entered public use. Indeed, most émigré properties were sold several times before returning to public ownership in the nineteenth or twentieth century. Today, these properties serve as a concrete reminder that if in principle it seems contradictory for old and new to coexist, in practice nothing is more natural.

Issues raised by the seizure process continued to pose challenges to French politics in the postrevolutionary era that extended through the nineteenth century. For example, political leaders continued to feel discomfort at the idea that property owners could behave badly, and this inspired harsh laws governing bankruptcy. The Constitution of 1795 included bankruptcy as a reason for suspending citizenship rights. Bankruptcy law in the nineteenth century focused on individual responsibility and carried harsh penalties, including imprisonment for debt.[5] In the case of bankruptcy, much like emigration, morally derelict behavior led to loss of rights. Similarly, the development of credit and capital made it harder to determine who owned what—the same issue administrators had struggled with as they processed émigré cases. Capital-based enterprises, such as banks or commercial firms, tended to associate several individuals together as a means of aggregating assets and distributing risk. In these situations, resolving ownership to a single individual was illusory at best, since the legal title holder might be insolvent, or there might be no single entity at all.[6]

Property and Family in Nineteenth-Century France

Revolutionary property reform took property out of the public realm of royal prerogative and caste, but it did not entirely separate it from public life. Nor did it entirely separate it from the realm of private life, which included family control. The state controlled property by gathering information about it: maintaining registers of transfers and liens, and requiring invasive declarations of income for tax purposes.

The new significance that revolutionary reform placed on property rights, and the conviction that property owners had a particular responsibility to the polity, justified a catastrophic level of intervention by the state in private affairs—at least as far as the émigrés were concerned. And yet, property took on new significance in the private realm as the economic expansion that characterized the eighteenth century continued in the nineteenth. Family control of property continued to be significant. In the nineteenth century, family-controlled businesses played an important role in economic development.[7] Even as legal reforms were intended to separate property from family control, the émigré confiscation process makes evident the ways that testamentary reform created new links between family members and property claims. Property remained enmeshed in the private concerns of dynastic wealth.

The nineteenth century has been characterized as a time when domestic and public life were divided into separate spheres of activity. This operation was primarily carried out through legal measures and social norms that kept middle-class women in the household. The economic expansion of the nineteenth century reinforced such a division: on the one hand, capital and credit markets developed, alongside industrialization; on the other hand, modes of consumerism became more expansive and more finely developed as manufacturing further expanded the variety of goods available, and retail outlets, notably the department store, enabled the activity of shopping. The world of markets and work were gendered male, whereas the realm of the home and consumption were gendered female.[8]

The experiences of the émigrés, however, undermine the clarity of such a separation. The ability to engage in the market by acting through property was not limited to those who actually owned assets, as we have seen in these pages. The nature of credit and the ability of property to be broken apart meant that people with limited access to capital could still make claims and leverage assets. This created opportunities for the propertied women who would become most subject to the strictures of domesticity to engage in operations involving property.

Individual property claims were enmeshed in familial claims. The ability of one person to raise capital from family wealth required the participation of family members who shared claims to the assets in question.[9] The Civil Code maintained a child's right to an inheritance, and French law also maintained the Revolution's preference for a marital property regime of communal assets. This meant that in marriages without a contract specifying otherwise, assets accumulated during a marriage were shared equally by the spouses upon dissolution of the marriage.

The actions of émigré families show the ways that the connection between family and patrimony could be used to defend assets from state intervention. Women who stayed in France defended family assets because they maintained claims on them—even when these claims were relatively weak, as in the case of Elisabeth Beauterne. These claims could slow or foil entirely the actions of administrators to seize the assets of a husband or son. For Henriette Becdelièvre, the inheritance claims of her daughter provided a starting point for an array of legal actions and negotiations with administrators. Even when no particular action was taken, webs of family claims to assets created difficulties for administrators seeking to separate out the assets of a particular family member.

The émigré confiscations, in other words, should encourage us to reexamine the relationship of the family to the market in nineteenth-century France. The Revolution did not break the networks of property ownership embodied by families under the Old Regime, and in some ways legal reform strengthened these networks. We must look for the influence of the family carefully, as weak claims may only have been asserted adversely, when family members sought to defend assets. Just as legal reform layered new political significance onto property—through its connection to citizenship in voting rights and in the rhetoric of social stability—so did economic change layer new possi-bilities for capital onto the dynastic functions property already served. For example, new types of assets and new opportunities for investment may have combined readily with the ability of complex family claims to shield assets from state intervention.

The émigré cases show the diverse ways that claims can be made and assets used, and highlight forms of use that may be less visible. We should look more deeply and more creatively at property ownership in the nineteenth century. Property ownership means making claims on property and making use of it in one way or another. A sexual divi-sion of labor may make it more difficult to recognize forms of owner-ship that do not look the way one might expect—in regard to asset holding.

Property and Capital

The image of property owners banding together to unseat a king and create a new form of polity is a central part of the origin story of mod-ern democracy—one that is shared by the French and American Revo-lutions. There is a neatness to the idea that the revolutionaries brought a new polity into being with a set of legal reforms. But rights, articu-lated in law, are only the beginning of a definition for property. The process of émigré property confiscation shows that core questions about what property was and should be continued to arise across the revolutionary period. Looking closely at the confiscation process allows us to recover the set of potentialities that lay within property in its vari-ous forms. The practicalities of how property was circulated and used show the ways social relations shaped the various forms of value that constituted property, and the ways that value could be captured by the state, or could escape it.

Revolutionary law used property to create separations, in the sense of delineating people from each other. The very concept of individual rights reflects this: property is attributed to discrete entities who are separated from each other by rights. The Civil Code describes the right to property as "absolute," echoing a principle of Roman law that evokes the idea of a clear line of separation. And yet, the practices revealed in the émigré confiscation process point to a very different dynamic, one of joining together. Property links people through shared interest, through the obligations of contract, and through shared understandings of value. Similarly, lawmakers considered property to be a source of stability, based on an idea of it being a solid and reliable source of monetary value. In practice, however, property proved to be malleable, easily broken apart, shared, and exchanged, either partially or wholly. Property was constantly in motion, in the marketplace and even when it was held within a family as dynastic patrimony.

These qualities of property—its ability to connect people and to circulate in part or in whole—suited it to an emerging marketplace that operated on credit and capital. This marketplace was, at least in some ways, hostile to law, to the extent that it permitted boundaries to be tested with innovative or unorthodox behavior.[10] Actions like Berthaud placing his goat on neighboring land or Cagnion taking down his wall infringed on the legal boundaries of property in ways that allowed these men to draw profit from property they didn't have a claim to. The confiscation process itself represented a legal innovation, whose legitimacy was dubious in the eyes of lawmakers who opposed it. The actions of many of the property owners we have seen in these pages, however, were not so much illegal as undesirable, from the point of view of administrators. The relatively *laissez-faire* approach of revolutionary property rights, which left a broad realm of action to the individual bearer of them, allowed for a space of action that was legal but did not fit the intentions of lawmakers.

The citizen property owner is thus in tension with the individual wielding property in the marketplace. Property was supposed to support a liberal, democratic order, but it did not, or did not do so entirely.

After all, a recurring concern about modern markets is that they encourage people to behave in selfish ways, a concern that is echoed by eighteenth-century theorists of democracy. There seems to be something naive in the idea that property could be the basis of a society of equals invested in the stability of their government, when one considers the inequality and borderlessness that characterize the modern, global market.

The unstable and plastic nature of property, however, is exactly what made it useful to those who engaged with it. It could be used in a variety of ways and repurposed creatively. Becdelièvre's collaboration on behalf of her daughter, the intricacies of the Balleroy family marriage contract, and the collaboration between Belzunce and his young cousins point to the diverse ways that property circulated in the family and the effects such circulation could have on family ties. The use of property to construct a social identity, like that undertaken by Ange-François Talaru in the Rue Saint-Fiacre, can in part be taken as engagement with the market through consumption. But the use to which he put his property, and to which the Domain was unable to put it, points to the way property facilitated practices of sociability that lay outside the formal realm of the market. Further, the repurposing of émigré houses and furniture for ministries of state, or the use of Cagnion's land for a public garden, points to the significance of property for the construction of cultural institutions and, by providing the *mise-en-scène* for ministers of state, for the construction of a national culture—in the sense of the state's self-presentation to its citizens and to foreign powers.

The way that property was used at the end of the eighteenth century was the product of a period of development and change that predated the Revolution by one hundred years. The change brought about by the Revolution, however, transformed the social context in which property circulated, creating new possibilities for exchange, leveraging, and the construction of consumer identities. The conjuncture of the

Revolution with economic change yielded a creative process of experimentation in law and society with unexpected outcomes. The regime of property that emerged maintained important links to the past, and yet the new political context created by the Revolution gave everything a new aspect. Revolutionary leaders wanted to transform property by giving it new significance, even as they expected it to continue doing some of the same things it always had. Property continued to play an influential role in social life, though in a society of equals, this role was changed; new political significance was placed on property by the reforms of revolutionary law and the creation of citizenship; meanwhile, the function of property as a financial tool was transformed by the development of credit and capital across the eighteenth century, a dynamic that revolutionary legal reforms aided.

Revolutionary leaders sought to reform property in order to bring about a new kind of society. They were successful, but not at all in the way they intended. The salient quality of property as it emerged from the Revolution was its adaptability and plasticity. The politics of the Revolution had to contend with this fact, and it continues to be an issue with which modern politics must contend. Property is not a source of order and stability. Quite the contrary, it is a source of change and novelty. The house in the Rue Saint-Fiacre, like the other property we've seen, served as a screen onto which a series of people and institutions projected their desires. Its solidity as a physical structure belies the fluidity with which ownership of it moved among claimants in the revolutionary years. The price for which property could be sold was only one means of measuring what it was worth to those claimants. In each of these cases, the state could have chosen to draw up a new title or even to execute the family—in other words, to do any of the things that regimes have done when seizing private property. This is perhaps where law shows its significance, as in every case the state continued to respect title throughout the course of the Revolution. In the émigré confiscation process, we glimpse the ideological power of property in action. Property rights and law reached the zenith of their strength through the medium of an asset. The nexus of the desires of various people, of the power of the law, of title, claims, and family lineage was funneled through an object worth money. Yet, to identify property merely as an object worth money is to look through the wrong end of the telescope.

NOTES

ACKNOWLEDGMENTS

INDEX

NOTES

The approach to citations adopted here limits references to only particularly relevant material, to allow for a nimbler and more accessible text in the face of the enormous body of literature relating to the French Revolution. Similarly, English editions are cited where available. All translations in the text are the author's own unless otherwise noted. Access to the text of revolutionary laws can be found in the excellent Université Paris 1 / ARTFL database, https://artfl-project.uchicago.edu/collection-baudouin. The Domain Bureau's spelling of proper names has been preserved throughout the text and index, even where this spelling obviously diverges from standard spelling, in order to accurately reflect the archival record.

Archival references begin with an abbreviated reference to the archive name (listed below), followed by the archival call number:

AN: Archives Nationales

AdP: Archives de Paris

Introduction

1. Archives de Paris (AdP) DQ10 708 Chab. "Chab" may reflect discrepancies in the spelling of the family name. This book preserves such discrepancies, reproducing names as they appeared in the dossiers.

2. AdP DQ10 169 Becdelièvre.

3. Women's access to property varied according to the different customary regimes in force across France at the end of the Old Regime. Dominique

Godineau provides a detailed overview in *Les femmes dans la société française, 16e–18e siècle* (Paris: Armand Colin, 2003), 18–23.

4. *Les origines de la France contemporaine*, vol. 2, *La Révolution* (Paris: Hachette, 1876), 386. Taine was part of a conservative tradition of interpretation of the Revolution, which also included Augustin Cochin; see *La Révolution et la libre-pensée: La socialisation de la pensée (1750–1789), la socialisation de la person (1789–1792), la socialisation des biens (1793–1794)* (Paris: Plon, 1924). Taine is contrasted here with the Marxist historians but could also be placed in opposition to the republican interpretative tradition. See, for example, Alphonse Aulard, *Histoire politique de la révolution française: Origines et développements de la démocratie et de la république (1789–1804)* (Paris: A. Colin, 1901); and Albert Mathiez, *La révolution française* (Paris: A. Colin, 1922).

5. William H. Sewell, *Work and Revolution in France: The Language of Labor from the Old Regime to 1848* (Cambridge: Cambridge University Press, 1980), 134. Sewell is part of the Marxist tradition of interpretation of the Revolution, along with George Rudé, *The Crowd in the French Revolution* (Oxford: Clarendon, 1959); Albert Soboul, *Les sans-culottes parisiens en l'an II: Mouvement populaire et gouvernement révolutionnaire, 2 Juin 1793–9 Thermidor An II* (Paris: Clavreuil, 1958); and Albert Mathiez, *La révolution française* (Paris: A. Colin, 1922). This interpretation of the Revolution on the Left can be placed in intellectual continuity with the republican tradition cited above.

6. The body of historiography on the French Revolution is enormous and politically charged. A useful, recent summary can be found in Dale Van Kley and Thomas Kaiser, eds., *From Deficit to Deluge: The Origins of the French Revolution* (Stanford, CA: Stanford University Press, 2011), 8–23.

7. Rafe Blaufarb, *The Great Demarcation: The French Revolution and the Invention of Modern Property* (New York: Oxford University Press, 2016). Another work that addresses property and considers the Revolution in its relationship to liberal democracy is Miranda Spieler, *Empire and Underworld: Captivity in French Guiana* (Cambridge, MA: Harvard University Press, 2012).

8. Rebecca Spang, *Stuff and Money in the Time of the French Revolution* (Cambridge, MA: Harvard University Press, 2015).

9. Partha Chatterjee makes a similar observation, contrasting civil society with governmentality as competing features of modern liberal states, in *The Politics of the Governed: Reflections on Popular Politics in Most of the World* (New York: Columbia University Press, 2004), 4.

10. Max Weber, "Bureaucracy," in *Economy and Society: An Outline of Interpretive Sociology*, ed. Guenther Roth and Claus Wittich (Berkeley: University of California Press, 1978), 956–1002; Michel Foucault, *Discipline and Punish: The Birth of the Prison*, trans. Alan Sheridan (first French ed. 1975; New York: Vintage,

1995), 135–139. For an overview of the social theory tradition that links these authors, see, for example, Alex Callinicos, *Social Theory: A Historical Introduction* (Cambridge: Polity Press, 1999).

11. The émigrés have been a perennial subject of interest. Émigré memoirs, published in the first half of the nineteenth century, recalled harrowing journeys and sparkling parties; see, for example, Henriette Lucie Dillon, Marquise de la Tour du Pin Gouvernet, *Escape from the Terror: The Journal of Madame de la Tour du Pin*, trans. Felice Harcourt (London: Folio Society, 1970) or Marie-Jeanne Roland, *The Memoirs of Madame Roland*, ed. and trans. Evelyn Shuckburgh (London: Barrie & Jenkins, 1989). The plight of the émigrés was recounted in greater detail in monographs of the early twentieth century. See Marcel Marion, "Quelques exemples de l'application des lois sur l'émigration, récits du temps de la Terreur," *Revue Historique* 107, no. 2 (1911): 272–284; and Ernest Daudet, *Histoire de l'émigration pendant la révolution française* (Paris: Hachette, 1905). The work of the next generation provided several now-standard treatments. See Donald Greer, *The Incidence of the Emigration* (Cambridge, MA: Harvard University Press, 1951); and Marc Bouloiseau, *Étude de l'émigration et de la vente des biens des émigrés (1792–1803); instruction: Sources, bibliographie, législation, tableaux* (Paris: Imprimerie Nationale, 1963). Over the past twenty years the émigrés have attracted a new round of interest. See Kirsty Carpenter, *Refugees of the French Revolution: Émigrés in London, 1789–1802* (Basingstoke: Macmillan, 1999); Doina Pasca Harsanyi, *Lessons from America: Liberal French Nobles in Exile* (University Park: Pennsylvania State University Press, 2010); Miranda Spieler, *Empire and Underworld: Captivity in French Guiana* (Cambridge, MA: Harvard University Press, 2012); Kelly E. Summers, "Healing the Republic's 'Great Wound': Emigration Reform and the Path to a General Amnesty, 1799–1802," in *Emigrants in Revolutionised Europe: Shared Histories and Memories*, ed. Juliette Reboul and Laure Philip (London: Palgrave Macmillan, 2019), 232–256; and Mary Ashburn Miller, "A Fiction of the French Nation: The Émigré Novel, Nostalgia, and National Identity, 1797–1815," *Historical Reflections* 44, no. 2 (2018): 45–66.

12. Michel Vovelle, *The Fall of the French Monarchy, 1787–1792*, trans. Susan Burke (first French ed. 1983; Cambridge: Cambridge University Press, 1983), 162–171.

13. In his detailed study of the emigration, Donald Greer tracks the flow of emigration against political events. See *Incidence of the Emigration*, 23–32.

14. Greer, *Incidence of the Emigration*, 70–71.

15. Greer, *Incidence of the Emigration*, 28.

16. Greer, *Incidence of the Emigration*, 28.

17. François Furet explains that "already the émigrés had occupied the place beyond the frontiers marked out for them in advance by *Qu'est-ce que le Tiers*

État?: they were the perfect embodiment of the nobility according to the revolutionaries, even before they began to fight alongside the enemies of the nation. Armed conflict would thus superimpose internal and external enemies, civil and foreign war, aristocracy and treason, democracy and patriotism, around the same images, feelings and values." *The French Revolution, 1770–1814* (Oxford: Blackwell), 103.

18. Lemontey, October 10, 1791, *Archives Parlementaires de 1787 à 1860: Recueil complet des débats législatifs et politiques des chambres français* (Paris: s.n., 1787–), 34:301.

19. A comprehensive overview of this literature is the subject of Bernard Bodinier and Eric Teyssier, *L'événement le plus important de la Révolution: La vente des biens nationaux dans les territoires annexés* (Paris: Editions du CTHS, 2000). See in particular Marc Bouloiseau, *Le séquestre et la vente des biens des émigrés dans le district de Rouen, 1792-An X* (Paris: Novathèse, 1937); and Anne Jollet, *Terre et société en Révolution: Approche du lien social dans la région d'Amboise* (Paris: CTHS, 2000). See also the classic studies, Marcel Marion, *La vente des biens nationaux pendant la Révolution française, avec étude spéciale des ventes dans la Gironde et dans le Cher* (Paris: Champion, 1908); Amédée Vialay, *La vente des biens nationaux pendant la Révolution française; étude législative, économique et sociale; ouvrage accompagné de deux plans* (Paris: Perrin, 1908); Ivan Vasil'evich Luchtiskii, *Propriété paysanne et ventes des biens nationaux pendant la Révolution française (principalement en Limousin)* (Paris: Champion, 1912).

20. See notably Anne Simonin, *Le déshonneur dans la République: Une histoire de l'indignité, 1791–1958* (Paris: Grasset, 2008), 264–319; and Spieler, *Empire and Underworld,* 21–31.

21. James Livesey, *Provincializing Global History: Money, Ideas, and Things in the Languedoc, 1680–1830* (New Haven, CT: Yale University Press, 2020), 17–51. These changes were notably brought about by the discovery of the New World and rising commercial competition between states; see J. G. A. Pocock, *The Machiavellian Moment: Florentine Political Thought and the Atlantic Republican Tradition,* Princeton Classics (Princeton, NJ: Princeton University Press, 2016), 462–506; Istvan Hont, *The Jealousy of Trade: International Competition and the Nation State in Historical Perspective* (Cambridge, MA: Belknap Press of Harvard University Press, 2005), 17–22. On the intellectual repercussions of eighteenth-century commerce in France, see in particular John Shovlin, *The Political Economy of Virtue: Luxury, Patriotism, and the Origins of the French Revolution* (Ithaca, NY: Cornell University Press, 2006); Anoush Terjanian, *Commerce and Its Discontents in Eighteenth-Century French Political Thought* (Cambridge: Cambridge University Press, 2013), 1–25; Paul Cheney, *Revolutionary Commerce: Globalization and the French Monarchy* (Cambridge, MA: Harvard University Press, 2010), 1–10.

22. Terjanian, *Commerce and Its Discontents*, 68–92.

23. Shovlin, *Political Economy of Virtue*, 49–79; James Livesey, "Agrarian Ideology and Commercial Republicanism," *Past and Present* 157 (1997): 94–121; Terjanian, *Commerce and Its Discontents*, 54–67.

24. See in particular Catherine Larrère, *L'invention de l'économie au XVIIIe siècle: Du droit naturel à la physiocratie* (Paris: Presses Universitaires de France, 1992), 231–260; Jean-Yves Grenier, "De la richesse à la valeur; les métamorphoses d'une notion au 18e siècle," in *Être riche au siècle de Voltaire, Actes du colloque de Genève (18–19 juin 1994)*, ed. Jacques Berchtold and Michel Porret (Geneva: Droz, 1996): 17–45; Shovlin, *Political Economy of Virtue*, 80–117.

25. On the dangers of financiers, see Michael Sonenscher, *Before the Deluge: Public Debt, Inequality, and the Intellectual Origins of the French Revolution* (Princeton, NJ: Princeton University Press, 2007), 4–11.

26. Shovlin, *Political Economy of Virtue*, 13–79.

27. It was also an important moment for the theorization of labor. See Michael Sonenscher, *Work and Wages: Natural Law, Politics, and the Eighteenth-Century French Trades* (Cambridge: Cambridge University Press, 1989), 7–39; Sewell, *Work and Revolution in France*, 138–149.

28. The Chabanais dossier, so prominent in this introduction, did not figure in the core sample.

29. See, for example, the use of the letter *B* in the Vernon sample, in Fabrice Boudjaaba, *Des paysans attachés à la terre? Familles, marchés et patrimoines dans la région de Vernon (1750–1830)* (Paris: Presses Universitaires Paris-Sorbonne, 2008). On issues surrounding the choice of surname first letter in constructing archival samples, see Jacques Dupâquier, "L'enquette des 3,000 familles," *Population* 39, no. 2 (1984): 380–383.

30. Lazard and Monin's *Sommier* is the best record of property seizure, but it is not complete. H. Monin and L. Lazard, *Sommier des biens nationaux de la ville de Paris, conservé aux Archives de la Seine*, 2 vols. (Paris: Cerf, 1920).

31. See, for example, AdP DQ10 226 Brancas Lauragnais, Director to Prefect, December 19, 1812.

32. Arlette Farge, *Fragile Lives: Violence, Power and Solidarity in Eighteenth-Century Paris*, trans. Carol Shelton (Cambridge, MA: Harvard University Press, 1993), 1–8.

33. Sarah Maza, *Private Lives and Public Affairs: The Causes Célèbres of Prerevolutionary France* (Berkeley: University of California Press, 1993), 10.

34. Law of March 28, 1793, IV.VIII.1.

35. Sewell argues as much in *Work and Revolution in France*, 113. Michael Sonenscher also finds that workers in the late eighteenth century were developing their own ideas about property. *Work and Wages*, 375.

36. Marx's sharpest critique of revolutionary values comes in "On the Jewish Question," published in 1844. Proudhon's most famous work, "What Is Property?," offers a systematic critique of the values of the Revolution on the basis of property. For Marx's inspiration of Third World Nationalism, see Frantz Fanon, *The Wretched of the Earth*, trans. Constance Farrington (New York: Grove Weidenfeld, 1991), 33–47.

37. Examples of this approach can be found in the analysis of time in postcolonial studies. See, for example, Partha Chatterjee, *The Politics of the Governed*, 3–8; Dipesh Chakrabarty, *Provincializing Europe: Postcolonial Thought and Historical Difference* (Princeton, NJ: Princeton University Press, 2000), 6–16, 47–71.

38. In the French case, see, for example, Ellen McLarney, "The Algerian Personal Statute: A French Legacy," *Islamic Quarterly* 41, no. 3 (1997); for the British case in India, see Julia A. Stephens, *Governing Islam: Law, Empire, and Secularism in Modern South Asia* (Cambridge: Cambridge University Press, 2018), 57–87.

39. See, for example, Mary Dewhurst Lewis, "Necropoles and Nationality: Land Rights, Burial Rites, and the Development of Tunisian National Consciousness in the 1930s," *Past & Present* 205 (November 2009): 105–141.

40. On the significance of such an approach, see Kenneth Lipartito, "Reassembling the Economic: New Departures in Historical Materialism," *American Historical Review* 121, no. 1 (February 2016): 101–139.

1. Property Law in Revolutionary Society

1. Rafe Blaufarb, *The Great Demarcation: The French Revolution and the Invention of Modern Property* (New York: Oxford University Press, 2016), 1–2.

2. The opposition is self-evident enough to historians, or was in the 1990s–2010s, that various works seek either to show that the two could be reconciled or to explain the origin of the opposition: Patrice Higonnet, *Goodness beyond Virtue: Jacobins during the French Revolution* (Cambridge, MA: Harvard University Press, 1998), 2; Dan Edelstein, *The Terror of Natural Right: Republicanism, the Cult of Nature, and the French Revolution* (Chicago: University of Chicago Press, 2009), 8–9.

3. On voting, see Patrice Gueniffey, *Le nombre et la raison: La Révolution française et les éléctions* (Paris: Editions de l'EHESS, 1993), 1–2, 18–19; and Pierre Rosanvallon, *Le sacre du citoyen: Histoire du suffrage universel en France* (Paris: Gallimard, 1992), 41–42. On taxation, see Michael Kwass, *Privilege and the Politics of Taxation in Eighteenth-Century France: Liberté, Egalité, Fiscalité*

(Cambridge: Cambridge University Press, 2000), 303–310; and François Hincker, *Les français devant l'impôt sous l'ancien régime* (Paris: Flammarion, 1971), 88–91.

4. On French customary law, see in particular Jean Hilaire, *La vie du droit: Coutumes et droit écrit* (Paris: Presses Universitaires de France, 1994); Paul Ourliac, *Droit romain et ancien droit* (Paris: Presses Universitaires de France, 1961); Jean Yver, *Egalité entre héritiers et exclusion des enfants dotés: Essai de géographie coutumière* (Paris: Sirey, 1966). In English, with specific regard to the Revolution, see Thomas Kaiser, "Property, Sovereignty, the Declaration of the Rights of Man, and the Tradition of French Jurisprudence," in *The French Idea of Freedom: The Old Regime and the Declaration of Rights of 1789*, ed. Dale Van Kley (Stanford, CA: Stanford University Press, 1994): 300–342; and Blaufarb, *Great Demarcation*, 15–47.

5. In French, the term *"ancien droit"* is used to distinguish Old Regime customary law from the "intermediate law" of the Revolution and the contemporary law of the Civil Code. Lacking this linguistic subtlety in English, the term "customary law" will be used, perhaps clumsily, to refer to Old Regime law. The salient characteristic in this context is that it is customary; its association with the Old Regime is evident.

6. Technically, sovereign rights exercised by the person of the lord were seigniorial rights, as opposed to the feudal rights that derived from the land itself. By the time of the Revolution, the two were generally confounded. See Marcel Garaud, *La Révolution et la propriété foncière*, vol. 2 of *Histoire générale du droit privé français* (Paris: Recueil Sirey, 1959), 16.

7. In theory, all land in France fell under the domain of a noble, but in practice some lands were free of feudal control. These lands, known as allodial property, were a subject of study and debate. See Kaiser, "Property, Sovereignty," 310–317.

8. On the "vaste champ d'application" of customary law, see François Olivier-Martin, *Histoire du droit français des origines à la Révolution* (Montchrestien: Editions Domat, 1948), 113–114.

9. On the relationship between the body politic and the body of Christ, see Ernst Kantorowicz, *The King's Two Bodies: A Study in Medieval Political Theology* (Princeton, NJ: Princeton University Press, 1957), 193–272.

10. Contrast this sacred human body with Hobbes's Leviathan, a monstrous body made up of thousands of individuals. See, for example, Patricia Springborg's pursuit of this contrast in "Hobbes and Schmitt on the Name and Nature of Leviathan Revisited," in *Thomas Hobbes and Carl Schmitt: The Politics of Order and Myth*, ed. Johan Tralau (London: Routledge, 2013), 39–58.

11. This tripartite division of society was common to Christendom. On its articulation in France, see Georges Duby, *Les trois ordres ou l'imaginaire du féodalisme* (Paris: Gallimard, 1978).

12. For other juridical distinctions among the orders, see Olivier-Martin, *Histoire du droit français,* 67.

13. Fully dismantling the body of feudal law was a more involved process, as Blaufarb shows. *Great Demarcation,* 48–118.

14. Garaud, *La Révolution et la propriété foncière,* 2.

15. Enslaved people were considered property, but even at the time this categorization was understood to be problematic, and, at the very least, the ability to own another person was an aberration within the French legal tradition. Laurent Dubois, *Avengers of the New World: The Story of the Haitian Revolution* (Cambridge, MA: Belknap Press of Harvard University Press, 2004), 60–90; and Nick Nesbitt, *Universal Emancipation: The Haitian Revolution and the Radical Enlightenment* (Charlottesville: University of Virginia Press, 2008), 41–80.

16. Jean-Louis Halpérin, *Histoire du droit des biens* (Paris: Economica, 2008), 185–186.

17. See, for example, the report by Merlin de Douai, April 20, 1790, *Archives Parlementaires de 1787 à 1860: Recueil complet des débats législatifs et politiques des chambres français* (Paris: s.n., 1787–), 13:156–158. See also Jean-Pierre Gross, *Fair Shares for All: Jacobin Egalitarianism in Practice* (Cambridge: Cambridge University Press, 1997), 54–66; Patrice Higonnet, *Goodness beyond Virtue: Jacobins during the French Revolution* (Cambridge, MA: Harvard University Press, 1998), 240–258. Higonnet points to the connection that would be made between selfishness and aristocracy, with important consequences for the émigrés. Guild regulation of food supplies offers an example of the challenge of balancing freedom of the market with the public interest of protecting the food supply.

18. Steven L. Kaplan, *Provisioning Paris: Merchants and Millers in the Grain and Flour Trade during the Eighteenth Century* (Ithaca, NY: Cornell University Press, 2018), 23–40; Judith A. Miller, "Politics and Urban Provisioning Crises in France: Bakers, Parlements and Police, 1750–1793," *Journal of Modern History* 64 (June 1992): 227–262.

19. See Sydney Watts, "Liberty, Equality, and the Public Good: Parisian Butchers and Their Rights to the Marketplace during the French Revolution," *Food and History* 3, no. 2 (January 2005): 105–117.

20. Pierre Rosanvallon, *The Demands of Liberty: Civil Society in France since the Revolution* (Cambridge, MA: Harvard University Press, 2007), 63–78; Edelstein, *Terror of Natural Right,* 15–17.

21. See, for example, Huri Islamoglu, "Towards a Political Economy of Legal and Administrative Constitutions of Individual Property," in *Constituting Modernity: Private Property in the East and West,* ed. Huri Islamoglu (London: I.B. Tauris, 2004), 3–34.

22. Pierre Rosanvallon, *Le peuple introuvable: Histoire de la représentation démocratique en France* (Paris: Gallimard, 1998), 18. Jedediah Purdy argues, similarly but from a neoliberal perspective, that private property offers the ideal means to reconcile the competing claims of individual and society, in *The Meaning of Property: Freedom, Community, and the Legal Imagination* (New Haven, CT: Yale University Press, 2010).

23. *Archives Parlementaires de 1787 à 1860,* 22:212 (Report on law of January 21, 1791). For an online database of this source, see the ARTFL project at the University of Chicago.

24. Bernard Edelman, *Le sacre de l'auteur* (Paris: Seuil, 2004), 187–190. Carla Hesse refers to a "revolution of the mind," *Publishing and Cultural Politics in Revolutionary Paris, 1789–1810* (Berkeley: University of California Press, 1991), 7.

25. Darrin McMahon, *Divine Fury: A History of Genius* (New York: Basic Books, 2013), 67–104.

26. Edelman claims authorship is based on patent; *Le sacre de l'auteur,* 190. Liliane Hilaire-Perez claims patent emerges by analogy with authorship. *L'invention technique au siècle des Lumières* (Paris: Albin Michel, 2000), 175–183.

27. Hilaire-Perez, *L'invention technique,* 71–73.

28. Hilaire-Perez, *L'invention technique,* 71–72.

29. Hilaire-Perez, *L'invention technique,* 52–59.

30. Liliane Hilaire-Perez, "Transferts téchnologiques, droit et territoire: Le cas français au XVIIIe siècle," *Revue d'histoire moderne et contemporaine* 44, no. 4 (1997): 547–579. For a more general treatment of the issue, see Istvan Hont, *The Jealousy of Trade: International Competition and the Nation-State in Historical Perspective* (Cambridge, MA: Belknap Press of Harvard University Press, 2005), 185–266.

31. Robert Darnton, *The Forbidden Bestsellers of Pre-revolutionary France* (New York: Norton, 1995), 3–21.

32. Frédéric Rideau, *La formation du droit de la propriété littéraire en France et en Grande-Bretagne: Une convergence oubliée* (Aix-en-Provence: Presses Universitaires d'Aix-Marseille, 2004), 169–174. See also Peter Baldwin, *The Copyright Wars: Three Centuries of Transatlantic Battle* (Princeton, NJ: Princeton University Press, 2014), 55–65.

33. Oddly, the outcome of the lawsuit is somewhat unclear, though the challenge it contained was perfectly evident to the printing industry. See Rideau, *La propriété littéraire,* 198.

34. Rideau, *La formation du droit*, 215; Edelman, *Le sacre de l'auteur*, 196. Much has been made of the divergent justifications of copyright in France and Britain / America. Traditionally, the difference is identified as a basis in natural right in France versus in monopoly in Britain and America. More recently, this dichotomy has been challenged in favor of an approach that highlights similarities and differences along a continuum. See, for example, Alain Strowel, *"Droit d'auteur* and Copyright: Between History and Nature," in Sherman and Strowel, *Of Authors and Origins: Essays on Copyright Law* (Oxford: Clarendon, 1994), 235; and Peter Baldwin, *The Copyright Wars: Three Centuries of Trans-Atlantic Battle* (Princeton, NJ: Princeton University Press, 2014), 53–81. This view is shared in France; see Rideau, *La formation du droit*, 20.

35. Hesse, *Publishing*, 120.

36. Darnton, *Forbidden Bestsellers*, xix.

37. Hesse, *Publishing*, 7–10.

38. Jane C. Ginsburg, "'Une Chose Publique'? The Author's Domain and the Public Domain in Early British, French and US Copyright Law," *Cambridge Law Journal* 65, no. 3 (2006): 655; Sarah Maza, *Private Lives and Public Affairs: The Causes Célèbres of Prerevolutionary France* (Berkeley: University of California Press, 1993), 121; see also Elizabeth Andrews Bond, *The Writing Public: Participatory Knowledge Production in Enlightenment and Revolutionary France* (Ithaca, NY: Cornell University Press, 2021), 6–15.

39. Rosanvallon explores the problem of "the people" as both an abstract ideal and social reality; see *Le peuple introuvable*, 12–19.

40. Keith Baker, *Inventing the French Revolution: Essays on French Political Culture in the Eighteenth Century* (Cambridge: Cambridge University Press, 1990), 224–251.

41. Gueniffey, *Le nombre et la raison*, 32. In addition to Keith Baker, both Lucien Jaume and Pierre Rosanvallon have explored the issues surrounding revolutionary sovereignty in great depth. See in particular Lucien Jaume, *Le discours Jacobin et la démocratie* (Paris: Fayard, 1989), 21; and Pierre Rosanvallon, *La démocratie inachevée: histoire de la souveraineté du peuple en France* (Paris: Gallimard, 2000), 43–66.

42. "The most perfect that can be conceived, since no superior authority exists that can modify or restrain it." Law of December 1, 1790.

43. *Archives Parlementaires de 1787 à 1860*, 22:212 (Report on law of January 21, 1791).

44. The particular commitment to transparency demonstrated by revolutionary regimes is explored in detail by Katlyn Carter, "Practicing Politics in the Revolutionary Atlantic World: Secrecy, Publicity, and the Making of Modern Democracy" (PhD diss., Princeton University, 2017). See also Gueniffey, *Le nombre et la raison*, 15–19. On legal transparency, see Jérôme Lasserre-Capdeville, *Le secret bancaire: Etude de droit comparé (France, Suisse,*

Luxembourg) (Aix-en-Provence: Presses Universitaires d'Aix-Marseille, 2006), 25–26.

45. On European ideas of privacy as a legal claim to respectability, see James Q. Whitman, "The Two Western Cultures of Privacy: Dignity versus Liberty," *Yale Law Journal* 113, no. 6 (April 2004): 1151–1221.

46. The significance of property to citizenship depended on the contentious principle of representation. From the perspective of all citizens exercising sovereignty equally, everyone should be allowed to vote. The model of direct democracy was, however, set aside almost immediately in favor of representative democracy. See Patrice Gueniffey, "Suffrage," in Furet and Ozouf, *A Critical Dictionary of the French Revolution*, trans. Arthur Goldhammer (Cambridge, MA: Belknap Press of Harvard University Press, 1989), 571–581, and Keith M. Baker, "Sovereignty," in Furet and Ozouf, *Critical Dictionary*, 844–859. See also Rosanvallon, *Le sacre du citoyen*, 47–55; and Peter Sahlins, *Unnaturally French: Foreign Citizens in the Old Regime and After* (Ithaca, NY: Cornell University Press, 2018), 220–224.

47. See, for example, Gueniffey, *Le nombre et la raison*, 52–54.

48. On representation, see Keith Michael Baker, "Representation," in *The Political Culture of the Old Regime*, vol. 1 of *The French Revolution and the Creation of Modern Political Culture*, ed. Keith Michael Baker (Oxford: Pergamon Press, 1987), 469–492; and Gueniffey, *Le nombre et la raison*, 36–40.

49. See, for example, Thouret, October 23, 1789, *Archives Parlementaires* 9:485.

50. *Réimpression de l'ancien moniteur* (Paris: n.p., 1840–1845), 25:92.

51. *Ancien Moniteur*, 25:93.

52. *Ancien Moniteur*, 25:93.

53. On the perdurance of this relationship after the Revolution, see Erika Vause, "'He Who Rushes to Riches Will Not Be Innocent': Commercial Honor and Commercial Failure in Post-revolutionary France," *French Historical Studies* 35, no. 2 (Summer 2012): 321–349.

54. *Ancien Moniteur*, 25:93.

55. Taxation was closely connected to citizenship by its very nature, as the idea that the people must consent to taxation was at the very core of the Revolution. See Hincker, *Les français devant l'impôt*, 88–90; Nicolas Delalande, *Les batailles de l'impôt: Consentement et résistances de 1789 à nos jours* (Paris: Seuil, 2011), 24–36.

56. Hincker points out that the Old Regime was already moving toward taxation based on capacity to pay. *Les français devant l'impôt*, 81. On the place of tax policy in the Revolution generally, see Michael Kwass, *Privilege and the Politics of Taxation in Eighteenth-Century France: Liberté, Egalité, Fiscalité* (Cambridge: Cambridge University Press, 2000), 253–310.

57. The wealthy would pay the same percentage of their income, which amounted to a greater sum in absolute terms. The idea of taxing the rich at a higher rate in order to redistribute wealth was rejected as a policy. Delalande, *L'impôt*, 34–37.

58. The *contribution mobilière* and *patente*. See Gueniffey, *Le nombre et la raison*, 52–55.

59. Philippe Sagnac, *La législation civile de la Révolution française (1789–1804)* (Paris: Hachette, 1898), 204–207; see Philip Hoffman, Gilles Postel-Vinay, and Jean-Laurent Rosenthal, *Priceless Markets: The Political Economy of Credit in Paris, 1660–1870* (Chicago: University of Chicago Press, 2000), 20.

60. Michel Buisson, "La publicité des hypothèques et des actes translatifs de propriété de l'ancienne France jusqu'à nos jours" (law thesis, Paris, 1962), 22, quoted in Serge Le Roux, *La mort du dernier privilège* (Paris: L'Harmattan, 2006), 59. For the principle outside the context of *hypothèque*, see Anne Patault, *Introductions historique au droit des biens* (Paris: Presses Universitaires de France, 1989), 174–175.

61. Lasserre-Capdeville, *Le secret bancaire*, 26 and 26n. Privacy has become the focus of positive law in France and in Europe generally more recently; on explicit protection of private life, see Monique Contamine-Raynaud, "Le secret de la vie privée," in *L'information en droit privé: Travaux de la conférence d'agrégation*, ed. Yvon Loussouarn and Paul Lagarde (Paris: LGDJ, 1978), 402–456.

62. Clare Haru Crowston, *Credit, Fashion, Sex: Economies of Regard in Old Regime France* (Durham, NC: Duke University Press, 2013), 96–138; Natacha Coquery, "Credit, Trust and Risk: Shopkeepers' Bankruptcies in 18th-Century Paris," in *The History of Bankruptcy: Economic, Social and Cultural Implications in Early Modern Europe*, ed. Thomas Max Safley (New York: Routledge, 2013), 52–71. See also Richard Bonney, "'Le secret de leurs familles': The Fiscal and Social Limits of Louis XIV's 'Dixième,'" *French History* 7, no. 4 (December 1993): 383–416; Charles Gavalda, "Le secret des affaires," in *Mélanges offerts à René Savatier* (Paris: Dalloz, 1965), 291–316. Commercial secrecy (*secret des affaires*) should not be confused with banking secrecy (*le secret bancaire*); one is a general prerogative of privacy in business dealings, while the other relates narrowly to the professional privilege that protects bankers from being forced to reveal what their clients confide in them. The latter is related to other forms of professional secrecy, including those exercised by lawyers and clergy. Lasserre-Capdeville, *Le secret Bancaire*, paras. 14, 21.

63. Gavalda, "Secret," 294n, 295. On the laws surrounding *secret des affaires*, see Marcel Cremieux, "Le secret des affaires," in Loussouam and Lagarde, *L'information en droit privé*, 457–468.

64. Adolphe Thiers, prime minister of France in 1840 and president of the Third Republic in the 1870s, expressed such views. Delalande, *L'impôt*, 64. Such fears were also expressed in the Old Regime, where the *secret des fortunes* and *secret des familles* were explicitly invoked in response to the prospect of revenue declarations for tax purposes. See Bonney, "Le secret de leurs familles," 383–416; see also Hincker, *Les français devant l'impôt*, 108.

65. Amalia D. Kessler, *A Revolution in Commerce: The Parisian Merchant Court and the Rise of Commercial Society in Eighteenth-Century France* (New Haven, CT: Yale University Press, 2007), 46. See also Craig Muldrew, *The Economy of Obligation: The Culture of Credit and Social Relations in Early Modern England* (Basingstoke: Macmillan, 1998), 97–101. On the personal nature of eighteenth-century Paris credit markets specifically, see Hoffman, Postel-Vinay, and Rosenthal, *Priceless Markets*, 96–113.

66. Patault, *Droit des biens*, 208–212.

2. The Émigrés and the Politics of Property

1. The usefulness of separating out the "'Terror" as a period has been questioned. See "Rethinking the French Revolutionary Terror," *H-France Salon* 11 (16), no. 1 (2019). For our purposes, it is significant as a period characterized by extralegal measures that stands in contrast with the attention to legality shown by the legislators who passed the first émigré confiscation laws.

2. Compare the account of the origin of the émigré confiscation laws, offered in the following pages, with the one offered by Ladan Boroumand, "Emigration and the Rights of Man: French Revolutionary Legislators Equivocate," *Journal of Modern History* 72, no. 1 (2000): 67–108. Boroumand reads the laws in continuity with the Terror, linking them together to show that the ideology of the Revolution tended toward extremism from the beginning; he also focuses on the émigrés as a perceived military threat as opposed to an economic one. See also Jean-Jacques Clère, "L'émigration dans les débats à l' Assemblée nationale constituante," in *Les droits de l'homme et la conquête des libertés, des Lumières aux révolutions de 1848, Actes du Colloque de Grenoble-Vizille 1986* (Grenoble-Vizille: Presses Universitaires de Grenoble, 1988): 156–162; Clère emphasizes the pressure of circumstances, in contrast to Boroumand, who explicitly rejects this interpretation. Finally, in a similar vein, see Jean d'Andlau, "Penser la loi et débattre sous la convention: Le travail du comité de législation et la loi sur les émigrés du 28 mars 1793," *Annales historiques de la révolution française* 396 (2019): 3–18; d'Andlau puts the debates around the émigré laws in the context of extralegal measures.

3. *Révolutions de Paris* 86, February 25, 1791, 373. Emigration was already taking place and had been discussed in the Constituent Assembly—the account here focuses on the run-up to the first law sequestering émigré property. For an account of debates and measures before February 1791, see Clère, "L'émigration dans les débats," 156–158; and Boroumand, "Emigration and the Rights of Man," 77–84.

4. As much was suggested on the floor of the Jacobin Club and heartily applauded. It was also reported in a newspaper run in part by Nicolas de Caritat, marquis de Condorcet, the *Chronique de Paris*. See François Alphonse Aulard, *La société des Jacobins: Recueil de documents pour l'histoire du club des Jacobins de Paris* (Paris: Librairie Jouaust, 1893), 2:90.

5. Jean Signorel provides a detailed account of the legislative debates over the émigrés, including this one, in the classic *Etude historique sur la législation révolutionnaire relative aux biens des émigrés* (Paris: Berger-Levrault, 1915), 2.

6. Le Chapelier, February 28, 1791, *Archives Parlementaires de 1787 à 1860: Recueil complet des débats législatifs et politiques des chambres français* (Paris: s.n., 1787–), 23:566 (hereafter cited as *AP*).

7. The royal family's departure inspired the first decree limiting free exit from France: the law of June 21, 1791, ordered that all persons exiting France be stopped, and specifically outlined what to do should the "famille royale" be among those crossing the border. During the October 20, 1791, debate on émigrés, Crestin noted that "the flight of the King recalled ideas that had been abandoned." *AP* 34:307. The flight to Varennes is understood to be a turning point of the Revolution, because it signaled the king's unwillingness to go along with the constitutional monarchy that nearly everyone had understood to be the likely outcome of the Revolution. See two noted works dedicated to the event and its consequences: Timothy Tackett, *When the King Took Flight* (Cambridge, MA: Harvard University Press, 2003); and Mona Ozouf, *Varennes: La mort de la royauté, 21 juin 1791* (Paris: Gallimard, 2005).

8. Laws of July 9, 1791, and August 1–6, 1791.

9. Until the rise of cultural history in the mid-twentieth century, the classic narratives of the French Revolution emphasized the influence of the émigrés on the growing political tensions in the fall and winter of 1791, as those sympathetic to the monarchy agitated for war in hopes of an easy victory for their allies, and radical revolutionaries sought war in hopes of consolidating the Revolution. As scholarly interest shifted from politics to political culture in the 1980s, the perceived significance of the émigrés to the progress of the Revolution waned. Mathiez argued that internal economic disruptions blamed on the émigrés inspired the more conservative Brissotin and Girondin fac-

tions to support laws against the émigrés. This is perhaps borne out by the Legislative Assembly's concern for merchants abroad on business. Albert Mathiez, *La Revolution Française* (Paris: Armand Colin, 1922), 1:179–199. For a more recent treatment of the politics surrounding the decision to legislate against the émigrés, see Patrice Higonnet, *Class, Ideology, and the Rights of Nobles during the French Revolution* (Cambridge, MA: Harvard University Press, 1981), 91–143.

10. The debate stretched over nine sessions in the course of four weeks: October 11, 15, 16, 20, 22, 25, 28 and November 8, 9, 1791.

11. Brissot, October 20, 1791, *AP* 34:312. The argument, arising from Roman law, could be linked either to natural right or to the French legal tradition. Two days later Arnail François, marquis de Jaucourt, reiterated that "toutes les opinions s'accordent pour proscrire le projet d'une loi contre l'émigration" because it would be "contraire au droit naturel, à notre Constitution." October 22, 1791, *AP* 34:354.

12. *AP* 34:305, 320. Baignoux and Dumas may have been inspired by an article in the *Révolutions de Paris* from the previous February. The article used almost the same language, arguing that food and cash could be stopped at the border "mais quant à lui, l'homme, vous ne pouvez l'arrêter, attendu qu'il n'est pas un produit de votre sol, mais un produit de la nature; or la nature habitable est le globe terrestre." No. 86, 378.

13. *AP* 34:301.

14. *AP* 34:399. The distinction between people and things held currency among members of the Assembly generally. See also Goupilleau *AP* 34:237. A petition from the Moselle, read by Pyrot, referred to "l'émigration des personnes et la sortie du numéraire," *AP* 34:351; Cavellier *AP* 34:399.

15. *AP* 34:405–406.

16. On the gnomic qualities of physiocracy, see Liana Vardi, *The Physiocrats and the World of the Enlightenment* (Cambridge: Cambridge University Press, 2012), 1–22. On the broad influence of physiocratic thought, see Catherine Larrère, *L'invention de l'économie au XVIIIe siècle: Du droit naturel à la physiocratie* (Paris: Presses Universitaires de France, 1992), 8–15. A particular example of the influence of physiocratic thought on revolutionary lawmakers can be found in François Hincker's discussion of tax reform; see *Les français devant l'impôt sous l'ancien régime* (Paris: Flammarion, 1971), 91.

17. François Crouzet, *La grande inflation: La monnaie en France de Louis XVI à Napoléon* (Paris: Fayard, 1993), 93–97, 108–114. See also John Bosher, *French Finances 1770–1795: From Business to Bureaucracy* (Cambridge: Cambridge University Press, 1970), 219–224.

18. Crouzet, *La grande inflation*, 212–217; François Hincker, "Emprunts," in *Dictionnaire historique de la Révolution française*, ed. Albert Soboul, Jean-René Suratteau, and François Gendron (Paris: Presses Universitaires de France, 1989).

19. *AP* 34:400.

20. Crestin, October 20, 1791, *AP* 34:308. Crestin was hardly the only one to describe the émigrés in terms of pride: Baignoux expressed the same sentiment, explaining to his colleagues that "des esprits ulcérés, honteux de survivre à leurs prérogatives, ont porte leur orgueil, ont ete ensevelir leurs regrets et leur desespoir dans des terres etrangeres," *AP* 34:305. The word was also invoked by Lequinio *AP* 34:299, 300 (twice); Chabot *AP* 34:318; Dumas *AP* 34:321; Aubert-Dubayet *AP* 34:353; Roujoux *AP* 34:394; Condorcet *AP* 34:397; Vergniaud *AP* 34:401; Lacombe-Saint-Michel *AP* 34:431; Lafon-Ladebat *AP* 34:480; Sissou *AP* 34:482, 483 (in conjunction with *honte*, shame); Baert *AP* 34:490; and Paganel *AP* 34:475. Other targets of the word included the Church and the Crown. Pride was an active concept in eighteenth-century religious discourse, whether Jansenist or the mainstream Catholic thought of Fénelon. See John McManners, *Church and Society in Eighteenth-Century France* (New York: Oxford University Press, 1998), 2:241–344; and Pierre Force, *Self Interest before Adam Smith: A Genealogy of Economic Science*, Ideas in Context 68 (Cambridge: Cambridge University Press, 2003), 169–204. Montesquieu associated *orgueil*, a negative quality, with monarchies, linking it to honor. See Céline Spector, "Vices privés, vertus publiques: *De la Fable des abeilles à De l'esprit des lois*," *SVEC* 2009:2, 127–157. Among the philosophes the issue was *amour propre*, not *orgueil*. For a useful overview of the literature debating Rousseau's attitude toward *amour propre*, see Michael Locke McLendon, "Rousseau, 'Amour Propre,' and Intellectual Celebrity," *Journal of Politics* 71, no. 2 (2009): 506–519.

21. Crestin *AP* 34:308.

22. In Old Regime France, the crime of *rapt* and seduction (i.e., the violation of a woman's honor) was punishable by marriage and, in the eighteenth century, became a perennial subject of novels, notably Jean-Jacques Rousseau's *La nouvelle Héloise* (1761) and Choderlos de Laclos's *Les liaisons dangereuses* (1782). On the influence of novel reading on other discourses, see Sarah Maza, *Private Lives and Public Affairs: The Causes Célèbres of Prerevolutionary France* (Berkeley: University of California Press, 1993), *263–312*; and Lynn Hunt, *Inventing Human Rights: A History* (New York: Norton, 2007), 35–69. Female sexual virtue was also a recurring theme in revolutionary discourse. See Suzanne Desan, *The Family on Trial in Revolutionary France* (Berkeley: University of California Press, 2004), 47–92, 178–219; and Joan Landes, *Visualizing the Nation: Gender, Representation, and Revolution in Eighteenth-Century France* (Ithaca, NY: Cornell

University Press, 2001), 1–6. The prospect of émigrés seducing others—in particular, émigré officers seducing their troops to emigrate—was also invoked by Lequinio *AP* 34:299 and Voisard *AP* 34:349.

23. See, for example, the speeches of Brissot, Dumas, and Gaston on October 20, 1791. *AP* 34:311, 318, 321.

24. Debates of October 11 and 16, 1791. See especially Chabot's speech, *AP* 34:173. The culmination of this debate was the law of November 9, 1791, vetoed by the king, which imposed a fine on frontier soldiers who crossed the border, and also stripped them of the rights of active citizenship.

25. Pépin d'Hegronette, October 22, 1791, *AP* 34:346.

26. October 15, 1791, *AP* 34:238.

27. In the subsequent February debate, Gohier referred to emigration as "a criminal desertion." *AP* 38:310.

28. The symbolic importance of oath swearing in the 1780s is reflected in Jacques-Louis David's iconic painting *The Oath of the Horatii*. Honor was a defining value of Old Regime nobility. See Jay Smith, *The Culture of Merit: Nobility, Royal Service and the Making of Absolute Monarchy in France, 1600–1789* (Ann Arbor: University of Michigan Press, 1996). But in the eighteenth century it came under debate, along with the role of the nobility itself. See John Shovlin, "Toward a Reinterpretation of Revolutionary Antinobilism: The Political Economy of Honor in the Old Regime," *Journal of Modern History* 72, no. 1 (2000), 35–66; Hervé Drévillon, "L'âme est à Dieu et l'honneur à nous. Honneur et distinction de soi dans la société d'Ancien Régime," *Revue Historique* 312, no. 2 (2010), 361–395. Honor overlaps with the republican value of virtue via their shared orientation toward the public interest. Anne Simonin argues that the Jacobins adopted notions of honor through the concept of civil degradation. See *Le déshonneur dans la république: Une histroie de l'indignité, 1791–1958* (Paris: Grasset, 2008), 39–89. See also the literature on postrevolutionary uses of honor: Robert A. Nye, *Masculinity and Male Codes of Honor in Modern France* (New York: Oxford, 1993); William M. Reddy, *The Invisible Code: Honor and Sentiment in Postrevolutionary France, 1814–1848* (Berkeley: University of California Press, 1997); Bernard Beignier, *L'honneur et le droit* (Paris: L.D.G.J., 1995). On Condorcet's proposal, see also Patrice Higonnet, *Class, Ideology, and the Rights of Nobles*, 74–75.

29. October 25, 1791, *AP* 34:395–396.

30. October 25, 1791, *AP* 34:396.

31. October 25, 1791, *AP* 34:399.

32. October 25, 1791, *AP* 34:400. The proposal recalled the idea of a balance between duties and rights that had first come up during the preparation of the Declaration of the Rights of Man. A declaration of duties was never written,

because the Assembly determined that a citizen's duties came down to up-holding the rights of his fellow citizens. The social compact depended on reciprocal rights among citizens, so it was impossible to fail in one's duties without endangering one's own rights. See "Droits de l'Homme," in *Dictionnaire Critique de la Révolution Française,* ed. François Furet and Mona Ozouf (Paris: Flammarion, 1988), 691.

33. Though Vergniaud was inspired by Rousseau, the American revolutionaries justified sequestering the property of defectors in nearly identical social contract terms, which were more likely derived from Locke. See Richard D. Brown, "The Confiscation and Disposition of Loyalists' Estates in Suffolk County, Massachusetts," *William and Mary Quarterly* 21, no. 4 (1964): 539.

34. AN ADXII 3, "Extrait des registres des séances du directoire du district de Saint Marcellin, Département d l'Isere." See also AN AD XII 3, "Extrait des registres des séances du Directoire du District de Saint Marcellin, Département de l'Isère," 29 Octobre 1790: "considérant qu'un plus long séjour des émigrants François dans les pays étrangers, seroit une infraction de leur part au pacte social." The importance of the social contract in political debate endured. See Boissy d'Anglas, "Motion d'ordre," 8 floréal V, 5 (AN AD XII 4a).

35. AN DIV 67, "Adresse tendante à la confiscation des biens des émigrés."

36. Bertrand Barère, *Opinion sur les mesures de police à prendre contre les émigrans* (Paris: Imprimerie Nationale, 1791), 6.

37. October 20, 1791, *AP* 34:317. A targeted law against princes and functionaries had been a perennial suggestion in debates since the émigré issue first came under discussion in the winter of 1790, so it would have represented a considerable de-escalation.

38. Law of November 9, 1791.

39. The émigré issue was debated again in the last week of November, on the 22, 27, and 29. On December 10 a petition from the citizens of Angoulême congratulating the Assembly on their decree against the émigrés was read on the floor. *AP* 35:717.

40. *AP* 38:303.

41. *AP* 38:304.

42. *Code des émigrés, condamnés et deportés ou, Recueil des décrets rendus par les Assemblées constituante, législative et conventionelle* (Paris: Imprimerie du Depôt des Lois, 1794–1795), 38–39.

43. Law of July 24–28, 1792.

44. *AP* 38:311.

45. September 2, 1792: "l'obstination de ces mauvais citoyens dans une désertion coupable"; September 12, 1792: "considérant que beaucoup de mauvais citoyens sont restés en France pour éviter le séquestre." The decree went on to

mention that "il serait injuste que les bons citoyens . . . fussent seules dans le cas de supporter les dangers."

46. Law of March 28, 1793, sec. 3–4; on wages, art. 44 and law of 1 floréal III (April 20, 1795), art. 7.

47. On legal limitations to women's property ownership in theory and practice, see, for example, Clare Crowston, "Family Affairs: Wives, Credit, Consumption, and the Law in Old Regime France," in *Family, Gender, and Law in Early Modern France*, ed. Suzanne Desan and Jeffrey Merrick (University Park: Pennsylvania State University Press, 2009), 62–100.

48. Women used their civil disabilities to argue for amnesty from the émigré laws. See Jennifer Heuer, *The Family and the Nation: Gender and Citizenship in Revolutionary France, 1789–1830* (Ithaca, NY: Cornell University Press, 2005), 99–120.

49. Bernard Bodinier overviews this phenomenon in "L'accès à la propriété: Une manière d'éviter les révoltes?," *Cahiers d'Histoire* 94–95 (2005): 59–68.

50. Thouret, October 23, 1789, *AP* 9:485.

51. See, for example, Robespierre on the *marc d'argent*, January 25, 1790.

52. See, for example, Lebrun, October 30, 1789; Viefville des Essarts, October 23, 1789; Vicomte de Mirabeau, October 30, 1789; Lamarck, October 31, 1789; Malouet, October 31, 1789; l'Abbé Maury, October 13, 1789.

53. Law of August 14, 1792.

54. Law of June 3, 1793. The provision ordering that property be distributed to dispossessed families appeared, incongruously, in the same law that asserted that émigré property would be sold to the highest bidder.

55. Law of February 21, 1793.

56. See John Shovlin, *The Political Economy of Virtue: Luxury, Patriotism, and the Origins of the French Revolution* (Ithaca, NY: Cornell University Press, 2006), 182–212.

57. Enjubault de La Roche, November 8, 1790, *AP* 20:323.

58. Rachel Hammersley addresses this divergence in the context of schools of republicanism, contrasting the Cordeliers Club's emphasis on agriculture with the Brissotin preference for commerce. *French Revolutionaries and English Republicans: The Cordeliers Club, 1790–1794* (Suffolk: Royal Historical Society, 2005), 41–55.

59. Camus, October 13, 1789, *AP* 9:418.

60. Paganel, October 28, 1791, *AP* 34:475.

61. Law of June 25, 26, 29 and July 9, 1790.

62. On the sale of Church lands, see the synthesis by Bernard Bodinier and Eric Teyssier, *L'évènement le plus important de la Révolution: La vente des biens nationaux (1789–1867)* (Paris: Société des Etudes Robespierristes: Editions du CTHS,

2000), 155–188. See also Georges Lefebvre, *Questions agraires au temps de la Terreur* (La Roche-sur-Yon: Potier, 1954), 10–32.

63. Peter McPhee, "'The Misguided Greed of Peasants'? Popular Attitudes to the Environment in the Revolution of 1789," *French Historical Studies* 24, no. 2 (Spring 2001): 247–269; Denis Woronoff, "La crise de la forêt française pendant la Révolution et l'Empire: L'indicateur sidérurgique," *Cahiers d'histoire* 24, no. 1 (1979): 3–17.

64. Marc Bouloiseau, *Le séquestre et la vente des biens des émigrés dans le district de Rouen, 1792-An X* (Paris: Novathèse, 1937), 177–179.

65. Marcel Marion argues that the Jacobins gave preference to partisans of the Revolution in the sale of émigré property because they were inspired by the egalitarianism of Rousseau; however, he cites only the August 1792 sale laws, which were suspended by the law of November 9–13, 1792. *La vente des biens nationaux pendant la Révolution française, avec étude spéciale des ventes dans la Gironde et dans le Cher* (Paris: Champion, 1908), 114. René Caisso corroborates Lefebvre's analysis in the district of Tours. *La vente des biens nationaux de seconde origine et les mutations foncières dans le district de Tours, 1792–1830* (Paris: Bibliothèque Nationale, 1977), 32–33.

66. Marc Bouloiseau relates the tension between local and national administrators that delayed the division of émigré property around Rouen into small lots. *Le séquestre et la vente des biens,* 212–217.

67. Assemblée nationale constituante, *Recueil des textes législatifs et administratifs concernant les biens nationaux* (Paris: E. Lreoux, 1926) 3:28. Girondin and Montagnard attitudes toward property were themselves fluid. See Marcel Dorigny, "Les Girondins et le droit de propriété," in *Bulletin de la Commission d'histoire économique et sociale de la Révolution française* 1980–1981, 15–31. See also Patrice Higonnet, "The Social and Cultural Antecedents of Revolutionary Discontinuity," *English Historical Review* 100 (1985): 513–544.

68. Lefebvre considered the notorious Ventôse decrees, which broadly demanded the confiscation of property from suspects, to have had little real significance. See *Questions agraires.* The entire work is dedicated to examining this point. Jean-Pierre Hirsch questions the radicalism of the decrees, suggesting that they were acts of "appropriation, not expropriation." See "Terror and Property," in *The French Revolution and the Creation of Modern Political Culture* (Oxford: Pergamon, 1994), 4:213. Hirsch's conclusion, that the revolutionaries remained fundamentally committed to defending property, is echoed by the legal scholars Jean-Philippe Lévy and André Castaldo, who find a consistent liberalism in revolutionary ideology even during the Terror. *Histoire du droit civil* (Paris: Dalloz, 2002), 456. See also Jacques Godechot, *Les institutions*

de la France sous la Révolution et l'Empire (Paris: Presses Universitaires de France, 1951), 406–408.

69. On the reduced enthusiasm for émigré auctions, see Bouloiseau, *Le séquestre et la vente des biens*, 253, and on graft surrounding the appraisal and sale process, 152.

70. See the suggestion by Echasseriaux jeune, AN ADXII 3, "Rapport fait au nom des comités de législation des finances, concernant la liquidation des créances & droits sur les biens nationaux provenant des émigrés, & de confiscations prononcées par les lois," an III (1794–1795).

71. Jean Signorel gives this value based on the discount rates for an inscription on the *Grand Livre*. See *Etude historique sur la législation révolutionnaire*, 103–104.

72. See, for example, Pardoux Borda's speech recommending that émigré liquidations be centralized in Paris. AN ADXII 3.

73. Eschasseriaux jeune, AN ADXII 4.

74. *Moniteur*, 3 germinal III, no. 183.

75. This culture expressed itself in a mixture of secular piety and economic liberalism. See, for example, Isser Woloch, *The New Regime: Transformations of the French Civic Order* (New York: W. W. Norton, 1994), 264–296; James Livesey, *Making Democracy in the French Revolution* (Cambridge, MA: Harvard University Press, 2001), 48–87. As these tendencies came together around property, see Suzanne Desan, "Reconstituting the Social after the Terror: Family, Property and the Law in Popular Politics," *Past and Present* 164, no. 1 (August 1999): 81–121. Compare this zeal for moral soundness with the quite similar Thermidorean attitude toward madness as explored by Jean-Luc Chappey, "Le nain, le médecin et le divin marquis: Folie et politique à Charenton entre le Directoire et l'Empire," *Annales historiques de la Révolution française* 4, no. 374 (2013): 53–83. See also Pierre Serna, *La république des girouettes: 1789–1815 et au-delà, une anomalie politique: La France de l'extrême centre* (Seyssel: Champ Vallon, 2005), 364–465.

76. Abbé Maury, in the context of the nationalization of Church property, a direct consequence of the debt crisis. *AP* 9:427. On public debt and speculation on *rentes viagères*, see François Crouzet, *La grande inflation: La monnaie en France de Louis XVI à Napoléon* (Paris: Fayard, 1993), 65–74. See also David R. Weir, "Tontines, Public Finance, and Revolution in France and England, 1688–1789," *Journal of Economic History* 49, no. 1 (March 1989): 95–124. The plight of the Compagnie des Indes also played a role in shaping attitudes. See Elizabeth Cross, "L'anatomie d'un scandale: L'affaire de la Compagnie des Indes révisitée (1793–1794)," in *Vertu et politique: Les pratiques des législateurs,*

  1789–2014, ed. Michel Biard, Alain Tourret, Philippe Bourin, and Hervé Leuwers (Rennes: Presses Universitaires de Rennes, 2015), 251–264.

77. James Livesey, *Provincializing Global History: Money, Ideas, and Things in the Languedoc, 1680–1830* (New Haven, CT: Yale University Press, 2020), 17–51. On networks of credit, see Laurence Fontaine, "Espaces, usages et dynamiques de la dette: Dans les hautes vallées dauphinoises (XVII-XVIIIe siècles)," *Annales: Histoire, Sciences Sociales* 49, no. 6 (December 1994): 1375–1391.

78. AN AD XII 3 Girod, "Rapport sur les déclarations à faire en vertu de la loi du 31 octobre, 2-3-10 et 25 novembre 1792."

79. "Extrait du décret qui déclare créanciers de l'Etat les créanciers des Émigrés, etc.," 1 nivôse III (December 21, 1794).

80. Laurence Fontaine, "Antonio and Shylock: Credit and Trust in France, c. 1680–c. 1780," *Economic History Review* 54, no. 1 (2001): 50–52.

81. Philip T. Hoffman, Gilles Postel-Vinay, and Jean-Laurent Rosenthal, "Information and Economic History: How the Credit Market in Old Regime Paris Forces Us to Rethink the Transition to Capitalism," *American Historical Review* 104, no. 1 (February 1999): 75–86.

82. On the different types of loan agreements available to borrowers and lenders, see Philip T. Hoffman, Gilles Postel-Vinay, and Jean-Laurent Rosenthal, *Priceless Markets: The Political Economy of Credit in Paris, 1660–1870* (Chicago: University of Chicago Press, 2000), 15–18.

83. Pardoux Bordas, "Rapport sur le mode de liquidation des dettes des émigrés, condamnés ou déportés fait au nom des Comités de Législation et des Finances." AN ADXII 3.

84. Bordas made this estimate in his report on the liquidation of émigré debt. AN ADXII 3. Whether or not it's accurate, it reflects the concern at the time that émigré creditors were quite numerous, and those with an interest in the debt yet more so.

85. "Réflexions sur le payements des rentes viagères dues aux émigrés," s.n., s.d. AN ADXII 4.

86. Law of March 28, 1793; *Circulaires de la régie de l'enrégistrement et du domaine national*, 2:387; no. 603.

87. AN ADXII 4, Villers, 7 frimaire V (November 27, 1795).

3. The Hands of the Nation

1. Pierre Rosanvallon, "La croissance de l'Etat comme problème," in *L'Etat et les pouvoirs*, vol. 2 of *Histoire de la France*, ed. André Bruguière and Jacques Revel (Paris: Seuil, 1989); Jean-Pierre Machelon, "L'administration entre

l'éxecutif et le législatif," in *L'administration de la France sous la Révolution,* Hautes études médiévales et modernes 69 (Geneva: Droz, 1992), 15–38.

2. This view is still held by scholars of French administration. Albert Lanza, *L'Expression constitutionnelle de l'administration française* (Paris: LGDJ, 1984), 390ff.

3. Michel Foucault, *Discipline and Punish: The Birth of the Prison,* trans. Albert Sheridan (New York: Vintage, 1995), 73–104. A recent, Foucauldian read of the Revolution focuses on bureaucracy. See Ben Kafka, *The Demon of Writing: Powers and Failures of Paperwork* (New York: Zone Books, 2012), 19–76.

4. For more on the implications of this, see Bruno Latour, *The Making of Law: An Ethnography of the Conseil d'Etat,* trans. Marina Brilman and Alain Pottage (Cambridge: Polity, 2010), 142–143, 167–168.

5. An excellent and developed body of work addresses administration in the Revolution. See in particular Clive Church, *Revolution and Red Tape: The French Ministerial Bureaucracy, 1770–1850* (Oxford: Clarendon, 1981); Howard G. Brown, *War, Revolution, and the Bureaucratic State: Politics and Army Administration in France, 1791–1799* (Oxford: Clarendon, 1995); John Bosher, *French Finances 1770–1795: From Business to Bureaucracy* (Cambridge: Cambridge University Press, 1970); Catherine Kawa, *Les ronds-de-cuir en Révolution: Les employés du ministère de l'intérieur sous la Première République, 1792–1800* (Paris: Edition du CTHS, 1996); Robert Descimon, Jean-Frédéric Schaub, and Bernard Vincent, eds., *Les figures de l'administrateur: Institutions, réseaux, pouvoirs en Espagne, en France et au Portugal, 16e–19e siècle* (Paris: Editions de l'Ecole des Hautes Etudes en Sciences Sociales, 1997); *L'administration de la France sous la Révolution* (Geneva: Droz, 1992); Pierre Serna, *La république des girouettes: 1789–1815 . . . et au-delà: Une anomalie politique, la France de l'extrieme centre* (Seyssel: Champ Vallon, 2005); André Burguière and Jacques Revel, eds., *L'etat et les pouvoirs,* vol. 2 of *Histoire de la France* (Paris: Seuil, 1989); Michel Erpeaux, *La naissance du pouvoir réglementaire, 1789–1799* (Paris: Presses Universitaires de France, 1991); Albert Lanza, *L'expression constitutionelle de l'administration française: Contribution à l'étude des constantes constitutionnelles* (Paris: Librairie Générale de Droit et de Jurisprudence, 1984).

6. On the Committee of Alienation, see Raymond Delaby, *Le rôle du Comité d'aliénation dans la vente des biens nationaux: D'après la correspondance inédite du Constituant Camus avec le Directoire du département de la Côte-d'Or (1790–1791)* (Dijon: Rebourseau, 1928), 3–6.

7. Laws of December 6, 1790, and January 2, 1791. At the time this ministry was known as Ministère des Contributions & Revenus publics; the term Ministry of Finances is used for clarity.

8. Law of March 28, 1793, articles 14–15. Perhaps the best testament to the multiplication of émigré lists is the law of 17 nivôse II (January 6, 1794) that ordered the list, previously produced in folio "et en gros caractère," to now be printed "*in*-8, et en petit caractère, afin de diminuer les frais d'impression."

9. Law of March 30, 1792, art. 1 sec. 7.

10. Marc Bouloiseau finds this to be the case in Rouen. See *Le séquestre et vente des biens des émigrés dans le district de Rouen, 1792-An X* (Paris: Novathèse, 1937), 37.

11. Law of 12 germinal II (April 1, 1794), art. 12; law of 29 germinal II (April 18, 1794).

12. The law of January 4, 1793, suppressed the Caisse, attributed its functions to the Treasury, and provisionally created the Administration des Domaines Nationaux, subsequently called the Administration Générale des Domaines Nationaux. The term "domaines nationaux" is similar to "biens nationaux," which refers only to Church and émigré property.

13. The law of April 11, 1793, for example, attributed it a budget and enumerated its employees.

14. Law of October 31, November 1, 3, 10, and 25, 1792, June 3, July 25, 1793, section IV.

15. As much is implied in a rather grumpy report, C 2682 "Suplément [*sic*] aux observations présentés par le département de Paris aux Comités des finances et de législation sur l'attribution à une commission particulière ou à un seul commissaire de la liquidation du passif des émigrés et condamnés," n.d. On the feud between the Convention and the city of Paris, see, for example, Marius Barroux, *Le departement de la Seine et la ville de Paris: Notions générales et et bibliographies pour en étudier l'histoire* (Paris: J. Dumoulin, 1910), 196–197. See also the classic, Albert Soboul, *The Sans-Culottes: The Popular Movement and Revolutionary Government,* trans. Rémy Inglis Hall (Princeton, NJ: Princeton University Press, 1980), 163–222. The Paris city government loomed large in national politics during the Terror, and with it the local Section assemblies that administered the neighborhoods of Paris played an important role in political mobilization. After the collapse of the Terror government on 9 thermidor (July 27, 1794), the new Directory government removed all oversight of *biens nationaux* from the municipal government and gave it to the Department as part of a larger reorganization that abolished Paris's government. The Constitution of the Year III further refined departmental authorities. The Constitution of the Year VIII rejiggered the Departments once again, installing a prefect at the head of the Department and also putting Paris under the surveillance of a prefect of police.

16. This was not unusual for, or particular to, the Régie. For example, Citizen Bayard, Inspecteur of the Garde-Meuble National, noted in a report, "A peine ais-je eu pris une connoissance exacte de cette gestion que le décret du dix Juin 1793 lui donna une forme absolumment différente." AN O2 470, "Garde Meuble National: Compte Rendu par le Cn Bayard, Ex-Inspecteur," 25 messidor an II (July 13, 1794).

17. Roland Mousnier, *Les institutions de la France sous la monarchie absolue* vol. 2 (Paris: Presses Universitaires de France, 1980), 226; François Olivier-Martin, *L'administration provinciale à la fin de l'ancien régime* (Paris: Loysel, 1988), 14–20, 44.

18. John Bosher, *French Finances*, 288.

19. Machelon, "L'administration entre l'exécutif et le législatif," 20.

20. Church, *Revolution and Red Tape*, 94–110.

21. Marcel Marion, *La vente des biens nationaux pendant la Révolution, avec etude spéciale dans les départements de la Gironde et du Cher* (Paris: Champion, 1908), 219.

22. Jacques Hillairet, *Dictionnaire historique des rues de Paris* (Paris: Minuit, 1963), 2:347.

23. Hillairet, *Dictionnaire*, 2:119.

24. H. Monin and Lucien Lazard, *Sommier des biens nationaux de la ville de Paris, conservé aux Archives de la Seine* (Paris: L. Cerf, 1920), 1:414.

25. Monin and Lazard, *Sommier*, 1:156.

26. AN F7 3330 Comité de Législation, "Mémoire: Lois contre les émigrés."

27. Jean-Louis Halpérin, *L'impossible Code civil*, 139–140, quoted in Anne Simonin, *Le déshonneur dans la République: Une histoire de l'indignité, 1791–1958* (Paris: Grasset, 2008), 316. Simonin notes that the first code issued in the Revolution, in 1791, was a penal code. *Le déshonneur*, 39.

28. AN F7 3330 "Question faites au ministre," 11 germinal 4.

29. Direction Générale de l'Enregistrement, des Domaines et du Timbre, *Circulaires de la Régie de l'enregistrement et du domaine national. 2e édition, corrigée et augmentée des circulaires qui n'ont été portées que par extrait sur la 1e édition*, 9 vols. (Paris: Bureau des Editeurs-Rédacteurs, s.d.).

30. G. Bosquet, *Dictionnaire raisonné des domaines et droits domaniaux, des droits d'échange, & de ceux de contrôle des actes des notaires & sous signatures privées* (Rennes: Vve. F. Vatar, 1783), 2. He referenced the "considerable" quantity of regulations in his 1763 edition; in 1783 he repeated this complaint. G. Bosquet, *Dictionnaire raisonné des domaines et droits domaniaux*, vol. 1 (Rouen: Jacques-Joseph Le Boullenger, 1763), iv. Of course, a handbook devoted to decoding legislation would have an incentive to overstate its complexity somewhat.

The problem of constantly changing hierarchies and authorities also endured into the nineteenth century. See Christophe Charle, *Les hauts fonctionnaires en France au XIXe siècle*, (Paris: Gallimard, 1980), 6.

31. C. P. Des Ormeaux, *Répertoire du domaniste, ouvrage nécessaire aux personnes qui se destinent à la partie des domaines, aux employés de cette partie* (Paris: Brun aîné, 1789); as C. P. Desormeaux, *Dictionnaire des domaines nationaux, des droits d'enregistrement, de timbre, d'hypothèques, de patentes* (Paris: Perronneau, an V). Editions were issued in 1789, 1796 (year V), 1797–1798 (year VI–VII), and 1802, as well as 1810 and 1817. On the phenomenon of administrative guides, see Ralph Kingston, *Bureaucrats and Bourgeois Society: Office Politics and Individual Credit: France, 1789–1848)*, 25–26.

32. The law of February 18, 1791, held officials responsible for the amount of any sums they failed to collect, but was suppressed by the law of 14 pluviôse II (February 2, 1794). The law of March 28, 1793, collated and reasserted existing émigré policy, and included the provision that "ceux qui seront convaincus d'infidélité dans l'exercice des fonctions relatives aux dispositions de la présente loi, seront punis de deux années de fers, & en outre responsables, sur tous leurs biens présents & à venir, des torts que leur infidélité aura occasionnés à la République ou aux particuliers," section X, art. 60.

33. AdP DQ10 168 Beaumarchais, Régisseurs to Director (Girard), 4 ventôse VI (February 22, 1798).

34. Clive Church finds strong continuity of employees in the Régie overall. *Revolution and Red Tape*, 94. Jean-Pierre Massaloux finds the same. *La régie de l'enregistrement et des domaines aux XVIIIe et XIXe siècles: Etude historique* (Geneva: Droz, 1989), 231–233.

35. Huguier appears in AN G2 137, a record of the Old Regime tax administration the Ferme générale, as a receiver in Ayraines, in the north of France; this is not the immediate Paris region, but a person named Huguier held the position of receiver in the Domain office in Paris from 1795 to 1804. The tenuousness of this link is exemplary of the records. The problem is not limited to Paris. See Léon Dubreuil, *La vente des biens nationaux dans le département des Côtes-du-Nord* (Paris: Champion, 1912), 209.

36. AdP DQ10 45, "Serment du 21 Janvier."

37. Pierre Robin, *Le séquestre des biens ennemis sous la Révolution française* (Paris: Spes, 1929), 171.

38. AdP DQ10 169 Bourgeois (Veuve de Claude Dufoy), 21 nivôse II (January 10, 1794), Director to Verifier (Pierret). "Il aurait fallu que vous eussiez rappellé les faits et établir une raisonnement."

39. See, for example, C 2682 "Suplément [*sic*] aux observations présentés par le département de Paris aux Comités des finances et de législation sur

l'attribution a une commission particulière ou à un seul commissaire de la liquidation du passif des émigrés et condamnés," unsigned, n.d. See also AN AD XII 3, Report by Pardoux Bordas, 18 prairial IV (June 6, 1796).

40. AdP DQ10 704 Bretignières de Courteille, unsigned and undated note and Directeur to Président du Département de Paris, 19 prairial II (June 7, 1794). He made the same request for two properties belonging to émigrés in ADP DQ10 704 Bochard de Champigny, Directeur to Département de Paris, 12 frimaire II (December 2, 1793).

41. AdP DQ10 709 Bernard and Delorme, Director to Department administrators, 3 floréal II (April 22, 1794).

42. AdP DQ10 169 Bouthillier, Lebrun to Administrators, 15 fructidor XI (September 2, 1803).

43. AdP DQ10 169 Bouthillier, Receiver to Director, 21 Pluviose XII (February 11, 1804). Another illusory inheritance, from the year XII (1803–1804), is reported in ADP DQ10 169, Bernard dossier.

44. AdP DQ10 704 Bolche, Unnamed to Director of the National Domain Agency, 21 germinal II (April 10, 1794). The Domain also learns of a property through its tenant in ADP DQ10 704 Bretony; through a neighborhood Revolutionary Committee in ADP DQ10 705 Breville; through an unnamed informant in ADP DQ10 704 Bretignières de Courteille.

45. Law of October 31, 1792, art. 2.

46. AdP DQ10 170 Brousse et Morel, letter from Lienard concierge, 24 germinal VI (April 13, 1798).

47. On the proliferation of inventories during the Revolution, see also Emma Rothschild, *An Infinite History: The Story of a Family in France over Three Centuries* (Princeton, NJ: Princeton University Press, 2021), 124–125.

48. Law of March 11 and 12, 1793.

49. AdP DQ10 168 Bellet (Mauleon Savaillant), Extract of Director's opinion dated 11 vendémiaire X (October 3, 1801). The house was located at 76 Rue des Tournelles. Monin and Lazard, *Sommier,* 2:471.

50. AdP DQ10 168 Bellet, letter from Receiver to Director (Eparvier), 9 frimaire X (November 30, 1801).

51. AdP DQ10 168 Bellet, Prefecture to Eparvier, 7 pluviôse X (January 27, 1802).

52. AdP DQ10 168 Bellet, Director to Durant, 13 germinal [X] (April 3, 1802).

53. Inventories of these documents can be found in AN T 1685–1688, "Etats de titres et pièces remis à la commission municipale (de Paris) chargée de la liquidation des créances de certains émigrés (2,200 dossiers environ). An II-1808."

54. AdP DQ10 172 Beziade, Bignon to Director, 15 gérminal II (April 4, 1794).

55. AdP DQ10 170 Baraumont, Verifier to Director, 5 jour complémentaire XI (September 22, 1803).

56. AdP DQ10 169 Boulainvilliers, Bignon to Director, 12 brumaire X (November 3, 1801).

57. AdP DQ10 173 Brisson, Bignon to Director, 15 floréal VIII (May 5, 1800).

58. AdP DQ10 709 Berbis Desmailly, Moncuit to Director, 6 nivose III (December 26, 1794).

59. AN AD XII 3, Report by Pardoux Bordas, 18 prairial IV (June 6, 1796).

60. AN T 1678 Ministère des Finances to Commission des Revenus Nationaux, "Copie du rapport des commissaires surveillant aux inventaires des papiers des émigrés, Bureau des Archives du Département de la Seine, Maison d'Uzès." The letter itself is undated but is filed with other documents dated brumaire / nivôse an IV (October–January, 1795–1796).

61. AdP DQ10 709 Berbis Desmailly, Moncuit to Directeur, 6 nivôse III (December 26, 1794).

62. AdP DQ10 709 Berbis Desmailly (Veuve), 9 nivôse III (December 29, 1794), Director to Verifier.

63. AdP DQ10 704 Brochet Saint Prest, Director to Gauthier, n.d.

64. AdP DQ10 704 Brochet Saint Prest, Director to Domain Bureau of Paris, 8 vendémiaire II (September 29, 1793).

65. AdP DQ10 704 Dubois de Lauzai and Duvergier, Director to Agence du Domaine National, 13 thermidor II (July 31, 1794). He made a similar request in the same terms in a letter recommending that architectural details belonging to a previous owner be sold from a house near the Arsenal because they were being damaged by tenants and "il serait avantageux pour les intérêts de la République qu'ils fussent vendus." See ADP DQ10 705 Bélissart, Directeur to Bureau du Département, 26 floréal III (May 15, 1795). See also ADP DQ10 173 Bergier veuve Bozonat, Director (Eparvier) to Verifier (Lachenaye), marginal response, 2 brumaire VII (October 23, 1798); ADP DQ10 704 Bousquet, Director to Bureau du Domaine Nationale 9 pluviôse III (January 28, 1795).

66. AdP DQ10 704 Brancas Villars, Director to Agence du Domaine National du Département de Paris 19 fructidor II (September 5, 1794).

67. AN T 1678, item 1442.

68. AdP DQ10 704 Boutin, Directeur to Balduc, 5 thermidor II (July 23, 1794).

69. AdP DQ10 169 Boulainvilliers, Administration Centrale du Département to Directeur, 24 Nivôse VII (January 13, 1799).

70. AdP DQ10 705 Balleroy (La Cour de), Director (Gentil) to Département, 27 nivôse II (January 16, 1794) and Président du Département to Directeur, 6 pluviôse II (January 25, 1794). The Department president made the same re-

quest again later that same year. See ADP DQ10 704 Bréville, Président du Département to Directeur, 5 messidor II (June 23, 1794).

71. AdP DQ10 704 Bochard de Champigny, Director to Visiteur des Locations (Balduc), marginal response, 12 frimaire II (December 2, 1793).

72. AdP DQ10 704 Bochard de Champigny, Administrateurs composant le Directoire du Département to Director (Gentil), August 24, 1793.

73. For an overview of political authority in the Old Regime, see Peter R. Campbell, "Absolute Monarchy," in *Oxford Handbook to the Ancien Régime* (Oxford: Oxford University Press, 2012), 11–38. For a much deeper dive into the concept of the king's will, see François Olivier-Martin, *Histoire du droit français des origines à la Révolution* (Paris: Domat, 1948), 17–19, 301–307. See also Keith Michael Baker, *Inventing the French Revolution: Essays on French Political Culture in the Eighteenth Century* (Cambridge: Cambridge University Press, 1990), 12–30.

74. Jean Bodin, *Les six lives de la république* (Paris, Fayard, 1986. First published 1576), chs. 11–14.

75. The point is made succinctly in book II, chapter 1. *The Social Contract and Other Later Political Writings*, Cambridge Texts in the History of Political Thought (Cambridge: Cambridge University Press, 1997), 57.

76. Law 16 ventôse III (March 6, 1795), "Décret qui adopte l'instruction présentée par le comité militaire, pour faire suite à la loi concernant l'organisation des commissaires des guerres," article X; Law of August 2, 1793.

77. On the concept of a modern public sphere, an idea Marx picked up from Hegel, see Jurgen Habermas, *The Structural Transformation of the Public Sphere: An Inquiry into a Category of Bourgeois Society*, trans. Thomas Burger and Frederick Lawrence (Cambridge, MA: MIT Press, 1989), 117–128. For a view on how the separation of public from private concerns property, see also Rafe Blaufarb, *The Great Demarcation: The French Revolution and the Invention of Modern Property* (Oxford: Oxford University Press, 2016), 1. The private sphere is also associated with gendered roles for women that were formalized in the Revolution; Suzanne Desan addresses and disputes this theory. *The Family on Trial in the French Revolution* (Berkeley: University of California Press, 2004), 12.

78. Karl Marx, *Critique of Hegel's 'Philosophy of Right,'* trans. Annette Jolin and Joseph O'Malley, ed. Joseph O'Malley (Cambridge: Cambridge University Press, 1970), 44–48.

4. Césarine's Inheritance

1. Natacha Coquéry, *L'espace du pouvoir: De la demeure privée à l'édifice public, Paris 1700–1790* (Paris: Sli Arslan, 2000), 9, 28.

2. Law of March 18 and 21, 1793 (see AN ADXII 3).

3. AN O2 434, 24 pluviôse III (February 12, 1795), Inventaire des meubles et effets de la maison Dusez [d'Uzès] rue Montmartre.

4. The catalog of the Mobilier National mentions these inventory marks; it also explicitly lists a number of pieces originating from owners condemned during the Revolution. "Mobilier Collections," Mobilier National, accessed May 12, 2022, http://www.mobiliernational.culture.gouv.fr/fr/collections-et-ressources/collection/mobilier.

5. Hôtel de Brienne Virtual Tour, Ministry of Defense, http://web.archive.org/web/20190525104722/; https://www.defense.gouv.fr/portail/mediatheque/visites-virtuelles/hotel-de-brienne; archived May 25, 2019.

6. "Le patrimoine de l'hotel de Matignon," Government of France, accessed June 10, 2022, https://www.gouvernement.fr/le-patrimoine-de-l-hotel-de-matignon. The author visited the property during Patrimony Days in 2010.

7. Peter Stearns offers a useful primer, Consumerism in World History, Themes in World History (New York: Routledge, 2006), 17–26. On global imports to Europe, see Maxine Berg, "Luxury, the Luxury Trades, and Industrial Growth," in The Oxford Handbook of the History of Consumption, ed. Frank Trentmann (Oxford: Oxford University Press, 2012), 185–188; John E. Wills Jr., "European Consumption and Asian Production in the Seventeenth and Eighteenth Centuries," in Consumption and the World of Goods, ed. John Brewer and Roy Porter (London: Routledge, 1993), 133–147.

8. For an overview, see Dominique Margairaz, "City and Country: Home, Possessions, and Diet, Western Europe 1600–1800," in Trentmann, Oxford Handbook, 192–210.

9. Jan de Vries offers an overview in The Industrious Revolution: Consumer Behavior and the Household Economy, 1650 to the Present (Cambridge: Cambridge University Press, 2008), 20–37. Daniel Roche examines the changing meaning of luxury in the face of expanding consumer goods, a fact taken for granted in his book A History of Everyday Things: The Birth of Consumption in France, 1600–1800 (Cambridge: Cambridge University Press, 2000), 72–78. See also T. H. Breen, "The Meanings of Things: Interpreting the Consumer Economy in the Eighteenth Century," in Brewer and Porter, Consumption, 249–260. Breen focuses on England and America, but as his reference to Habermas telegraphs, he has a broader European context in mind (257).

10. Amalia D. Kessler offers a useful overview on bills of exchange and other negotiable instruments in A Revolution in Commerce: The Parisian Merchant Court and the Rise of Commercial Society in Eighteenth-Century France (New Haven, CT: Yale University Press, 2007), 188–237. See also Philip T. Hoffman, Gilles Postel-Vinay, and Jean-Laurent Rosenthal, Priceless Markets: The Political Economy of Credit in Paris, 1660–1870 (Chicago: University of Chicago Press,

2000), 18. Gérard Béaur tracks changes in the real estate market in *Le marché foncier à la veille de la Révolution: Les mouvements de propriété beaucerons dans les régions de Maintenon et de Janville de 1761 à 1790* (Paris: Editions de l'Ecole des hautes études en sciences sociales, 1984), 278, 332.

11. James Livesey explores the social breadth of these investors in the Languedoc region in "Les réseaux de crédit en Languedoc au XVIIIe siècle et les origines sociales de la Révolution française," *Annales historiques de la Révolution française* 359 (January 2010): 29–51. Michael Sonenscher considers the political implications of this social diversity in *Before the Deluge: Public Debt, Inequality, and the Social Origins of the French Revolution* (Princeton, NJ: Princeton University Press, 2007), 173–253.

12. Philip T. Hoffman, Gilles Postel-Vinay, and Jean-Laurent Rosenthal, "Revolution and Evolution: Notarial Credit Markets in France (1780–1840)," *Annales: Histoire Sciences Sociales* 59, no. 2 (March 2004): 387–424.

13. Clare Crowston, *Credit, Fashion, Sex: Economies of Regard in Old Regime France* (Durham, NC: Duke University Press, 2013), 2–17.

14. On the role of enslaved labor in French political economy, see Manuel Covo, "Baltimore and the French Atlantic: Empires, Commerce, and Identity in a Revolutionary Age," in *The Caribbean and the Atlantic World Economy: Circuits of Trade, Money and Knowledge, 1650–1914,* ed. Adrian Leonard and David Pretel (Basingstoke: Palgrave Macmillan, 2015), 87–107; and Robert Louis Stein, *The French Sugar Business in the Eighteenth Century* (Baton Rouge: Louisiana State University Press, 1988), 93–105. On the presence of enslaved people in Paris, see Miranda Spieler, "The Vanishing Slaves of Paris: The *Lettre de Cachet* and the Emergence of an Imperial Legal Order in Eighteenth-Century France," in *The Scaffolding of Sovereignty: Global and Aesthetic Perspectives on the History of a Concept,* ed. Zvi Ben-Dor Benite, Stefanos Geroulanos, and Nicole Jerr (New York: Columbia University Press, 2017), 230–245.

15. Locke's move to situate ownership in work falls in this vein, as it is humanity's ability to cultivate and tame nature that creates a claim to ownership. *The Second Treatise of* Government, V, in *Two Treatises of Government,* ed. Peter Laslett (Cambridge: Cambridge University Press, 1988), 285–302. Marxist theory has pointed out the dominion over nature most explicitly in Marx's concept of species being and in Max Horkheimer and Theodor Adorno's dialectic of enlightenment. See Karl Marx, *Economic and Philosophical Manuscripts of 1844,* XXIV, in Karl Marx, *Selected Writings,* ed. Lawrence H. Simon (Indianapolis: Hackett, 1994), 62–64; Max Horkheimer and Theodor Adorno, *Dialectic of Enlightenment,* trans. Edmund Jephcott (Stanford, CA: Stanford University Press, 2002), 1–34.

16. Michael Xifaras, *La propriété: Etude de philosophie du droit* (Paris: Presses Universitaires de France, 2004), 12.

17. Walter Benjamin explores the symbiotic relationship between owner and object in his writing on collectors, drawing out what is particular about ownership within a regime of consumerism; see in particular *The Arcades Project*, trans. Howard Eiland and Kevin McLaughlin (Cambridge, MA: Belknap Press of Harvard University Press, 1999), 203–227. In book 1 of *Capital*, Marx considers the particular regime of value brought about by capitalist production. See Martha Campbell, "The Objectivity of Value versus the Idea of Habitual Action," in *On the Constitution of Capital: Essays on Volume I of Marx's 'Capital,'* ed. Riccardo Bellofiore and Nicola Taylor, International Symposium on Marxian Theory, 2002, Università di Bergamo (Basingstoke: Palgrave, 2004), 63–87.

18. The archival materials generally identify individuals by all three or four of their given names; the number has been reduced here for clarity.

19. Deported priests were given émigré status by the law of 29–30 vendémiaire II (October 20–21, 1793). Ange-François is referred to as "voluntarily deported" in the sources; as a clergyman who refused to take an oath to the Revolution, he was eligible for deportation to Guyana. See Spieler, *Empire and Underworld*, 20–44.

20. This information is related in a judgment issued by the Domain, 29 germinal V (April 18, 1797), AdP DQ10 169 Becdelièvre veuve Talaru, and corroborated in Emile Campardon, *Les guillotinés de la Terreur* (Paris: Publications Henri Coston, 1988), 130. Those condemned by the Revolutionary Tribunal were given the status of émigrés. The law of March 10, 1793, ordered the confiscation of their property. They began to be rolled into the émigré laws in December 1793 and January 1794. Their property was returned to their heirs by the law of 18 prairial III (June 6, 1795) while the émigré seizure process was still otherwise in effect.

21. *Archives Parlementaires de 1787 à 1860: Recueil complet des débats législatifs et politiques des chambres français* (Paris: s.n., 1787–), 34:305 (October 20, 1791).

22. *Archives Parlementaires de 1787 à 1860*, 34:238 (October 15, 1791).

23. The seller bought the land on which the house sat as part of a larger package five years earlier. Details of the sales are related in an arrêté dated 13 floréal XI (May 3, 1803).

24. AdP DQ10 169 Becdelievre veuve Talaru, Auget Montyon subdossier. Probably Antoine Auget de Monthion; the spelling used by the Domain has been maintained.

25. Hoffman, Postel-Vinay, and Rosenthal, *Priceless Markets*, 14–18; James Livesey, *Provincializing Global History: Money, Ideas, and Things in the Languedoc, 1680–1830*

(New Haven, CT: Yale University Press, 2020), 17–51. On the growing real estate market, see Gérard Béaur, *Le marché foncier*; and Fabrice Boudjaaba, *Des paysans attachés à la terre? Familles, marchés et patrimoines dans la région de Vernon (1750–1830)* (Paris: Presses Universitaires de France, 2008).

26. Henriette-Jeanne-Elie de Becdelièvre de Cany, married to Louis-François vicomte de Talaru July 22, 1767. Their two children were Louis-Justin-Marie vicomte de Talaru and Césarine-Marie-Louise de Talaru. The family is Talaru de Chamazel (also spelled Chalmazel).

27. On the gender dynamics of emigration and the strategic use of divorce, see Jennifer Heuer, *The Family and the Nation: Gender and Citizenship in Revolutionary France, 1789–1830* (Ithaca, NY: Cornell University Press, 2005), 99–120.

28. Law of October 31, 1792. On the problem of "necessary" items, see Colin Jones and Rebecca Spang, "Sans-culottes, *sans café, sans tabac*: Shifting Realms of Luxury and Necessity in Eighteenth-Century France," in *Consumers and Luxury: Consumer Culture in Europe, 1650–1850*, ed. Maxine Berg and Helen Clifford (Manchester: Manchester University Press, 1999), 37–62.

29. AdP DQ10 169 Becdelièvre, letter without heading or signature, 12 messidor V (June 30, 1797).

30. AdP DQ10 169 Becdelièvre, *Régisseurs* to Director, 6 thermidor VII (July 24, 1799).

31. *Prospectus de la (1re et 2e) loterie nationale de maisons, bâtiments et meubles nationaux, établie en vertu des décrets de la Convention nationale, des 29 germinal et 8 prairial an III* (Paris, Year III), 17. For insight into the Paris wine market of the time, see Jean-Pierre Poussou and Philippe Bertholet, "Les vins que buvaient les notaires Parisiens, du règne de Louis XIV à la Monarchie de juillet," *Revue du Nord* 2, nos. 400–401 (2013): 351–371.

32. Yves Durand, *Les fermiers généraux au XVIIIe siècle* (Paris: Presses Universitaires de France, 1971), 338–346; David Garrioch, *The Making of Revolutionary Paris* (Berkeley: University of California Press, 2002), 84–111. The composition of elites and the behaviors that distinguished them varied regionally and depended on divisions within the nobility and between types of elites, such as nobles, financiers, and merchants. These distinctions were in flux by the end of the eighteenth century and are the subject of a rich literature; for a recent overview in English, see Crowston, *Credit, Fashion, Sex*, 21–55.

33. Natacha Coquéry, *L'hôtel aristocratique: Le marché du luxe à Paris au XVIIIe siècle* (Paris: Publications de la Sorbonne, 1998), 194–195. The house was purchased from an architect, which suggests it was recently built and Ange-François was the first occupant. The interior disposition of homes in Paris also changed over the course of the eighteenth century, a point not explored here. See Youri Carbonnier, *Maisons parisiennes des lumières*, Collection

du Centre Roland Mousnier (Paris: Presses Universitaires de la Sorbonne, 2006), 280–291.

34. AdP DQ10 169 Becdelievre veuve Talaru, 26 fructidor VII (September 12, 1799), Régisseurs to Director (Girard).

35. On speculative building in Paris before the Revolution, see Allan Potofsky, *Constructing Paris in the Age of Revolution* (Basingstoke: Palgrave, 2009), 65–67.

36. Coquéry, *L'espace du pouvoir,* 194–195.

37. AdP DQ10 709 Boulogne, Agent des Domaines to Director, 6 prairial II (May 25, 1794); architect's report, 3 prairial II (May 22, 1794).

38. AdP DQ10 Bertrand Kanguen, Director to Architect (Aubert), 4 messidor VII (June 22, 1799).

39. AN C 2682, Extrait d'un arrêté du Directoire, 24 vendémiaire II (October 15, 1793). Marc Bouloiseau found problems of graft and theft in Rouen as well. Marc Bouloiseau, *Le sequestre et la vente des biens des emigres dans le district de Rouen, 1792—an X* (Paris: Novathese, 1937), 152.

40. Law of October 24, 1792.

41. *Rapport fait au nom de la Commission des Finances par Defermon,* 7 vendémiaire V (September 28, 1796).

42. The Commission des Revenus Nationaux, a body of the Convention, noted that guardianship costs could eat up the whole profit of property sale. AN F7 3330, letter to Commission de Révision des Loix, 27 messidor II (July 15, 1794).

43. Circular no. 23, November 17, 1793, in Augustin Cochin and Charles Charpentier, eds., *Les actes du gouvernement révolutionnaire* (Paris: A. Picard, 1920), 1:421–424.

44. AN F7 3328, March 9, 1793, Circular letter, Minister of Interior to Department Administrators. He was reiterating the law of September 27, 1792, and the circular letter to Department administrators from October 12. As early as September 1792 the Convention called for the seals on émigré and ecclesiastical properties to be lifted so that anything that might benefit troop encampments could be removed (law of September 27, 1792). Horses had been requisitioned in the law of August 15, 1792.

45. Law of 25 vendémiaire III (October 16, 1794).

46. Cochin and Charpentier, *Les actes du gouvernement révolutionnaire,* 1:93.

47. The law of October 10, 1792, reserved fine arts from émigré property auctions. The law of April 4, 1793, art. 8, stipulated that "tous les objets d'arts et sciences, tableaux, statues, estampes, dessins, bronzes, vases, porcelaines, médailles, meubles, précieux" should not be sold in individual émigré auctions but rather grouped together and sold after the publication of a special catalog.

48. AdP DQ10 171 Baudouin, Architect (Bourla) to Director, 17 floréal VIII (May 7, 1800).

49. AdP DQ10 171 Baudouin, Régisseurs to Director (Girard), 28 floréal VIII (May 18, 1800).

50. AN C 2722, Ministre de la Guerre to Commission des Dépenses, 27 pluviôse V (February 15, 1797). See, relatedly, the exchange about a potential public garden, AN Q 2 196, Ministre de l'Intérieur, 30 Messidor IV (July 18, 1796), and Ministre de l'Intérieur to Administration Municipale du 1er Arrondissement (undated), in which the minister rejects the idea of keeping a property as a public garden, in part on the grounds that the buildings "qui ont été construits avec une parcimonie si voisine du luxe, ne valent presque rien."

51. Similar issues of account reconciliation during the liquidation of an estate can be found in the following dossiers: AdP DQ10 89 Babaud Lachaussade, Bethune Charost; DQ10 168 Bailly, Bailleul; DQ10 169 Brizard heirs Gouesmel, Boulainvilliers; DQ10 172 Beziade, Baron, Benjamin; DQ10 173 Bergier veuve, Becquet, La Bourdennais.

52. The "Décret des deux tiers," 5 fructidor III (August 22, 1795).

53. This information is related in a letter from Cornebize, a receiver, to the director, dated 24 Brumaire IX (November 15, 1800).

54. AdP DQ10 169 Becdelievre, Cornebize to Director, 25 fructidor VIII.

55. AdP DQ10 169 Boulainvilliers, Régisseurs to Director, 13 fructidor VI (August 30, 1798).

56. AdP DQ10 169 Boulainvilliers Sapinault, Barbier, Radel to Director, 2 jour complémentaire VI (September 18, 1798).

57. AdP DQ10 704 Bonneval, Commis principal in the Bureau des Locations (Saladin) to Director, October 16, 1792.

58. For dossiers that deal primarily with tenant issues, see, for example, AdP DQ10 89 Barre; DQ10 89 Blottefier; DQ10 131 Bouthilliers; DQ10 168 Beauvais; DQ10 170 Bachelier; DQ10 170 Baraumont; DQ10 704 Bossu d'Alsace; DQ10 705 Beauvilliers Saint-Aignan; DQ10 705 Bellepeaume; DQ10 705 Bélissart; DQ10 709 Bérard; DQ10 709 Boucher d'Argis; DQ10 711 Beaune; DQ10 751 Planoy (Bochard Champigny); DQ10 225 Boudet; DQ10 131 Breuillard; DQ10 170 Brousse et Morel; DQ10 168 Bouvrain. Nearly as many deal with repairs and construction, which were usually requested by tenants.

59. AdP DQ10 704 Bouthillier, Director to Bureau du Domaine National du Département de Paris, 8 frimaire III (November 28, 1794).

60. France, Convention nationale Comité de salut public, *Recueil des actes du Comité de salut public: Avec la correspondance officielle des représentants en mission et le registre des représentants en mission et le registre du Conseil executif provisoire* (Imprimerie nationale, 1903), 15:398.

61. AdP DQ10 704 Bouthillier, Bureau du Domaine National to Director, 23 frimaire III (December 13, 1794).

62. AdP DQ10 704 Bouthillier, Director to Bureau du Domaine National, 3 nivôse III (December 23, 1794).

63. AdP DQ10 704 Bouthillier, Director to Administrateurs du Département, 7 messidor II (June 25, 1794).

64. News of her request is transmitted in a letter from the director to the general liquidator of the public debt dated 5 pluviôse X (January 25, 1802).

65. The arrangement is related in an opinion by the director, 13 floréal XI (May 3, 1801).

66. Michel Xifaras points out the way that the dichotomy of person and thing breaks down when property is studied from the perspective of its social functions. *La propriété*, 82.

5. Property, Family, and Patrimony

1. The ownership and disposition of mirrors in seized properties was a major issue: mirrors figure in eleven of the dossiers in the sample, or about 10 percent. As we saw in Chapter 4, seized objects were frequently used in public buildings. See also AdP DQ10 Bouvrain, mirrors removed to furnish the office of the Directeur Général des Droits Réunis, a tax authority. On mirrors being moved for various purposes, see also AN O2 470.

2. ADP DQ10 172 Jacob Benjamin, Administrators of the 1st Division to the Director of the Domain, n.d.

3. ADP DQ10 172 Jacob Benjamin, Verifier to Director, 22 Nivose year X (January 12, 1802).

4. On revolutionary reforms and the family, see in particular Suzanne Desan, *The Family on Trial in Revolutionary France* (Berkeley: University of California Press, 2004); Jennifer Ngaire Heuer, *The Family and the Nation: Gender and Citizenship in Revolutionary France, 1789–1830* (Ithaca, NY: Cornell University Press, 2018); and Anne Verjus and Denise Davidson, *Le roman conjugal: Chronicles de la vie familial à l'époque de la Révolution et de l'Empire* (Seyssel: Champ Vallon, 2011).

5. Desan, *Family on Trial*, 40–92.

6. An extensive literature explores the nature of these changes in France; for a recent overview of changing attitudes toward family life in the eighteenth century, see Meghan K. Roberts, *Sentimental Savants: Philosophical Families in Enlightenment France* (Chicago: University of Chicago Press, 2016), 102–135. See also the classic works: Annick Pardailhé-Galabrun, *La naissance de l'intime: 3000 foyers parisiens XVIIe-XVIIIe siècles* (Paris: Presses Universitaires de France, 1988); and David Denby, *Sentimental Narrative and the Social Order in France*

(Cambridge: Cambridge University Press, 1994). See also Dena Goodman, "Marriage Choice and Marital Success: Reasoning about Marriage, Love, and Happiness," in *Family, Gender, and Law in Early Modern France*, ed. Suzanne Desan and Jeffrey Merrick (University Park: Pennsylvania State University Press, 2009), 26–61. Similar changes took place across Europe, as a significant body of literature traces. For an overview of these works, see Sarah Maza's introduction to a special issue on the topic: "Only Connect: Family Values in the Age of Sentiment: Introduction," *Eighteenth-Century Studies* 30, no. 2 (Spring 1997): 207–212. See also the classics: Jean-Louis Flandrin, *Familles, maison, sexualité dans l'ancienne société* (Paris: Flammarion, 1976); and Leonore Davidoff and Catherine Hall, *Family Fortunes: Men and Women of the English Middle Class, 1780–1850* (1987; reissue, London: Hutchinson, 2002), 321–356.

7. Desan, *Family on Trial*; Heuer, *Family and the Nation*, 23–43; Verjus and Davidson, *Le roman conjugal*.

8. Law of 7–11 Mars 1793. See Desan, *Family on Trial*, 141–177. This is still the case in France today, per the Civil Code, Article 914.

9. Suzanne Desan argues that the Civil Code's approach to family law, a departure from that of the Revolution, did not represent a return to Old Regime values so much as "a new alliance between state, father, and conjugal family." *Family on Trial*, 297.

10. Denise Z. Davidson and Anne Verjus, "Generational Conflict in Revolutionary France: Widows, Inheritance Practices, and the 'Victory' of Sons," *William & Mary Quarterly* 70, no. 2 (April 2013): 399–424. See also François-Joseph Ruggiu, *L'individu et la famille dans les sociétés urbaines anglaise et française (1720–1780)*, Collection du Centre Roland Mousnier 30 (Paris: Presses Universitaires de la Sorbonne, 2007); David Warren Sabean, Simon Teuscher, and Jon Mathieu, eds., *Kinship in Europe: Approaches to Long-Term Development (1300–1900)* (New York: Berghahn Books, 2007).

11. AN F7 3328 Ministre de l'Intérieur aux Administrateurs des Departements, December 4, 1792.

12. AN ADXII 3, Report by P. Bordas, 18 prairial IV (June 6, 1796).

13. On the use of marriage contracts and their legal bearing, see, for example, Hannah Callaway, "A Contested Inheritance: The Family and the Law from the Enlightenment to the French Revolution," *Law & History Review* 37, no. 2 (2019): 61–87.

14. AN T 240–242.

15. ADP DQ10 173 Brisson, Régisseurs to Director, 29 thermidor 7 (August 16, 1799).

16. On the La Cour de Balleroy family, sword nobles from Normandy, see Gustave Chaix d'Est Ange, *Dictionnaire des familles françaises anciennes ou notables*

à la fin du XIXe siècle (Evreux: Charles Hérissey, 1913), 12:110–112; and Mathieu Marraud, *La noblesse de Paris au XVIIIe siècle* (Paris: Seuil, 2000), 136.

17. His parents were Charles Auguste de la Cour de Balleroy and Adélaïde Elisabeth Sophie de l'Epineau.

18. Marriage contracts have been quite well studied, from the perspective of both professional and family strategies. They were by no means the exclusive province of the wealthy, as artisanal and professional families also used them to protect and manage family assets. See Julie Hardwick, *The Practice of Patriarchy: Gender and the Politics of Household Authority in Early Modern France* (University Park: Pennsylvania State University Press, 1998), 51–76; Robert Forster, *Merchants, Landlords, Magistrates: The Depont Family in Eighteenth-Century France* (Baltimore: Johns Hopkins University Press, 1980), 51–76, 111–127; and Verjus and Davidson, *Le roman conjugal*, 173–241. On marriage itself as a contract, see James F. Traer's classic *Marriage and the Family in Eighteenth-Century France* (Ithaca, NY: Cornell University Press, 1980), 22–47. For an overview of European marriage strategies, see Margareth Lanzinger, "Parenté et genre: Des mariages par alliance," in *Genre femmes, histoire en Europe: France, Italie, Espagne, Autriche,* ed. Anna Bellavitis and Nicole Edelman (Paris: Presses Universitaires de Paris Ouest, 2011), 233–254. The Balleroy-Vaupalière contract is a fine specimen of the genre.

19. On the tendency of military nobility to live with their wives' families, see Marraud, *La noblesse de Paris,* 135–136.

20. Her brother, Charles-Auguste, married his son Philippe-Auguste to Elisabeth-Jacqueline Maignard de la Vaupalière in the marriage contract discussed above.

21. AN T 243 La Cour de Balleroy, "Mémoire instructif," n.d.

22. AN T 243 La Cour de Balleroy, Délégation.

23. Grandmothers, and the elderly more generally, were an important part of family life and enjoyed a distinct improvement in status over the course of the eighteenth century. See David Troyansky, *Old Age in the Old Regime: Image and Experience in Eighteenth Century France* (Ithaca, NY: Cornell University Press, 1989), 8–26; and Vincent Gourdon, "Are Grandparents Really Absent from the Family Tradition?," *History of the Family* 4, no. 1 (1999), 77–91.

24. Philippe-Antoine Merlin, *Répertoire universel et raisonné de jurisprudence* (Paris: Garnery, 1812), 2:548.

25. On widow's rights or *douaire,* see Scarlett Beauvalet, *Etre veuve sous l'ancien régime* (Paris: Belin, 2001), 200–204.

26. AdP DQ10 170 4 Baraumont. 15 germinal VIII (March 28, 1800) Cornebize to Director.

27. Law of 12 September 1792; law of 17 frimaire II (December 7, 1793).

28. Denise Z. Davidson and Anne Verjus argue that sons benefited at the expense of elderly women in particular. See "Generational Conflict in Revolutionary France."

29. Law of 17 frimaire II (December 7, 1793).

30. Law of March 28, 1793, section II, art. 5.

31. AN DIII 336, Antoinette-Madaleine Jeanne Portail, Veuve Louis-Gabriel Conflans to Committee of Legislation, n.d.

32. AN DIII 237–238 22 pluviôse II (February 10, 1794), Citoyen Carbonnet Canily to Committee of Legislation.

33. AN F7 3330 18 Fructidor II (September 4, 1794), André, Verificateur de l'enregistrement et des domaines nationaux du département de l'Hérault to Ladère, deputé de l'Hérault.

34. AN DIII 237–238, letter to Ministre de l'Intérieur, pluviôse II (January / February 1794).

35. Law of 1 floréal III (April 20, 1795), law of 9 floréal III (April 28, 1795).

36. AN F7 3330, August 26, 1793.

37. AN F7 3330, 25 Brumaire III (November 15, 1794).

38. Law of 1 floréal III (April 20, 1795). The law of 18 pluviôse VI (February 6, 1798), which dealt with émigré creditors, also included provisions for employees of émigrés. Article 44 of the law of March 28, 1793, had already given protected status to servants' wages.

39. Sarah Maza, *Servants and Masters in Eighteenth-Century France: The Uses of Loyalty* (Princeton, NJ: Princeton University Press, 1983), 170–173.

40. Circular 417 *bis*, May 31, 1793, "Terres appartenant à la nation, qui sont délaissés, à faire cultiver. Fermiers des biens nationaux dont les baux sont expirés, doivent jouir de la récolte de l'année."

41. Law of June 3, 1793.

42. See, for example, AdP DQ10 704 Bochard de Champigny, a doorkeeper named Gallery; DQ10 704 Dubois de Lauzai, a doorkeeper named Guillhamont; DQ10 709 Bernard et Delorme, a doorkeeper named Redy.

43. For recent work on the expansion of credit instruments, see in particular Rebecca Spang, *Stuff and Money in the French Revolution* (Cambridge, MA: Harvard University Press, 2015), 19–56; and James Livesey, *Provincializing Global History: Money, Ideas, and Things in the Langudeoc, 1680–1830* (New Haven, CT: Yale, 2020), 17–51.

44. AN AD XII 3 Pardoux Bordas, "Rapport sur les moyens les plus surs et les plus économiques de terminer la liquidation générale des dettes des émigrés," 18 prairial IV (June 6, 1796).

45. AN AD XII 4a Crenière, "Sur la resolution du conseil 500 du 24 nivôse dernier, portant que les copartageants avec la République ne seront pas tenus

solidairement des dettes communes, & ne pourront être poursuivis que pour le paiement de la portion desdites dettes, proportionnée a la part qu'ils auront prise dans les biens," II germinal V (March 31, 1797).

46. AN AD XII 4a Bonnières, "Rapport sur les poursuites dirigées contre les cautions des émigrés reconnus solvables," 4 messidor V (June 22, 1797).

47. AN AD XII 4A, L. Barreau, "Sur la résolution relative au paiement des dettes des succession indivises, ou partagées avec la République, comme représentant des émigrés," Conseil des Anciens, 10 Germinal V (March 30, 1797).

48. AN AD XII 4A, "Opinion de Brothier sur la resolution relative aux co-partageants, co-obliges & cautions des émigrés solvables," Conseil des Anciens, 6 messidor VI (June 24, 1798).

49. Anciens. S. J. H. Bonnesoeur (Manche) Sur la resolution relative aux dettes solidaires entre la république représentant des Émigrés, et d'autres co-partageants. 12 germinal V (June 24, 1798).

50. Adolphe Robert and Gaston Cougny, *Dictionnaire des parlementaires français: Depuis le 1er mai 1789 jusqu'au 1er mai 1889* (Geneva: Slatkin, 2000), 1:389.

51. Philippe-Antoine Merlin, *Répertoire universel et raisonné de jurisprudence*, 5th ed. (Brussels: Tarlier, 1828), 31:337–339.

52. Raymond-Théodore Troplong, *Commentaire des privilèges et hypothèques*, vol. 1 (Brussels, 1844–1848), para. 44, *The Making of the Modern World*, Gale. The issue of property rights and debt came up over the issue of repossession for debt, something that was itself profoundly enmeshed in émigré property sales and the paper currency that depended on them. See Judith A. Miller, "The Aftermath of the Assignat: Plaintiffs in the Age of Property, 1794–1804," in *Taking Liberties: Problems of a New Order from the French Revolution to Napoleon*, ed. Judith Miller and Howard Brown (Manchester: Manchester University Press, 2002), 70–91.

53. Quoted in Troplong, *Commentaire*, para. 85.

54. Report by Grenier, March 17, 1804, summarized in Troplong, *Commentaire*, para. 157.

55. See in particular Colin Jones and Rebecca Spang, "Sans-Culottes, *sans café, sans tabac*: Shifting Realms of Necessity and Luxury in Eighteenth-Century France," in *Consumer Culture in Europe, 1650–1850*, ed. Maxine Berg and Helen Clifford (Manchester: Manchester University Press, 1999), 37–62; see also William H. Sewell Jr., "The Sans-Culotte Rhetoric of Subsistence," in *The Terror*, ed. Keith Baker, *vol. 4* of *The French Revolution and the Creation of Modern Political Culture* (Oxfordshire: Pergamon Press, 1994), 249–270.

56. The Marxist historian Georges Lefebvre is more forceful on this point, but the liberal political theorist Pierre Rosanvallon also emphasizes the Jacobins' commitment to property rights. Work that finds the Revolution to be illiberal

frames the question differently, focusing on the revolutionary state's failure to defend individual rights after recognizing them. Georges Lefebvre, *Questions agraires au temps de la Terreur* (La Roche-sur-Yon: Potier, 1954), 73–79; Pierre Rosanvallon, *Le sacre du citoyen: Histoire du suffrage universel en France. Bilbiothèque des histoires* (Paris: Gallimard, 1992), 55. The concept of a "traditional" moral economy that was abandoned, at great price and great resistance, in favor of "modern" market values recurs. For a discussion of such narratives as regards peasant economies, see Philip T. Hoffman, *Growth in a Traditional Society: The French Countryside, 1450–1815*, (Princeton, NJ: Princeton University Press, 1996), 12–20.

57. This separation is examined—and challenged—by scholars through women's relegation to a domestic sphere. See Karen Offen, *The Woman Question in France, 1400–1870* (Cambridge: Cambridge University Press, 2017), 6–7; see also Davidoff and Hall, *Family Fortunes*, xiii–xviii, 13–35.

6. By Iron or Nail

1. James Livesey, "Agrarian Ideology and Commercial Republicanism," *Past and Present* 157 (1997): 94–121; John Shovlin, *The Political Economy of Virtue: Luxury, Patriotism, and the Origins of the French Revolution* (Ithaca, NY: Cornell University Press, 2006), 182–212.

2. For a recent, standard characterization of the Directory, see, for example, Peter McPhee, *Liberty or Death: The French Revolution* (New Haven, CT: Yale University Press, 2016), 297–320; see also William Doyle, *The Oxford History of the French Revolution*, 3rd ed. (Oxford: Oxford University Press, 2018), 319–320. For particular consideration of the politics of the Directory and its conservatism, see Pierre Serna, *La république des girouettes: 1789–1815 et au-delà une anomalie politique: la France de l'extrême centre* (Seyssel: Champ Vallon, 2005), 394–397.

3. *Réimpression de l'ancien moniteur* (Paris: n.p., 1840–1845), 25:92.

4. Livesey, "Agrarian Ideology and Commercial Republicanism"; Pierre Rosanvallon, *Le sacre du citoyen: Histoire du suffrage universel en France* (Paris: Gallimard, 1992), 99–100.

5. The term comes from Louis Bergeron's study of the landed notability who supported the Napoleonic regime, *Les 'masses de granit': Cent mille notables du Premier Empire* (Paris: Editions de l'Ecole des Hautes Etudes en Sciences Sociales, 1979).

6. The conflict between the poor and the revolutionary state is foregrounded, classically, by Georges Lefebvre in *The Coming of the French Revolution*, trans. R. R. Palmer (Princeton, NJ: Princeton University Press, 1989). Subsequent

authors who have modified elements of the Marxist interpretation have none-theless retained this element, such as Jack A. Goldstone, "The Social Origins of the French Revolution Revisited," in *From Deficit to Deluge: The Origins of the French Revolution*, ed. Thomas E. Kaiser and Dale Van Kley (Stanford, CA: Stanford University Press, 2011), 67–103. Studies of property in the Revolution are linked to an interpretation of the Revolution that foregrounds such conflict, as they have traditionally focused on land and are associated with Marxist interpretations of the Revolution, and because of their interest in whether property seizure did, in fact, lead to redistribution. Bernard Bodinier and Eric Teyssier overview generations of such scholarship in *L'événement le plus important de la Révolution: La vente des biens nationaux* (Paris: Société des études robespierristes et Éditions du CTHS, 2000), 41–102. Marcel Marion falls outside the Marxist tradition with his classic, *La vente des biens nationaux pendant la Révolution française, avec étude spéciale des ventes dans la Gironde et dans le Cher* (Paris: Champion, 1908). For a recent work that interrogates the traditional categories, see Anne Jollet, *Terre et société en Révolution: Approche du lien social dans la région d'Amboise* (Paris: CTHS, 2000). Closely associated in the Marxist tradition are studies of rural peasant movements, particularly the classic of Anatoli Ado, *Paysans en Révolution: Terre, pouvoir et jacquerie 1789–1794* (Paris: Société des Etudes Robespierristes, 1996). A related vein of literature considers the economic impact of the Revolution on French agriculture; for an overview of this literature, see Peter McPhee, "The French Revolution, Peasants, and Capitalism," *American Historical Review* 94, no. 5 (December 1989): 1265–1280.

7. On the particular role of popular subsistence crises and social unrest in the Directory, see Jeremy D. Popkin, *A New World Begins: The History of the French Revolution* (New York: Basic Books, 2019), 459–462; McPhee, *Liberty or Death*, 301–320.

8. With regard to the French case in particular, see James Livesey, *Provincializing Global History: Money, Ideas, and Things in the Languedoc, 1680–1830* (New Haven, CT: Yale University Press, 2020), 1–16.

9. On real estate markets, see Gérard Béaur, *Le marché foncier à la veille de la Révolution: Les mouvements de propriété beaucerons dans les régions de Maintenon et de Janville de 1761 à 1790* (Paris: Editions de l'Ecole des Hautes Etudes en Sciences Sociales, 1984); Fabrice Boudjaaba, *Des paysans attachés à la terre? Familles, marchés et patrimoines dans la région de Vernon (1750–1830)*, Collection du Centre Roland Mousnier (Paris: Presses Universitaires de Paris Sorbonne, 2008); Anne Jollet, *Terre et societé en révolution: Approche du lien social dans la région d'Amboise* (Paris: Comité des Travaux Historiques et Scientifiques, 2000). On credit, see Livesey, *Provincializing Global History*, 17–51; Philip T. Hoffman,

Gilles Postel-Vinay, and Jean-Laurent Rosenthal, *Priceless Markets: The Political Economy of Credit in Paris, 1660–1870* (Chicago: University of Chicago Press, 2000), 96–113; Laurence Fontaine, "Espaces, usages et dynamiques de la dette: Dans les hautes vallées dauphinoises (XVII-XVIIIe siècles)," *Annales: Histoire, Sciences Sociales* 49, no. 6 (December 1994): 1375–1391.

10. The Revolution has long been understood to have slowed French economic development, in part because the revolutionary wars decimated the economy and in part because the social revolution prevented the kinds of exploitation that helped launch Britain on the path of economic development. While it seems clear that the Revolution had a negative impact on the economy, the idea that France "failed" to develop in comparison with the British model has been discredited. Recent work has focused on articulating the specificity of the French model. See the classic, Patrick O'Brien and Çağlar Keyder, *Economic Growth in Britain and France, 1780–1914: Two Paths to the Twentieth Century* (London: G. Allen & Unwin, 1978); more recently, see Jeff Horn, *The Path Not Taken: French Industrialization in the Age of Revolution, 1750–1830* (Cambridge, MA: MIT Press, 2006).

11. This chapter's emphasis on practices follows an approach that has been used to study credit, as articulated by Craig Muldrew, *The Economy of Obligation: The Culture of Credit and Social Relations in Early Modern England*, Early Modern History (New York: St. Martin's Press, 1998), 8. See also Clare Haru Crowston, *Credit, Fashion, Sex: Economies of Regard in Old Regime France* (Durham, NC: Duke University Press, 2013), 2–3; and Amalia D. Kessler, *A Revolution in Commerce: The Parisian Merchant Court and the Rise of Commercial Society in Eighteenth-Century France* (New Haven, CT: Yale University Press, 2007), 2–8.

12. AdP DQ10 89 Brousse. The lease began September 25, 1794.

13. In a similar situation, the Domain canceled a sale when it was determined to have occurred after the émigré owner had her rights reinstated. AdP DQ10 704 Bourgevin Vialart de Moligny.

14. A similar claim was made by a tenant named Bohet. See AdP DQ10 169 Bohet.

15. AdP DQ10 89 Brousse, Receiver to Director, 19 germinal VIII (April 9, 1800); Receiver to Director, 25 brumaire IX (November 15, 1800). The letter was finally located in the prefect's office, as related by Director to Receiver, 25 pluviôse IX (February 14, 1801).

16. AdP DQ10 89 Brousse, Berthaud to unknown, 30 prairial IV (June 18, 1796).

17. Lynn Hunt discusses the political implications of transparency and publicity in *Politics, Culture, and Class in the French Revolution* (Berkeley: University of California Press, 1984), 43–46. Keith Michael Baker discusses the articulation

of these values in the Declaration of the Rights of Man in "The Idea of a Declaration of Rights," in *The French Idea of Freedom: The Revolution and the Declaration of Rights of 1789*, ed. Dale Van Kley (Stanford, CA: Stanford University Press, 1994), 154–196.

18. See Décret sur le rachat des rentes foncières, December 18, 1790, and Décret sur les déclarations foncières, 9 messidor III (June 27, 1795).

19. On the varying types of investments, see Hoffman, Postel-Vinay, and Rosenthal, *Priceless Markets,* 12–25. Robert Forster examines one family's strategies in depth over generations in *Merchants, Landlords, Magistrates: The Depont Family in Eighteenth-Century France* (Baltimore: Johns Hopkins University Press, 1980).

20. Probably Jean Bochart de Champigny; see François-Alexandre Aubert de la Chesnaye-Desbois, *Dictionnaire de la noblesse,* 2nd ed. (Paris: Veuve Duchesne, 1771) 2:570. The spelling used by the Domain has been retained here.

21. AdP DQ10 751 Planoy (Bochard Champigny), Planoy to Andouille par Angerville la Gaste, Département de Seine et Oise, 18 frimaire II. (December 8, 1793). The letter was redirected to Paris; Planoy may have addressed the letter to the bureau where she knew Bochard's primary residence was located; émigré property was handled by the bureau where it was located, not at the home of the owner.

22. AN Minutier Central Répertoire LVII 12–13.

23. AdP DQ10 751 Bochard Champigny, Planoy to unnamed official, 18 frimaire II (December 8, 1793).

24. AdP DQ10 751 Planoy (Bochard Champigny), unsigned, undated note in Director's hand. The scrap mentions papers served on 10 nivôse IV (December 31, 1795), which fits with its position in the folder with respect to other letters and allows for a relative sense of the date.

25. AdP DQ10 751 Planoy (Bochard Champigny), Domaine Nationale to Rugeot, 28 messidor IV (July 16, 1796).

26. This was consistent with other Domain decisions from the same period: Gentil had refused to entertain a similar appeal to emotions in September 1794, when an elderly widow asked for her lease to be canceled so she could be near her family. See AdP DQ10 704 Bochard de Sarron, Gentil to Francfort, 4 vendémiaire III (July 16, 1796).

27. Ronen Steinberg, *The Afterlives of the Terror: Facing the Legacies of Mass Violence in Postrevolutionary France* (Ithaca, NY: Cornell University Press, 2019), 72–78.

28. The National Lottery offered two drawings, in 1795 and 1797. Ostensibly a means of distributing seized émigré property, the cost of tickets was prohibitively expensive. See Jean Leonnet, *Les lotteries d'état en France aux XVIIIe et XIXe siècle* (Paris: Imprimerie Nationale, 1963), 38–51.

29. AdP DQ10 172 Bertez, Director to Bachellery (receiver), 16 fructidor XI (September 3, 1803); the phrase also appears in DQ10 172, Jacob Benjamin, Régisseurs to Girard (director), 24 thermidor VII (August 11, 1799).

30. AdP DQ10 172 Bertez, Directeur to Bachellery, Receveur, 16 fructidor XI (September 3, 1803).

31. Pothier, "Traité des personnes et des choses," part 2, section 1, para. 242.

32. The *Sommier* reveals that the date of the lease was 7 Fructidor VI (August 24, 1798). AdP DQ13 294. The presence or absence of mirrors in a confiscated property caused endless problems for the Domain. See DQ10 171 Bergeret Frouville; DQ10 172 Benjamin et Cie; DQ10 172 Berckmeyer; DQ10 172 Benjamin; DQ10 172 Jacob Benjamin; DQ10 172 Bertez; DQ10 172 Baron; and DQ10 172 Bazonat veuve Forceville Méricourt. The question of who should pay for repairs to confiscated properties was also a common theme in the dossiers. See DQ10 88 Le Camus / Bourbon; DQ10 89 La Haye (Hôtel de Bazancourt); DQ10 168 Bellet; DQ10 169 Beaurepaire; DQ10 170 Brousse et Morel; DQ10 172 Blondel d'Azincourt; DQ10 709 Boulainvilliers.

33. AdP DQ10 168 Bouvrain, Daubigny to Director, 12 brumaire XIII (November 3, 1804).

34. AdP DQ10 168 Bouvrain, Prefect to Director, 26 fructidor XII (September 13, 1804); repeated by Director to Daubigny, 4 vendémiaire XIII (September 28, 1804).

35. AdP DQ10 168 Bouvrain, Daubigny to Director, 11 thermidor XII (July 30, 1805).

36. AdP DQ10 168 Bouvrain, Daubigny to Director, 11 thermidor XII (July 30, 1805).

37. The rental value of a property had an impact on total value, because this was generally calculated by multiplying the annual revenue by a coefficient that depended on a host of factors, including the type of property.

38. The word is used by the notaries who inventoried his collections. AdP DQ10 170 Baillet St Julien, Inventory, November 15, 1787.

39. He explained his intentions in the act of donation that transferred the lands to his relatives. AN Minutier Central LI 1163 Donation 6 Mars 1783; the act is also cited in full in AdP DQ10 170 Baillet St Julien, Donation, March 6, 1783.

40. The women were the daughters of his cousin Jeanne-Marguerite Baillet, herself the daughter of his uncle Lazare Baillet, older brother of his father Mathurin Baillet de Saint-Julien. See Louis Alexandre Expilly, *Dictionnaire géographique, historique et politique des Gaules et de la France* (Paris: Libraires Associés, 1761), 702.

41. Marguerite's daughter, Madeleine-Susanne, emigrated with her husband, Anne-Charles Sigismond de Montmorency-Luxembourg, triggering the

involvement of the Domain. Marguerite's husband, Antoine-René, was the son of the political theorist René-Louis de Voyer de Paulmy, Marquis d'Argenson.

42. We find another case of a relative donating his estate to his heirs in exchange for a life annuity in AdP DQ10 172 Beauharnais *père*.

43. The contract was signed in Paris before Arnault, January 17, 1784. Its details are related, accurately, in a letter in AdP DQ10 190 Baillet Saint-Julien, Brulé to Director, 19 frimaire IX (December 10, 1800).

44. The donation agreement mentions the rental. Courteilles lived northwest of Paris in the Eure department before emigrating, so it is likely she maintained the lease.

45. AN F7 5835 Belzunce Antoine Louis. On the flow of people between Paris and the colonies, see in particular Miranda Spieler, "The Vanishing Slaves of Paris: The *Lettre de Cachet* and the Emergence of an Imperial Legal Order in Eighteenth-Century France," in *The Scaffolding of Sovereignty: Global and Aesthetic Perspectives on the History of a Concept,* ed. Zvi Ben-Dor Benite, Stefanos Geroulanos, and Nicole Jerr (New York: Columbia University Press, 2017), 230–245.

46. On separations in Old Regime France, see Julie Hardwick, *Family Business: Litigation and the Political Economies of Daily Life in Early Modern France* (Oxford: Oxford University Press, 2009), 20–56. Roderick Phillips offers a brief, useful overview of separations in *Family Breakdown in Late-Eighteenth-Century France: Divorces in Rouen, 1792–1803* (Oxford: Clarendon, 1980), 4–11.

47. This operation is summarized in the documentation of Pierre-Elisabeth de Fontanieu's estate. AN Minutier Central LIII 597, Griveau, December 20, 1784, "Transaction et Arrangements de famille entre les heritiers de M. de Fonantanieu."

48. AN Minutier Central LXXVII 438, Havard, July 5, 1791, *Vente*.

49. His Tuscan origins are referenced throughout the Domain dossier, as well as his address in Hanover Square, in the tony Mayfair district of London. In addition to Belzunce and Baillet Saint-Julien, we find a case of real estate being paid for with life annuities in AdP DQ10 171 Bergeret Frouville.

50. Fumel may have been an acquaintance of Belzunce's. Both men served as aides de camp in the royal army and were members of the Royal Order of Saint-Louis. Belzunce also held the title of governor of the Agen region, while Fumel was the lieutenant of the Bourdelais, immediately to the north. Both men also lived in the same parish in Paris, attending church at La Madeleine. Their titles and addresses are listed in the act of sale. AN Minutier Central LII 603, Chavet, March 22, 1786, *Vente*.

51. AdP DQ10 Prefect to Director, December 18, 1806.

52. Law of 21 frimaire III (December 11, 1794); the law of 17 prairial (June 5, 1796) stipulated the procedure for indemnifying dispossessed owners.

53. The projected street ran along a piece of land that had belonged to Monsieur; this was the reason for the Domain's involvement. The issue of providing alternative access to a buyer of *biens nationaux* also appears in AdP DQ10 169 Bacot, Architecte to Administration des Domaines, 3 brumaire XI (October 25, 1802).

54. AdP DQ10 226 Bailly et Cagnion, Guillaumot to Administrateurs du département de la Seine, 24 brumaire 6, quoted in Administrateurs to Bureau central de Paris, 24 brumaire VI (November 14, 1797).

55. AdP DQ10 226 Bailly et Cagnion, Administrators to Bureau central, 24 brumaire VI (November 14, 1797).

56. AdP DQ10 226 Bailly et Cagnion, avis du Directeur, Arrêt du Prefet, 25 pluviôse IX (February 14, 1801).

57. AdP DQ10 226 Bailly et Cagnion, Receveur to Directeur, 7 germinal IX (March 28, 1801); Directeur to Prefect, 21 germinal IX (April 11, 1801); Bourla to Directeur, 25 germinal IX (April 11, 1801).

58. AdP DQ10 226 Bailly et Cagnion, Bourla report, 18 / 27 prairial, 6 messidor IX (June 25, 1801).

59. The architects' assessments are included in the contract between Cagnion and the republic for the three additional properties. This agreement was signed 28 Messidor VI (July 16, 1798) but is filed with the previous agreement, dated 12 Frimaire V (December 2, 1796). AN Minutier Central LXXVIII 1013, Guillaume le jeune, 12 Frimaire V (December 2, 1796), Échange.

60. AN Minutier Central LXXVIII 1013, Guillaume le jeune, 12 Frimaire V (December 2, 1796), Échange.

61. AN Minutier Central LXXVIII 1013, Guillaume le jeune, 12 frimaire V (December 2, 1796), Échange, maison Rue du Temple, "charges relatives à ladite maison."

62. AdP DQ10 226 Bailly et Cagnion, Cardon to Director, February 12, 1821. Laffon-Ladebat is likely the Revolutionary representative of the same name.

63. AN Minutier Central XCVII 626, Lefebure Saint Maur, 22 pluviôse IX (February 11, 1801), *Vente de maisons.*

64. A game whose rules are unequal; Michel de Certeau's schema of "strategy" versus "tactic" describes the unequal playing field in which such maneuvering takes place: *The Practice of Everyday Life*, trans. Steven Randall, vol. 1 (Berkeley: University of California Press, 1984), 34–39.

Conclusion

1. See Kelly Summers, "Healing the Republic's 'Great Wound': Emigration Reform and the Path to a General Amnesty, 1799–1802," in *French Emigrants in Revolutionised Europe: Connected Histories and Memories,* ed. Philip Laure and Juliette Reboul (Cham, Switzerland: Springer, 2019), 235–255. An exhaustive account of the indemnity can be found in André Gain, *La restauration et les biens des émigrés; la législation concernant les biens nationaux de seconde origine et son application dans l'Est de la France (1814–1832)* (Nancy: Société d'impressions typographiques, 1928).

2. Law of 23 nivôse III (January 12, 1795); Law of 18 prairial III (June 6, 1795).

3. The family's experience was not unusual for Paris, where the majority of seized property was restored, but this was not the fate of the émigré property outside of Paris. How much was lost varied greatly by region. For a succinct overview, see Robert Forster, "The Nobility during the French Revolution," *Past & Present* 37 (July 1967): 71–86. For information on the restoration of assets in Paris, see H. Monin and L. Lazard, eds., *Sommier des biens nationaux de la Ville de Paris, conservés aux Archives de la Seine* (Paris: Cerf, 1920); n.b. this source covers only three quarters of the city.

4. Delacroix, November 10, 1791, *Archives Parlementaires de 1787 à 1860: Recueil complet des débats législatifs et politiques des chambres français* (Paris: s.n., 1787–), 34:238.

5. Erika Vause, "He Who Rushes to Riches Will Not Be Innocent': Commercial Values and Commercial Failure in Postrevolutionary France," *French Historical Studies* 35, no. 2 (2012): 321–349.

6. Tyson Leuchter, "Solidarity, Liability, and the New Regime of Corporate Property in Post-revolutionary France," *La Révolution Française* 15 (2018); Erika Vause, *In the Red and in the Black: Debt, Dishonor, and the Law in France between the Revolutions* (Charlottesville: University of Virginia Press), 91–118.

7. See in particular Harold James, *Family Capitalism: Wendels, Haniels, Falcks, and the Continental European Model* (Cambridge, MA: Harvard University Press, 2006), 41–72; Luciano Segreto, "Carving out a Place in International Markets: Success and Failure in European Family Papermaking Firms (1800–2010)," in *Family Multinationals: Entrepreneurship, Governance, and Pathways to Internationalization,* ed. Christina Lubinski, Jeffrey Fear, and Paloma Fernàndez Pérez (New York: Routledge, 2013), 151–168; Andrea Colli, *The History of Family Business, 1850–2000* (Cambridge: Cambridge University Press, 2003), 50–64.

8. For the French context, see in particular Bonnie Smith, *Ladies of the Leisure Class: The Bourgeoises of Northern France in the 19th Century* (Princeton, NJ: Princeton University Press, 1981), 34–52; a relevant European context is offered

by Leonore Davidoff and Catherine Hall, *Family Fortunes: Men and Women of the English Middle Class, 1780–1850*, 2nd ed. (1987; London: Routledge, 2002), 272–316. See also Jan de Vries, *The Industrious Revolution: Consumer Behavior and the Household Economy, 1550 to the Present* (Cambridge: Cambridge University Press, 2008), 186–237.

9. Davidoff and Hall explore this dynamic in the British case in *Family Fortunes*, 198–228.

10. See, for example, Johan Mathew, *Margins of the Market: Trafficking and Capitalism across the Arabian Sea* (Oakland: University of California Press, 2016), 1–2.

ACKNOWLEDGMENTS

This book is the product of many years of research and writing. As a result, I have the pleasure of acknowledging many people and institutions that helped me bring the book into being. I look to the origins of my formation as a historian and my interest in property in the hazy past, and I am grateful to the teachers and mentors who influenced me: Ann Johnson, Carl Weiner, Susannah Ottaway, and Jean-Pierre Bardet.

I am grateful to the institutions that made my research possible: the Fulbright Commission US Student Program, the Social Science Research Council, the Center for European Studies at Harvard, and the Harvard History Department supported research in Paris; the Krupp Foundation and the Committee on Degrees in Social Studies at Harvard supported subsequent writing and research. Librarians and library collections in France and the United States made my research possible, particularly the Bibliothèque nationale de France, Archives Nationales, Archives de Paris, Harvard Widener Library, and the Harvard Law School Library.

This book was vastly improved by the generosity and insight of the anonymous reviewers of Harvard University Press and by my brilliant and generous editor, Emily Silk. I am grateful to everyone at HUP who assisted in the publication of this book.

To the teachers and mentors who shaped my thinking and inspired me to produce whatever is useful and good in this work, I owe the deepest gratitude. Patrice Higonnet dared me to write this, and I am grateful to him for that and for his wisdom, mentorship, and conversation over many years at Harvard and in Paris. Jim Livesey has been a mentor, inspiration, and valued interlocutor. Pierre Serna, my supervisor in *co-tutelle* at the Institut d'Histoire de la Révolution Française, offered insight and guidance at key moments. Faculty at Harvard and beyond encouraged this project, particularly Ann Blair, David Armitage, John Shovlin, Emma Rothschild, Jennifer Heuer, and Mary Lewis. I appreciated the collegiality of Rebecca Spang and Rafe Blaufarb as we worked on projects that seemed, at times, very similar.

Friends who shared similar journeys sharpened my thinking and kept me company along the way: Mira Siegelberg, George Gallwey, Julia Stephens, Elizabeth Cross, Erik Linstrum, Eddie Kolla, Claire Cage, Josh Lobert, Erika Vause, Katie McDonough, Caroline Creson, Gregory Clines, Andrew Bellisari, Sofia Grachova and the late Stephen Walsh, Heidi and Michael Tworek, Nimisha Barton, Sreemati Mitter, Jesse Howell, and many others. Friends and colleagues in Paris made the time I spent there much sweeter: my cousin Christopher Manning, Annika Cederfeldt, Molly Gower, Miranda Spieler, Michelle Kuo and Albert Wu, Coraline Lambert, the Grange family, Clyde Plumauzille, Virginie Martin, and Manuel Covo.

The years I spent in the Committee on Degrees in Social Studies were transformative, and for that I am indebted to Anya Bernstein Bassett and Jim Kloppenberg. I am grateful to the friends there who read portions of the manuscript and discussed the ideas with me, particularly Ryan Acton and Alvin Henry, Will Selinger, Angela Maione, Ana Keilson, and Justin Reynolds.

Revising the manuscript would have been a much bleaker undertaking without the love and laughter of Cavan Curran.

I would not have wanted to undertake this project without the entourage of my family, and especially my parents, Mary (her blue pencil always sharp but wielded with love) and Jamie Callaway.

INDEX

Please note that *italicized* page numbers in this index indicate illustrative material.